Employment Security in Action

Pergamon Titles of Related Interest

Amara/Lipinski Business Planning For an Uncertain Future: Scenarios
& Strategies

Guzzo/Bondy A Guide to Worker Productivity Experiments in the United
States 1976-81

Lundstedt/Colglazier Managing Innovation: The Social Dimensions of
Creativity, Invention and Technology

MaCoy/Morand Short-Time Compensation: A Formula for Work Sharing

O'Brien/Dickinson/Rosow Industrial Behavior Modification:
A Management Handbook

Zager/Rosow The Innovative Organization: Productivity Programs
in Action

Work in America Institute Policy Studies:
Employment Security in a Free Economy
Productivity Through Work Innovations

Related Journals

Long Range Planning
Omega
The Wharton Annual
Work in America Institute Studies in Productivity
World of Work Report

Employment Security in Action

Strategies That Work

HD
5708.45
.U6
G88
1985

Jocelyn F. Gutchess

Economic Consultant

Pergamon Press
New York • Oxford • Toronto • Sydney • Paris • Frankfurt

Pergamon Press Offices:

U.S.A.	Pergamon Press Inc., Maxwell House, Fairview Park, Elmsford, New York 10523, U.S.A.
U.K.	Pergamon Press Ltd., Headington Hill Hall, Oxford OX3 0BW, England
CANADA	Pergamon Press Canada Ltd., Suite 104, 150 Consumers Road, Willowdale, Ontario M2J 1P9, Canada
AUSTRALIA	Pergamon Press (Aust.) Pty. Ltd., P.O. Box 544, Potts Point, NSW 2011, Australia
FRANCE	Pergamon Press SARL, 24 rue des Ecoles, 75240 Paris, Cedex 05, France
FEDERAL REPUBLIC OF GERMANY	Pergamon Press GmbH, Hammerweg 6, D-6242 Kronberg-Taunus, Federal Republic of Germany

Copyright © 1985 Pergamon Press Inc.

Library of Congress Cataloging in Publication Data
Gutchess, Jocelyn F.
    Employment security in action.

    (Pergamon Press/Work in America Institute series)
    1. Job security--United States--Case studies.
I. Title. II. Series.
HD5708.45.U6G88   1985   331.25'96'0973   84-25444
ISBN 0-08-031594-1

Printed in the United States of America

Pergamon Press/Work in America Institute Series

Work in America Institute, Inc., a nonprofit, nonpartisan organization, was founded in 1975 to advance productivity and quality of working life. Through a series of policy studies, education and training programs, an extensive information resource, and a broad range of publications, the Institute has focused on the greater effectiveness of organizations through the improved use of human resources. Because of its close working relationships with unions, business, and government, the Institute is sensitive to the views and perspectives of all parties and is recognized as an objective source of information on issues of common interest.

The Pergamon Press/Work in America Institute Series is designed to explore the role of human resources in improving productivity in the workplace today and to identify the trends that will shape the workplace of the future. It will focus primarily on the issues of:

- *Quality of working life* through work innovations that encourage employee participation in decision making and offer recognition to employees for their contributions.
- *Productivity* through the more effective management of human resources.
- *Interaction between people and technology* to achieve a more satisfactory transition to the workplace of the future.
- *Labor-management cooperation* to solve mutual problems in the workplace, to achieve improved quality of product, and to make organizations work better.
- *National labor-force policy* as it relates to productivity and the quality of working life.

Contents

Preface

Unemployment incurs staggering economic, social, and political costs, well documented by recent history. Policies that enhance and sustain employment, on the other hand, provide major benefits to employers, employees, the community, and the economy. This timely volume describes the efforts of both companies and unions—as well as entire communities—to stabilize employment in a changing economy. A companion to Work in America Institute's policy study report *Employment Security in a Free Economy*, it details over 30 specific cases in which organizations have taken positive action to assure the continuity of employment for their work forces. These diverse programs and policies support the proposals set forth by the policy study report and provide the practical experience on which its 26 recommendations are based. In effect, this book links the policy process to successful employment security practices currently in place in the United States, Canada, and Western Europe.

The case studies are grouped under six different headings: guarantees and other no-layoff policies, employment buffering techniques, voluntary work-force reductions, worker–oriented adjustment strategies, easing the adjustment to technological change, and job replacement strategies. But one characteristic is common to all: they are a response to economic change, whether due to the introduction of new technology, economic recession, or the increase in foreign competition.

It is the belief of Work in America Institute that in the world economy of the 1980s, economic performance requires keeping up with the accelerated rate of change and that "keeping up" depends, first and foremost, on the cooperation of the employees who operate the business day in and day out. Employees are generally not averse to change, but when it carries with it the threat of job loss, they will resist it, overtly or covertly. With their future secured, however, employees feel free to participate enthusiastically and even to initiate change. Although most of the business community still doubts that employment security is a practical option, organizations that have actually tried it have found that employment security releases the creative energies and ideas of employees—responses that offer the enterprise a clear competitive advantage over companies operating in the conventional mode. Case after case in this book proves the point.

Employment Security in Action: Strategies That Work has been supported by grants from the Andrew W. Mellon Foundation, the Charles Stewart Mott Foundation, and, for European coverage, The German Marshall Fund of the

United States. The statements made and views expressed, however, are solely the responsibility of Work in America Institute.

The Institute wishes to express its appreciation to the author, Jocelyn F. Gutchess, for a fine job in reporting on and interpreting employment security measures in both the United States and Western Europe. Her expertise and broad experience in the field of employment policy is reflected throughout. Gutchess was assisted in these efforts by Jill Casner-Lotto in the section on California's Employment Training Panel, and by Ramelle MaCoy in the sections on Motorola, Signetics, Advanced Micro Devices, and Hewlett-Packard. Robert Zager, Work in America Institute's vice-president for Policy Studies and Technical Assistance, worked closely with Gutchess to integrate the casebook with the policy study, and Beatrice Walfish, editorial director, provided editorial guidance. Frances Harte, managing editor, directed the production of the book. Work in America Institute is proud of their achievements in bringing these significant case studies to the attention of the American public.

Jerome M. Rosow
President
Work in America Institute, Inc.

1.
Employment Security:
Promise and Practice

To some people employment security connotes a kind of protectionism, a rigidity on the part of both managers and workers, and an unwillingness to change. In this book, however, the opposite view is taken. Good employment security practice almost always involves change and recognition that change is necessary. What employment security is all about is finding practical and positive ways for companies to adapt to change. Providing employment security for employees does not require lifetime employment—the kind of security available to a favored portion of the work force in Japan. Nor does it require an employer's guarantee that every worker will be able to stay in the same job forever. Employment security, as it is discussed here, results from the positive actions taken by companies and/or unions to assure that the people associated with them—employees of a company or members of a union—have an opportunity to continue working in a productive job, if that is what they want to do, for as long as they want to do it.

More and more corporate managers have come to recognize that employment security for their employees is an important and, indeed, expedient element in human-resource management. As international competition increases and becomes more rigorous, and as the pace of technological change quickens, managers are taking a new look at their personnel-management policies. Many are coming to regard their employees not only as a valuable resource, replaceable only at considerable cost, but also as a form of capital, human capital, to be protected and conserved if at all possible.

Change is natural in a free economy. Today, however, the coincidence of three global trends—(1) the increasing industrialization of many Third World countries, (2) the computer-led technological revolution, and (3) the increasingly frequent, convulsive, and often unpredictable swings in national and international economies—have made adjustment to change both more difficult and more urgent. Policies which enhance employment security allow corporate managers to maximize the skills, technical know-how, and creativity of their workers. Such policies may also encourage worker loyalty, thus helping the companies adjust to change and stay on top. A good employment security program will help to smooth the adjustment process, to the economic

1

and social benefit of the company, the workers, and society as a whole. Much has been written about the economic costs of unemployment—lost production, wasted resources, and the increased taxes necessary to support the jobless. There are social costs as well—the devastating effect on the lives and health of the people directly affected by long periods of involuntary idleness and dependency. It is not the purpose here to argue the benefits of a good employment security policy. Rather, the intent is to describe some interesting and sometimes innovative responses by the private sector to deal with the issue.

This book presents a number of cases describing the experiences of several companies and some other private-sector organizations that have successfully coped with a perceived need to provide employment security for workers. To identify examples of good employment security practice here in the United States and in Western Europe, several methods have been used, including a search of the literature and many conversations with leaders in industry and the labor movement, government officials concerned with labor-management relations, specialists in the academic world, and journalists familiar with the general field.

Work in America Institute's National Advisory Committee on Employment Security in a Free Economy provided valuable insights and many good leads. In addition, a questionnaire was sent to all the U.S. companies on *Fortune* magazine's list of the top 1,000 industrial companies, asking about their employment security policies and inviting them to take part in this project. The results of these efforts led to the identification of many more cases than those presented here. Selection for inclusion was based on a desire to present examples of a variety of approaches to the problem of employment security. We make no claim that the cases included in the book represent the best employment security practice, only that they are examples of good practice.

Information on the cases themselves was obtained, for the most part, from interviews with officials of the companies and unions. A grant from The German Marshall Fund of the United States enabled the author to visit Great Britain, France, and West Germany to collect firsthand information on employment security policies and practices in Western European countries.

Six general approaches or strategies have been identified. The individual cases described here have been assigned to one or another of these approaches, each of which is handled in a separate chapter. Although companies and other private-sector organizations actively pursuing policies to strengthen employment security are apt to utilize more than one strategy—in fact, most of them usually make use to some extent of all six approaches—assignment was made to a particular chapter either because that strategy predominates in the company's employment security program or because the company's experience is especially illustrative of the problems involved in its implementation.

The six strategies are:

- guarantees and other no-layoff policies
- employment buffering strategies
- voluntary work-force reductions
- worker-oriented adjustment strategies
- easing the adjustment to technological change
- job-replacement strategies

There is a kind of natural progression here, with *guarantees and other no-layoff policies* at one end of the spectrum, providing perhaps the surest avenue to employment security. *Employment buffers* are preplanned measures which allow a company to expand or contract its available work-force hours and, at the same time, protect the employment security of a core work force. *Voluntary work-force reductions* are, more often than not, temporary in nature. The assumption is that things will return to normal and that, therefore, special measures to protect employment security need only last a short time. Voluntary early retirement is included in this group, and although the effect is permanent for the participants, the inducement offer made by the employer is usually a limited one. Whereas buffering strategies and work-force reductions usually stem from a desire on the part of the employer to keep a work force more or less in place, riding out the ups and downs of the business cycle, *worker-oriented adjustment strategies* assume that there has been or will be a displacement. The objective is to ease the transition for the worker, to help him or her move to a different job, sometimes, although certainly not always, with a different employer. *Strategies aimed at easing the adjustment to technological change* are also worker-oriented, but there is a recognition that the change is definite and permanent. Finally, *job-replacement strategies* are applicable when there is a loss of employment; the old job is gone and a new one must be created. Employment security in this instance is not an uninterrupted state of affairs, but a promise of a better prospect for the future than would be the case without a job-replacement effort.

GUARANTEES AND OTHER NO-LAYOFF POLICIES

It may come as a surprise to many Americans that there are companies in the United States that guarantee continuous employment for their workers. Indeed, some companies even offer employees a written guarantee, although more often the guarantee takes the form of an implicitly understood no-layoff policy. Generally, companies with no-layoff policies require something in return from their workers, and most often that something is greater flexibility in the way tasks are assigned and work schedules arranged. No-layoff guarantees occur in both union and nonunion situations. Many unions have negotiated no-layoff clauses in their collective-bargaining agreements, the quid pro quo again being concessions or give-backs from the union, flexibility for management, or both.

Unless it is part of a collective-bargaining agreement, a no-layoff guarantee is never completely sacrosanct. There are instances in which a company has for years been able to go without ever having to lay off any of its employees, and then one day finds itself unable to honor its pledge. Companies that have no-layoff policies, however, do make every effort to protect employment security through thick or thin and whether the promise is in writing or not.

Many large European companies also have no-layoff policies. French and West German companies, particularly, often pride themselves on their ability to protect the employment security of their workers. However, these companies usually make a very careful distinction between a layoff and the kind of work-force reduction that they all allow and even encourage to take place by attrition and other means. In Europe too, it must be noted, layoffs for economic reasons are much harder to accomplish than in the United States. An employer wishing to lay off a portion of the work force must not only provide substantial advance notice, but also must get permission from the government employment agency to do it. The workers must also be paid substantial redundancy payments.

Five cases are presented here to illustrate the use of guarantees and other no-layoff policies to protect employment security: Donnelly Corporation, a manufacturer of automotive mirrors and other glass-coated products, guarantees its workers, in writing, against technological layoffs; Materials Research Corporation, a medium-sized company in the semiconductor industry, started with a "closet" no-layoff policy and moved to an explicitly stated written guarantee; Advanced Micro Devices, also in the semiconductor business, has a written policy; Hewlett-Packard, the computer industry giant, does not actually guarantee employment, but it has managed to avoid layoffs since the mid-1960s; and Nucor, the country's tenth largest steel company, has an implicit no-layoff policy backed by considerable management flexibility in work-force utilization. Despite the problems facing smokestack industries, Nucor has earned a profit every year, in part, it claims, because of its no-layoff policy.

EMPLOYMENT BUFFERING STRATEGIES

Management can use many different employment buffering options to keep its principal work force productively occupied despite cyclical shifts in demand or structural changes resulting from the introduction of new technology or other market shifts. Buffering usually starts from the premise that there is a core work force which must be protected—for which employment security is a must. Companies adopting a buffering strategy generally reflect a management philosophy that regards the employees as an important, if not the most important, resource the company has—an investment to be realized and not be wasted.

Companies that use buffering techniques tend to use them in conjunction with one another and not to rely on only one or two of the possible options. Such buffering techniques often begin with a program of deliberate understaffing, "staffing lean," thereby identifying the core personnel that is to be protected. In some instances, the staffing target is overtly stated, say at 70 percent to 85 percent of the level deemed necessary to meet normal demand. In many other cases, however, understaffing is more a "seat-of-the-pants" decision. In any case, the object is to use other methods, other employment categories— the buffers—to build up to full capacity in terms of human resources, with the expectation that if and when there is a downturn in the company's fortunes, the buffers will be expendable, thus leaving the core group intact. Such buffering techniques include the regularly scheduled use of overtime; hiring (and dismissal) of temporary staff; internal job assignment shifts; subcontracting (to outside vendors when things are going well, with the option to call the work back in-house when they are not); above- or below-average inventory building; and rescheduling of deliveries.

The experience of four American companies is described here. The companies are: International Business Machines (IBM), perhaps the company best known in the United States for its employment security record; Control Data Corporation, the computer industry multinational, which has developed several innovative approaches to employment security; McCord, a smaller company supplying parts for the automotive industry, whose successful employment security program impacts on, and has the support of, the entire community in which the company is based; and Honeywell, Inc., a high-technology engineering and manufacturing company that is working toward increasing the employment security of its employees throughout its many diverse and decentralized operations.

VOLUNTARY WORK-FORCE REDUCTIONS

Several kinds of voluntary work-force reductions as a means of bolstering employment security are considered. One is the use of work sharing, the reduction of work hours and pay, with or without short-time compensation. Another is the lending-out of temporarily surplus workers, internally to different parts of the company or externally to other employers either in the public or private sector. A third is voluntary early retirement, the standard staff reduction technique used throughout Western Europe today.

Work sharing with short-time compensation (STC) is a government-authorized program under which an employer can reduce the number of weekly hours worked by the company's employees, spreading the resulting unemployment evenly over the entire work unit, but with the affected workers being compensated for the lost work time through the unemployment insurance system. Very popular in Europe, work sharing with STC takes place in this country in only seven states—California, Arizona, Oregon, Florida, Illinois, Washington, and Maryland. Work sharing also occurs without government involvement and without compensation for lost time. By asking everyone to share the hardship of a temporary work shortage and to accept fewer hours of work and reduced pay during a slump is, in fact, how some companies make good on their no-layoff pledges. Lending out of surplus employees during a downturn in business is much more apt to be in the form of interim internal transfers than in the form of temporary external placements with outside employers. One can find examples of the use of such a strategy, but the practice is not widespread.

The cases illustrating temporary reductions include Motorola, a leader in the electronics industry, which was instrumental in getting Arizona's short-time compensation program established; and Signetics, a relatively new semiconductor manufacturer located in Silicon Valley, which has benefited from California's short-time compensation law. Another case, that of the West German automotive company Daimler-Benz, illustrates the fairly extensive and systematic use of intracompany lending of temporarily surplus workers.

European voluntary early-retirement programs are also described, with specific reference to particular companies where such programs have proved especially effective in providing employment security for the remaining workers. It should be noted, however, that voluntary early-retirement programs are not always voluntary: In many countries, they have gained a reputation of being "an offer that cannot be refused."

WORKER-ORIENTED ADJUSTMENT STRATEGIES

In business and industry, the ability of a company to respond quickly and efficiently to shifts in the market is the name of the game. Companies often switch to new and different products, redefine their particular markets, or make changes in what they do and how they do it in order to retain or regain profitability and stay ahead of the competition. Some companies with a strong commitment to employment security for their workers utilize the market itself to support their full-employment policies. Sometimes this means forgoing a market advantage. For example, several well-known companies restrict their acceptance of government contracts to avoid an exceptional expansion that could not be sustained over a long period and thus would necessitate laying off workers sometime in the future. Other companies have found a way to successfully exploit the market by pioneering new techniques or processes that allow them to produce at a low cost.[1]

There are times, however, when even the most astute and dedicated managers cannot forever forestall or completely mitigate the impact of market changes on their business. As workers are displaced by unavoidable and unrelenting structural changes in demand due to shifts in world trading patterns, technological change, or other market factors, employment security policies can be, and often are, directed at helping the workers themselves adjust to the new situation. Retraining programs feature importantly among the adjustment techniques that companies support in the name of employment security. Unions have been especially interested in retraining programs, sometimes underwriting such efforts on their own but more often negotiating with employers to make retraining available to their displaced members. However, retraining is not the only adjustment strategy that is utilized. Redeployment of staff to different positions, usually accompanied by a company-supported training program, is another. A third technique is outplacement, in which a company supports a program that generally includes intensive counseling, job-search assistance, job development and placement, and in some cases, relocation to distant jobs. Here the government can and sometimes does play an important role, providing direct financial support in some cases, more often contributing specialized expertise through its local employment-service agencies.

Planning in advance for adjustment, of course, makes the process easier. Some companies put a high priority on such planning. Whereas most worker-adjustment strategies presuppose that the workers already have been or are about to be displaced, in Canada and Sweden some interesting programs have been developed to prevent unemployment by getting the adjustment measures in place and under way before a layoff occurs.

Examples of all of these adjustment techniques are included. Two cases are presented describing retraining as an adjustment measure. The first is the program being carried out as a result of a negotiated agreement between the United Automobile Workers (UAW) and the Ford Motor Company. The jointly run UAW-Ford Employe Development and Training Program, supported by a negotiated per-hour-worked contribution from the company, is making it possible for laid-off Ford workers to take training courses to better equip themselves for reemployment. The program also provides support for outplacement efforts, including counseling, development of job-finding skills, support for increased mobility, and some job development and placement. A second example of training to support employment security is a relatively new California program, under which a portion of the tax that private-sector employers pay to support the federal/state unemployment insurance system is set aside in a separate fund for training and retraining. It is administered by the Employment Training Panel, which is drawn entirely from the private sector and includes representatives of both business and labor. At the present time California is the only state with such a program, but a similar one is currently under consideration by the state of Delaware.

The experience of the Dana Corporation, an important manufacturer in the automotive industry, provides a good illustration of a successful outplacement program during a plant shutdown. British Airways, the nationalized British airline, used redeployment as its principal adjustment technique when the company had to slim down and restructure in order to meet its competition.

Canada's Manpower Consultative Service and the Swedish Employment Security Council are interesting examples of multiservice adjustment agencies. Although the Canadian program is government-operated, the key element in its success is a tripartite committee—including representatives of both the company and the employees, but headed by an outside chairperson—which develops an adjustment program specifically tailored to each particular situation. The Swedish program is the result of a negotiated agreement between the white-collar unions and the Federation of Swedish Employers. A trust fund, supported by employer contributions, is used to develop and carry out appropriate adjustment programs in individual situations on a case-by-case basis.

EASING THE ADJUSTMENT
TO TECHNOLOGICAL CHANGE

Because the introduction of new technology is taking place at such a rapid pace and on such a large scale, affecting so many industries in both the United States and in Western Europe (and, indeed, throughout the industrialized world), measures to ease the process of adjustment for workers affected by such changes have been treated separately from other employment security strategies. Like the adjustment strategies described in the preceding section, these are also worker-oriented. For the most part they are also very progressive in that the managers and unions supporting them not only accept the future but embrace it. Four cases are described here.

The first is a joint company/union program, the UAW-Buick Employe Development Center. This program, like the UAW-Ford program, is supported by a negotiated company contribution to a jointly managed fund. It was developed by the company and union working together and provides up to two years of retraining for Buick workers who will be displaced by the introduction of new technology (for example, robots) designed to maintain the company's ability to compete in international markets.

A second case describes the initiative taken by the Amalgamated Clothing and Textile Workers Union to develop a new technology for the apparel industry, which will permit U.S. companies and workers to compete successfully with foreign imports. Supported jointly by the union and several large employers in the industry, introduction of the new technology will no doubt result in some job displacement, but without it, the union is convinced, there might not be any jobs at all.

In both of these cases, the union and management have worked together in a cooperative and forward-looking manner to prepare for the future. Another case where the unions' posture might be described as more defensive is the development of new-technology agreements (NTAs) in Great Britain. Many such agreements have been negotiated in recent years. Particularly successful in protecting the employment security of the workers without impeding technological progress has been the Job Security Agreement negotiated by the British Post Office and the Post Office Engineering Union, the union that represents most of the employees of British Telecom, the telecommunications part of the Post Office. This agreement establishes a detailed buffering plan to be used as technological displacement occurs and sets up a jointly managed mechanism for implementing the buffer system.

The last case is the Ruhr Coal Corporation in West Germany, the large state-supported monopoly that operates in an industry where new technology is an ongoing and ever-present challenge to managers. Ruhr Coal uses a long-established comprehensive work-force planning program to bring to bear all of the company's considerable resources on assuring employment stability for its employees, not only for the present but far into the future.

JOB-REPLACEMENT STRATEGIES

As the pace of change has quickened, many companies have faced the need to shed large numbers of their workers or to close down plants or processing facilities entirely. It is well known that sometimes the decision to close a plant or other facility is based on questionable or shortsighted management practices and does not truly represent a do-or-die, fold-or-fail situation for the company. In this book, we are not concerned with such cases but have focused on those situations in which the need for drastic restructuring is genuine—the kind of situation that is especially prevalent today among companies in older industries. Many European companies in this kind of situation have turned to job-replacement strategies to protect the employment security of their former workers. This strategy involves the utilization of company funds, as well as its expertise, to help new enterprises get started in locations affected by plant closures. The objective is to create new jobs to replace those lost by the cutback or closure. Sometimes the new jobs are taken by the dislocated employees, but often they are taken by other persons in the community. Whichever occurs, the community as a whole benefits as economic activity in the area increases.

Two kinds of job-replacement strategies are presented. In the first group are job-creation efforts that are initiated and supported directly by the companies undergoing restructuring. The experiences of two French companies are described: Rhone-Poulenc, the giant French chemical and pharmaceutical company; and Thomson, the multinational electric and electronics manufacturer.

In measures that are typical of big French companies, each has established a separate, wholly owned subsidiary to develop and encourage the establishment of new businesses in areas affected by the company's employment cutbacks. Each of these companies makes a special effort to provide jobs for its own workers, and with some degree of success. In Great Britain, a subsidiary of British Steel, BSC Industry, has been doing much the same kind of thing as the French companies for the last ten years, but its principal focus is the improvement of the economy of the area. BSC Industry has pioneered in the establishment of workshops, often using its own abandoned facilities to provide inexpensive space and a "nursery" environment for budding entrepreneurs.

In a unique Swedish program, Landskrona Finans, the local governments, a nationalized shipbuilding company, the union, and other employers in the area have joined together to capitalize and operate a development and finance agency to establish new businesses on the site of a shipyard that was being closed. Some national government support was also involved, since the shipyard was owned by Swedyard, the nationalized shipbuilding company, but for the most part, the new venture is a private-sector initiative. By developing and implementing a plan before the yard was completely closed, Landskrona Finans has been able to help maintain the level of economic activity in the area, and by itself has been responsible for the replacement of about 30 percent of the lost jobs.

Another kind of job-replacement activity is sponsored by community-based agencies, rather than directly by the companies responsible for the displacement. The Downriver Community Conference provides the single U.S. example of a job-replacement strategy. Downriver is a consortium of 16 local governments, located "downriver" from the Detroit area. With dynamic leadership and a dedicated and imaginative staff, this organization has moved from being a provider of government-funded training programs to being a community catalyst, which brokers the development of new job-creating business, including defense contracts, for companies in the area. Another interesting community-sponsored job-creation initiative, this one the result of joint actions on the part of the unions and the local government, is an informal employment council in Munich, West Germany. The council includes representatives of all of the major institutions concerned with employment and unemployment in the area: employers, unions, educators, and local and federal government. By sharing information and coordinating efforts, the council is finding ways to ensure employment security for the Munich-area labor force. A final case describes the growth of local enterprise agencies in Great Britain. These agencies, established with the help of Business in the Community (BIC)—itself a voluntary association of large British employers—combine the resources and talents of all elements of a local community to support the development of new enterprises. One highly successful agency is the New Work Trust in Bristol.

THE FOREIGN EXPERIENCE

The European experience requires a special word of explanation. Employment security policies as they are carried out in the private sector necessarily reflect the context in which companies and unions operate. Since employment practices and industrial relations in Western European countries differ markedly from those in the United States, employment security practice and policies also reflect those differences.

In most Western European countries government plays a much more significant role in the conduct of business and employment practices than is the case in this country. The prevalence of government-subsidized or nationalized industries in these countries results in greater government involvement and control of employment practices. But even in the private sector, government regulation affects managerial decisions, for example, by inhibiting the freedom of employers to hire and fire workers, particularly if the dismissal is for economic reasons. Government is also more involved in training and retraining than is the case in the United States. In France, employers are *required* to spend an amount equal to 1.5 percent of revenues for retraining purposes. West Germany supports a substantial vocational education system with close ties to business and industry. The system provides training both for new entrants into the labor force and for adults retraining for new or different occupations. Sweden subsidizes employers to train workers who might otherwise be unemployed. In the United Kingdom, the government's Manpower Services Commission has launched several new training programs to place young people in job-training situations with employers and to enable small employers to adopt new technologies. One retraining program of special interest to Europeans is the Fiat Company's program in Italy, which, with the help of government, provides displaced Fiat workers with up to two years' leave with full pay and benefits, to acquire whatever training is necessary to equip themselves for new careers and reemployment.

Collective bargaining and the conduct of industrial relations in European countries also differ from the norm in the United States. The West Germans have their system of codetermination, which provides for labor participation in corporate management. In Sweden, almost the entire labor force is organized by the trade unions, and collective bargaining takes place on a national basis between associations of unions and the confederation of employers. Similarly, France has a relatively high degree of unionization, although bargaining in that country is often carried out in the political arena. Industrial relations in Great Britain are closer to the American pattern, but even there unionization is greater and relations between employers and unions more confrontational than in this country.

Finally, the European economies appear to have been harder hit by world recessions, particularly the last recession, which is still going on in some countries. Unemployment is high, and in some countries was continuing to rise even in 1984. Many industries are staggering. In all of Western Europe, companies in the older industries, spurred by their governments, are facing the need to adopt new technologies, slim down, and restructure their operations. The issue uppermost in the minds of many European employers at the moment is not employment security for current workers but, as they put it, "managed redundancy." They are looking for ways to shrink their work forces, not to safeguard jobs. Luncheon conversation among industrial managers is more apt to be an exchange of boasts concerning how many workers each has shed, or will be able to shed, rather than an exchange of ideas about how to preserve the employment opportunities of those workers who are still on the payroll. Even the unions, or at least some of them, appear to have accepted the need to streamline work forces in order to become more competitive and are concentrating on getting the best possible deal for the members who must be let go.

Despite the economic climate, most Europeans have not lost interest in employment security. Indeed, their concern may even be strengthened. Interesting developments are taking place. New ways are being found and tried to support and improve the employment security of European workers. It is true that the context is not the same, but good ideas can be made to work in different situations, even if they are modified somewhat in the transfer process.

Webster's dictionary defines security as both "the condition of being protected or not exposed to danger" and as "a feeling of confidence, assurance." The implicit promise in employment security policies as they are carried out today by U.S. and Western European employers and in the current practices described in this book incorporates both meanings. For employers, good employment security practice provides protection against loss of work-force skills and all of the hazards and costs of repetitive hiring and firing. Similarly, workers who are the beneficiaries of good employment security practices are protected against the worst effects of the changes in a free-market economy. The feelings of confidence and assurance that stem from an effective employment security program also do not discriminate between employers and employees. Both benefit; both emerge stronger, more resilient, more willing to experiment and to change. Both become less defensive, less rigid. In the end, of course, it is society as a whole which is the winner.

NOTES

1. Fred K. Foulkes and Anne Whitman, "Full Employment Marketing Strategies and Other Considerations," an unpublished paper commissioned by Work in America Institute, February 1984.

2.
Guarantees and
Other No-Layoff Policies

One of the first companies to give its employees a guarantee against layoff was the meat-packing and food-processing company Hormel, of Austin, Minnesota. Although the guarantee was not in the form of a written promise never to lay off any workers for economic reasons, Hormel did and still does guarantee an annual income to its employees in return for a certain flexibility in scheduling work time. Hormel's guarantee was the subject of a special amendment to the federal Fair Labor Standards Act, which limits the number of hours that can be worked without the payment of overtime to eight per day and forty per week. Adopted in the late 1930s, the so-called "Hormel exception" provides a waiver in situations where employees have agreed through collective bargaining to calculate work hours on an annualized basis in return for a guaranteed income. To qualify, a company must guarantee the workers an annual income equal to at least 1,840 work hours per year. Overtime rates must be paid when the number of hours worked exceeds 2,080 hours a year. The income guarantee is still in effect at Hormel, assuring Hormel workers pay for at least 36 hours of work per week, or 1,872 hours per year. For Hormel, the ability to schedule irregular working hours made it possible to overcome the problems of seasonality, a characteristic of the meat-packing industry, and to offer its employees a degree of employment security not often found in that business. Hormel puts a high priority on employment security and is known to do things in very unorthodox ways, even sacrificing profit in order to maintain an adequate level of work for its employees.

Another company with a history of interest and concern with employment security is Caterpillar, the multinational giant in the farm- and heavy-equipment industry. Caterpillar has long prided itself on its employment security record, even though world recessions and international competition have forced the company to cut back its employment and even shut down some plants in recent years. As late as 1977, no one could be dismissed at Caterpillar, not even a sweeper, without the specific approval of the chief executive. Since first-line supervisors are generally not anxious to deal directly with the CEO, the result was that very few employees were ever laid off.

The agreement between American Airlines and the Transport Workers Union (TWU) is a more recent case involving a trade-off between an employer and employees to achieve a work guarantee. In 1983 the members of the TWU reached an agreement with American Airlines in which the union members accepted certain changes in work rules and concessions in wages in return for a no-layoff guarantee and lifetime job security. The three-year contract called for moderate wage increases and guaranteed TWU workers full-time jobs until they reached retirement age. In return, American Airlines won the right to hire new workers at a lower starting rate, increase the number of part-time workers who could be hired, and change the work rules to allow the company to use ground crew and maintenance workers in other jobs. Being able to shift workers into other jobs as needed has proved particularly beneficial to the company and has helped American Airlines maintain its ability to compete. Although many union members were at first skeptical about the job-shifting arrangements, the new flexibility is apparently now well regarded by both sides. A spokesperson for the workers has stated that not only do the workers generally feel more secure, but job satisfaction has increased. With the addition of more tasks, "there is a feeling that we are more important, more valuable to the airline." In the same newspaper account, a company spokesperson is quoted as saying, "It increases the productivity of everybody. . . . The bottom line is that we are finishing the work with fewer people."[1]

In this chapter the experiences of five companies which have instituted and followed policies guaranteeing their workers against layoff for economic or technological reasons are described. Understandably, such guarantees do not protect workers against dismissal based on poor performance. Nor are the guarantees always all-inclusive. For example, in one case—the Donnelly Corporation, a manufacturer of automotive mirrors and other coated glass products—the guarantee protects workers against technological displacement but does not cover layoffs for economic reasons. Donnelly, however, has tried hard to assure continuous employment for its employees and, in fact, has been remarkably successful in promoting employment stability by adapting its marketing policies to changing economic fluctuations.

In three of the cases described here, the company's no-layoff guarantee is openly stated and even put in writing. In addition to the Donnelly Corporation, there is the case of Materials Research Corporation, a New York company in the electronics industry, which at first followed an implicit no-layoff policy but at a later date decided to go public insofar as its own employees were concerned and put its guarantee clearly on record. Another company in the same industry, Advanced Micro Devices, located in California's Silicon Valley, also found it more advantageous for the company to make its no-layoff guarantee overt, explicitly stated, and publicly recorded. In both of these companies, the guarantee provides protection against layoff for either economic or technological reasons.

Two other companies, Hewlett-Packard, one of the largest companies in the electronics industry, and Nucor, the tenth largest U.S. steel company, follow a no-layoff policy in practice but have not put it on record. Since the mid-sixties, Hewlett-Packard has had no significant economic layoffs and is well known for the imaginative, resourceful, and successful efforts it makes to keep all of its employees working. Nucor also has an enviable record, not having had a single layoff for economic reasons in more than 14 years. This is a remarkable achievement for a company operating in the steel industry, where shutdowns and layoffs during the recession affected as many as half of all steel workers.

DONNELLY CORPORATION

Donnelly Corporation is a privately owned manufacturing company with four plants in Holland, Michigan, and one in the Republic of Ireland. It employs approximately 1,000 people and has specialized for over 75 years in glass processing.[2] A principal supplier of mirrors for the automotive industry, Donnelly also produces glass products for the marine, aircraft, photographic projection, commercial refrigeration, and electronics display markets. It has pioneered technologies in glass processing, coating, and plastic molding. With annual sales of over $56 million for 1983, the company is a strong competitor in U.S. and international markets. Donnelly's plant in Ireland allows the company to market its products in the European Common Market on a competitive basis. With such close ties to the automotive industry, it might be expected that Donnelly's employment practices would follow the pattern typical of that industry, with employment levels shifting up and down in concert with "boom-or-bust" cyclical swings and with frequent large-scale layoffs and recalls. At Donnelly, however, such is not the case. Governed by a management philosophy that gives high priority to employment security, Donnelly has been able to maintain its employment at fairly steady levels. John F. Donnelly, chairman of the company, explains it this way: "I believe that most employers do not relish laying people off. . . . If we really felt the pain layoffs cause, we would not wait until recession was upon us before thinking about the bad results of layoffs and how to prevent them. . . . There are very practical benefits to employers if we can stabilize employment. Almost all of the benefits can be measured in dollars, and very significant numbers of dollars. . . . If we really looked at our people in terms of their potential, we would see a vast and untapped reservoir of responsibility, cooperation, initiative, and creativity. Properly organized, this reservoir can make our companies stronger and more competitive." To paraphrase, Donnelly pursues its employment security policies to avoid pain for both the managers and the employees, to reduce costs and reap the benefits of employment stability, and to make the company stronger and better able to compete.

Donnelly's employment security record has been good. The company was not able to insulate itself entirely from the impact of the devastating recession that hit the U.S. auto industry in the early 1980s but, in the four years preceding that period, Donnelly had not had a single involuntary layoff that involved people with five or more years of seniority. The company has an enviable reputation. To achieve this record, John Donnelly developed a three-step plan to raise the level of performance of the company and also to gain a larger measure of employment security for the workers. The first step focuses on serving the customer, thereby enabling the company to strengthen its market position and thus be better able to afford the up-front costs of employment security. In Donnelly's view, customer service is the key to a successful employment security policy. A company whose business is in a precarious position clearly will have difficulty establishing and maintaining a solid employment security program.

The second step in the Donnelly plan is to make certain that all parts of the company and all employees understand the importance of both good customer service and working together to achieve that goal. Communication plays an important role in the Donnelly program, and great efforts are made to assure that the message is clearly understood by everyone. The company's workers are organized into teams of approximately ten, with each team responsible for its own production and for setting its own standards and goals. Donnelly workers know that they share the responsibility for discovering new and better ways to produce Donnelly products. Regular open meetings of both management and workers are held to discuss ways service to the company's customers can be improved. In addition, the Donnelly Committee, which consists of elected representatives from all levels—one representative is elected for a two-year term for every 35 workers—meets monthly to consider grievances and to discuss compensation, benefits, and other equity issues. Communication and employee participation are the accepted way of life at Donnelly, but the goal is always to make the company stronger, to do it better, to serve the customers.

The third step of the Donnelly plan involves recognition of the principle that people should share in the benefits that accrue to the company from working "harder and smarter." As the company becomes stronger and more prosperous through the joint efforts of management and the employees, and thus able to better serve its customers, equity and fairness demand that all should share in whatever benefits result from that effort. At Donnelly this principle is implemented through a productivity gain-sharing plan that has been in operation for more than 30 years and that rewards employees for productivity improvements. Bonuses based on profitability are paid monthly.

Employment security is, of course, another kind of reward offered to Donnelly employees. Says John Donnelly, "This three-step program of customer service, employee participation, and systemwide equity should make the company stronger, and a strong company is basic to any plan for employment security." He continues, "We have to anticipate the fact that our plan for market leadership and employee participation in this effort should lead to better results and that these results should be shared, not only with customers and shareholders, but with employees. . . . We should look ahead to what employees want in return. If employment security is one of the items, then we should be trying to work out a plan that factors this into the total compensation picture."

At Donnelly the plan that has been in place since 1964 is this: All employees are guaranteed, in writing, against technological layoffs. Any person whose job is eliminated by technological changes or other work rationalization process can keep his or her job at the old rate of pay for six months. During that time, the employee can seek other work in the company, with the right to the first bid on any suitable job openings, even those that pay more than the old job. Workers who have been with the company for five years or more also enjoy an annual income guarantee equal to 90 percent of their base rate of pay.

In John Donnelly's view, forward planning is essential to the success of the company, and to its employment stability program. Planning is involved in every aspect of the company's business. It starts with the company's customers, its market. The strategy at the Donnelly Corporation has been to try to isolate the section of the market where it "will be able to excel." Then, Donnelly continues, "We commit ourselves to serving our customers so well that they will have to rely on us. . . . We work to get them to rely on us, to turn to us" so that the company will be more likely to have work and jobs when and if a recession hits. In looking ahead to meet the future needs of its customers, and not just its current ones, Donnelly prepares itself ahead of time to meet new demands, new needs. "We try always to have some work coming in," he says. Obsolete products and plants are scheduled for gradual phasing out in periods when new products are coming into production and new jobs are being created to which employees can be transferred.

Like many other companies that try to protect employment during periods of downturn, Donnelly has several strategies to avoid layoffs. During slow periods, the company produces for inventory and carries out extensive maintenance projects that are not usually undertaken when plants are operating at full capacity. Donnelly also takes advantage of downtimes to retrain its employees to keep up with changing technology. At the same time, Donnelly keeps an eye on the interests of its shareholders. "We want not only to be fair to employees, but also to shareholders. We want both sets of people to continue to invest in the company willingly," says Chairman Donnelly.

Planning precepts are also applied to the company's personnel management. John Donnelly feels strongly that "Our job is to run the business in such a way that people know ahead of time that they will share equitably if the company prospers, and then we must organize to make it prosper." He tells this anecdote to illustrate the point. Several years ago when the company's management was putting together a plan that called for a 20 percent increase in sales for the next year, it had listed all the equipment needed, inventory levels, additional lines of credit, and some key positions to be filled. Donnelly asked his colleagues, "What would you think of adding a goal to hire 15 percent more people?" After some moments of stony silence, someone asked, "Why would we want to do that?" His answer was that since the personnel plan called for hiring about that many people, the increase should be included as part of the company's stated goals. By so doing, the company would be putting itself clearly on record and letting its employees know that it considered job creation an integral part of the company's goals.

Apparently Donnelly employees do know and understand that the company is indeed interested in job creation and does, in fact, regard employment security as an important goal in itself. Its reputation is well known, and people flock to its doors to become employed there. Donnelly is one of the companies named in the recently published book *100 Best Companies to Work for in America*.[3] Despite the layoffs of 1982, Chairman Donnelly reports that the trust between employees and management that the company has worked so hard and long to build "is still there."

MATERIALS RESEARCH CORPORATION

"For a long time we were a company with a closet no-layoff policy, but now our no-layoff policy is up front." This is the way Dr. Sheldon Weinig, chairman and chief executive officer of Materials Research Corporation describes his company's present employment security policies. How and why the change was made, and with what results, provides an interesting contrast to the experience of some other companies with no-layoff, guaranteed-employment policies.[4]

Materials Research Corporation (MRC) is a medium-sized, nonunion company in the electronics and semiconductor industry. At the present time it employs about 1,000 people in five plants in and around Orangeburg, New York. From a labor-market point of view, it is high-tech country. IBM's main offices are located about 50 miles away, and there are many other companies involved in the computer and electronics industry in the same general area. MRC also has plants in France and, in August 1983, opened a new plant in the southern part of Japan, so it is a burgeoning multinational. However, it is the domestic operation which is the focus here.

The company was established 25 years ago by Weinig, a metallurgical engineer who decided to resign his position as a professor of metallurgy and to go into business for himself. Although it started as a consulting firm, the company soon grew into a more elaborate research operation through its work on U.S. government contracts. Finally, in the late 1960s, it became what it is today: a full-fledged materials and equipment production company dedicated to serving the electronics industry. Weinig was then—and is still—convinced that a key element in the advancement of electronic technology is the materials required to make devices. The company continues to be involved in research and development of such materials and has become an important supplier of the materials to the electronics and computer industries. It manufactures processing equipment and materials to make silicon-integrated circuits called chips. Its customers include such giants of electronics as IBM, Texas Instruments, Motorola, the Thomson Group (in France), and Siemens (in West Germany).

From the beginning, the company has had a no-layoff policy, but it was never advertised as such and never really discussed. Steady growth and expansion throughout the 1960s and 1970s made it easy to adhere to the policy. No one was ever laid off for economic reasons, and it was generally understood by the workers that a no-layoff policy did in fact exist. The basis for the policy was Weinig's firm belief that "People are very expensive assets, and you should always protect the assets of a company." Unlike some companies, concern with increased productivity was not a primary motive for adopting the no-layoff policy. More likely, it was simply an outgrowth of Weinig's management style. He clearly prefers an open, cooperative relationship with his employees. "Fair, but firm," he says, "that's the only way to be."

By the late 1970s, Weinig had decided that it was time to consider a change: to make a public commitment to the no-layoff policy and even put it in writing. The matter was discussed at one of the company's regular think-tank sessions for the senior staff where, in addition to routine corporation business matters such as budgets, plans, and marketing decisions, time was reserved in the evenings for more general sessions concerning management philosophy and style. Weinig recalls that on the evening when he brought up the no-layoff issue, there was a "hot discussion," with many of the senior executives strongly opposed. Their chief concern was that to give up the escape hatch implicit in an unwritten policy could not only be expensive for the company, but might also be ruinous. However, after listening to all the arguments, Weinig decided to go ahead. He did so for two reasons. First, he reasoned that, in fact, the so-called escape hatch was a mirage; it did not really provide an escape at all. If there truly was an understanding among the employees that such a policy existed, then to abandon it when it proved convenient or necessary to lay off workers would be just as upsetting to the workers as if there were no policy at all. They would feel just as vulnerable, just as angry, just as exploited as any other laid-off workers. And the company would never have the benefits, whatever they might be, of having had a no-layoff policy. The experience of Eastman Kodak illustrates his point. For many years Kodak had an unwritten no-layoff policy, and it was clearly understood by Kodak workers that employment with the company was employment for life. When increased competition and the recession forced Kodak to finally use its escape hatch and lay off hundreds of its workers, the Kodak workers—and indeed the entire community of Rochester—were shocked, hurt, and resentful. Weinig felt that he really had nothing to lose by an explicit policy.

Secondly, Weinig knew that he himself would feel better with a publicly stated no-layoff policy. "I would like to be counted for the things that I stand for," he said. Having reached this conclusion, he announced it to the entire work force at the annual pre-Christmas meeting at which the company's past performance and future prospects were reviewed. At the conclusion of that meeting, every employee left the hall with a new employee handbook in which the no-layoff policy was clearly and unequivocally stated. But instead of smiles, relief, or jubilation, the announcement was met with indifference. In fact, there was no apparent reaction at all. Employees were much more concerned with the more pressing issues of wage increases and future work schedules than with whether the no-layoff policy was in writing or not. No wonder, since at that time—in 1978—the company was still expanding and no threat, or even a hint, of a downturn was on the horizon.

By 1981, however, things had changed, and the worldwide recession forced the company to face a different sort of reality for the first time. Business slowed and MRC found itself with approximately 100 surplus workers out of the existing work force of about 700. The no-layoff policy was in place, in writing, but no specific planning had been done as to how to make good on the promise. Weinig and his managers, therefore, had to set out on an un-charted sea, undertaking a series of actions to implement the employment guarantee, more or less as the situation and logic demanded. Mistakes were made, and as Weinig says, "I wish I knew then what I know now."

The steps they took to protect employment were not earthshaking, not even particularly unusual. What made them different was the spirit in which they were undertaken. A commitment, a determination to fulfill the no-layoff pledge, is what made it possible to succeed.

The obvious first step was to stop hiring, in the hope that through attrition the work force would self-reduce to a manageable level. But in so doing, the MRC management discovered what might be called "Weinig's Law," that is, "When business turns down, attrition approaches zero." There was a lot of hoping and praying but very few voluntary quits. Clearly something more had to be done. Therefore, the second step was to find other work for the surplus employees to do. At that time, MRC subcontracted its three principal maintenance services to outside entrepreneurs. These services were the security services in the five plants, building maintenance and cleaning services, and the upkeep of the grounds. All three were on relatively short-term contracts and could be shed without too much difficulty. At that time, the company was organized into seven divisions: four production divisions, sales, marketing, and accounting. Each division manager was instructed to assign some of his surplus staff to the service operations, now set up as separate departments of the company. They did so, but in a very short time it became apparent that the program was not working. The managers were taking the opportunity to dump personnel that, for one reason or another, they wanted to get rid of, and this led to trouble. The workers so assigned felt stigmatized and, therefore, angry. Also, the managers were being given a chance to avoid the consequences of their own mistakes rather than being required to correct them. The result was that the system was changed. The service assignments were made on a 90-day rotating basis, with everybody, including supervisors, eligible for rotation. By including them in the rotation group, any potential resistance of the supervisors to a break-up of their own work groups was circumvented. The pay of workers on rotation assignment was fully protected; no one had to take a pay cut. Since everyone was taking his or her turn at the rotation assignment, no one had grounds for complaints. In fact, the entire system was called "KP" after the military method of rotating some not-so-pleasant assignments.

Over the one and one-half years that the system was in effect, several hundred employees took part. Only two left the company rather than accept the assignment. At the end of the 90-day period, the workers went back to their original jobs, or they could bid for whatever alternative openings were available at the time. Open bidding is the normal practice in the company. As it turned out, some individuals liked their rotation assignment so much that they bid for permanent jobs in the service departments at the end of the rotation period. Of course, these jobs were usually at the lower end of the company's pay scale. Obviously, in those cases where the previous wage level of such a worker was way out of line with the service department's wage scale, the company could not accept the burden of protecting the worker's salary on a permanent basis. Thus, a rule was adopted that limited the protection in such cases to 120 percent of the regular pay scale for the particular service job.

With these adaptations, the rotation program proved to be a success, but it was not enough. The company still had more workers than it needed to fill its orders. At this point, the management took a third step and turned to the use of task-force groups. These were temporary groups of between 15 and 40 people, mostly engineers and scientists, drawn from different parts of the organization and assigned to perform a specific task that needed to be done but which the company had not had the time or staff to do when business was booming. For example, one task group was assigned to make a much-needed inventory of all company equipment. Another group called on MRC customers to verify that the equipment supplied by the company was working properly—with the unexpected result that a few surprised customers then placed additional orders. It was important that the work be really necessary and not even perceived as make-work. To assure that this was so, each task force was given a deadline for completing the assignment; depending on the task, deadlines varied from several weeks to several months. In addition, to make the task-force approach more acceptable to the division managers, the costs were borne by the corporation and not charged to the divisions. This helped to assuage any worries these managers might have concerning the impact of such assignments on the bottom-line performance of their respective divisions.

Finally, when business got even worse for the company, some of the available time was used for education. Materials Research Corporation has always had a generous policy of support for further education of its employees. Any legitimate educational course employees want to take, whether directly work-related or not, is paid for by the company. About 15 percent of MRC's employees normally take advantage of this policy, three to four times the rate of participation typically found for such programs. In Weinig's view, further education of his employees is a useful and effective way of increasing the value of the company's human resources. So it was natural that education should also be regarded as a productive way to use excess time in implementing the no-layoff policy. It was decided to make the in-house educational program available to everyone just as outside courses are. Four classes were offered: public speaking, a management course for supervisors, a basic electronics and metallurgy course, and a course in interviewing. The last was added with the thought that when business picked up, the company would be hiring again, and therefore would need people with interviewing skills. The company turned to its staff to find the instructors but purchased the necessary curricula from established educational sources.

Altogether the employment security, no-layoff policy cost the company from $3 to $5 million over a two-year period. No exact accounting has been made. That was a lot of money to spend at a time when the company's profits dropped from over $4 million on $71 million in sales in 1980 to only $728,000 on $60 million in sales in 1982. The first half of 1983 was still bad, but by the end of the year, the worst was over; sales were up to $63 million and rising. As expected, there was considerable anxiety and some dissatisfaction among the stockholders, which showed up in the company's stock market performance. But on balance, Weinig believes that the no-layoff policy was worth the cost.

Two clear benefits have emerged. First, the company now has a much easier time recruiting and hiring the personnel it needs. Wages and salaries are competitive with the other high-tech industrial companies in the area. MRC is apparently regarded as a desirable place to work. The word is out, and as evidence to prove it, the company is now getting many unsolicited employment seekers. The no-layoff policy is even paying dividends for the company in its new venture in Japan. American companies that establish plants in Japan often have difficulty recruiting workers, especially blue-collar workers, who have heard that the layoff is normal practice in the United States in contrast to the Japanese system of lifetime employment. Materials Research

Corporation was able to assure potential recruits in Japan that the company has never laid off anyone and has a written policy to that effect.

The second major benefit concerns the attitudes of MRC employees, the issue of employee loyalty and its value to the company. Weinig does not kid himself about this. He does not credit the no-layoff policy with any miraculous transformation of the work force. In his view, those employees who were skeptical about the commitment of the company and the value of its employment security policy remain skeptical. As he says, "The U.S. worker is a natural born skeptic. It's really hard to get people to believe." But he also feels that the employees who already were comfortable with MRC, who "liked our style," became even more so, and in fact worked better and maybe harder. One group of workers was so moved by the company's commitment to the no-layoff policy that they offered to work every other Saturday, without compensation, to repay the company for its support of them during the crisis. The offer was gratefully acknowledged and refused, but "it was nice to get it."

Was the program successful because of any particular characteristics of the work force? Apparently not. Although many skilled professional and technical people are employed by the company, it also employs semiskilled workers. Nor is there any particular concentration of workers by age or sex. The work force includes young and old, men and women, workers from two-earner families, and those who are the only support of their families. People still leave for other jobs, of course. "We're not changing the migratory nature of the U.S. worker," says Weinig.

What would have happened if the company had even more severe problems and there were an even greater number of surplus workers? Weinig is not sure. Some layoff-avoidance measures often used by other companies were not used and, in fact, were never considered. For example, the company never went to a shortened workweek. Nor did it consider work sharing. The possibility of a pay cut was also ruled out, in part because the problem was not competition but a lack of orders which, in turn, was the result of the general recession affecting the entire industry. Cutting costs to beat the competition would not have helped—the competition was also in trouble.

Would the company staff lean, that is, at a lower level than necessary to meet normal demand, in the future? Weinig admits that this is probably already the case, at least unconsciously. One employment buffer that the company has used from time to time is the hiring of temporary workers to meet sudden expansions in demand. However, to guard against their misuse, the company has a strict limitation of only six months' employment for them. Thus, there was never any question of using temporaries to protect the permanent work force.

Weinig reports that people regard him as being totally committed to the company's employment security policy. And he is. But, as he says, "I'm no fool. I won't commit suicide." Recognizing that there is no way to foresee all possible future contingencies, Weinig believes that a flexible approach, based on trust and cooperation, is the only way to manage. "When there is a problem," he says, "we will work our way out of it together." Pointing to his experience in the last recession, he says, "We survived."

ADVANCED MICRO DEVICES

A stable work force and a family of loyal employees is an ideal to which virtually every company pays at least lip service. Loyal employees who identify their own interests with those of the company are presumed to be better motivated and productive. At the same time, the costs of recruiting, orienting, and training new employees to replace those who leave are known to be costly, although difficult to measure precisely.

Advanced Micro Devices (AMD), headquartered in Sunnyvale, California, has—like other companies in the semiconductor industry concentrated in California's Silicon Valley—special and immediately urgent reasons for valuing employee loyalty.[5] In the first place, there is within the relatively new and burgeoning industry fierce competition for a limited supply of creative engineering talent. Secondly, and perhaps more important, the industry is heavily dependent on ideas and technical know-how, and it is inevitable that employees take some of these ideas and knowledge with them when they depart.

AMD pays more than lip service to the ideal of company loyalty and, like other companies in the industry, is able to make a heavier-than-average investment for two reasons. First, it is a growing and profitable industry. Second, and perhaps more important, labor is a relatively small component of the industry's products. Rumor in the industry has it, by way of example, that there are only two hours of labor (at least, human labor—automation is big and growing) in a new and widely advertised computer that bears a $2,500 retail price tag. While the rumor may or may not be precisely accurate, it is undoubtedly true in a general and comparative sense, and it underscores the negligible importance of hourly labor costs for that particular product. It explains, at least in part, why AMD—in the absence of union pressure in an almost totally unorganized industry—automatically provides attractive salaries, a thick package of fringe benefits, and profit sharing.

AMD, however, needs a degree of employee loyalty that it suspects cannot be bought with high wages or fringes or even profit sharing. Company spokesperson Elliott Sopkin, vice-president for Communications, says: "You cannot buy loyalty with a paycheck. It doesn't work. To earn its employees' loyalty, the company itself must exhibit loyalty." Within that philosophy lies the genesis of AMD's no-layoff policy.

AMD rather informally instituted its no-layoff policy in January 1980 and, even in the absence of any explicit commitment, stuck to the policy throughout the recession, relying primarily on a partial hiring freeze to absorb the shock of the recession. Even the freeze, however, was flexible and not total: In anticipation of better days, the company continued to hire engineers throughout the recession. It also filled other key, nonengineering jobs, whether created through attrition or growth.

By 1983, the company had weathered what it deemed to be, and what turned out to be, the worst of the recession with its no-layoff policy intact. Although AMD Board Chairman and President W. J. Sanders III, had referred to the company's no-layoff policy frequently in newspaper articles, speeches, and memos to employees, it had not yet been formalized by inclusion in the company's written policy. The time was now ripe for such a statement, and it took the form of a terse, single paragraph in the policy book. All employees on the payroll at the time were guaranteed continuing employment as long as they continued to meet company performance standards. Currently, the policy applies to new employees after they complete one year of satisfactory service, and it applies in all the company's departments and plants and to all employees, including, in theory at least, the board chairman and president.

The company's decision to formalize the no-layoff policy reflected, in part, satisfaction with the policy. ("While it couldn't be measured, it was obvious," says Sopkin, "that something was happening. Production reflected it.") In part, it probably also reflected the young and growing company's relative freedom from much necessity for layoff. In its 15-year history it had resorted to layoff just once—in 1974, when some 150 employees (a considerable portion of the work force at the time) were furloughed.

Founded in 1969, the company has seen its sales grow from $25.8 million during the year ending March 1975 to $583 million for the year ending in March 1984. This, the company claims, makes it the fastest growing company in the semiconductor industry, the fifth largest U.S. company in the industry, and the ninth largest worldwide.

AMD has 14,000 employees in plants and sales offices around the world, including manufacturing facilities in Manila, Singapore, and Penang, as well as in Austin and San Antonio, Texas, and Sunnyvale and Santa Clara, California. A major assembly plant is under construction in Bangkok. More than a third of its employees work in Sunnyvale, but the company has been taking what it terms a "Texas tilt." AMD employees tend to be young and well-educated; perhaps more than half, including production workers, have had at least some college. Minorities and women appear to be fairly well represented.

Sopkin credits Sanders with articulating and fostering what he calls a "caring-about-people philosophy," which led to the no-layoff policy, and claims that the policy enjoys the unanimous support of supervisors as well as top management because "it makes their jobs easier." The benefits of the no-layoff policy were most dramatically demonstrated, according to Sopkin, during the recent recession. He says: "You have to realize just how awful the recession was. Other plants in the area and in the industry were announcing layoffs—almost daily, sometimes over plant loudspeakers. By reducing hiring, we stuck to our policy and suddenly found ourselves witnessing dramatic improvements in production. It is hard to resist the conclusion that the increased efficiency was directly attributable to appreciation for our no-layoff policy. Certainly, it was due in large measure to that increased efficiency that we were able to come through it without showing a loss in any quarter. Equally certain, we came through the recession with our production teams intact and able to take advantage of improved demand. Sure, it may have cost some money to keep everyone on the payroll at the trough of the recession, but it was an investment that we had to make in order to avoid losing qualified people."

The company is anxious to reduce turnover among production workers, but the people AMD is most eager to hang on to are engineers, because they are the hardest to recruit. Somewhat ironically, this is the group to whom the no-layoff policy probably means least in any practical sense. Their skills are in great demand, and they tend to be not much concerned about security. AMD seeks to win their loyalty—indeed, in a sense, their partnership—by supplementing the no-layoff policy with stock ownership plans and options. In addition, the company offers the tax advantages of deferred salary options, educational reimbursements of up to $2,500 per year, and a closed-circuit television link to Stanford University's Honors Cooperative Program. Engineers also benefit from the profit-sharing plan, which distributes 10 percent of pretax earnings to the entire work force, partly in cash and partly in retirement fund credits. In June 1984, for example, the company distributed $8 million for the six-month period ending in March 1984.

One percent of pretax profits is earmarked for charities of the company's choice and definition. Half the charitable contributions are reserved, for admittedly self-serving motives, for engineering scholarships. The company allots the remaining half to "charities that touch our people." Libraries are frequent recipients.

AMD has not estimated the dollar value to the company of the no-layoff policy in reducing the cost of turnover. The company is very much aware, however, of the cost of turnover and the effect of layoffs in increasing that cost. Sopkin says: "Losing people is not cheap." The more highly skilled employees are thought not to reach peak production for two years and, even at the lowest skill level, that of hand assemblers, maximum production is not attained for at least six to eight weeks. Automation is eliminating many of the lower-skilled jobs and thus has the effect of increasing the skill level of the work force as a whole. The ultimate effect, the company feels, is to increase the cost of turnover and, additionally, to enhance the value of the no-layoff policy.

Except for reducing hiring, as it did during the recent recession, the company has no strategies for maintaining its no-layoff posture in the face of hard times more severe than those already successfully weathered. Sopkin readily concedes, however, that modification or abandonment of the no-layoff policy, while seen as totally unlikely, is not unthinkable: "Our first responsibility is to the stockholders, and we are just not going to threaten the viability of the corporation. But I cannot now envision any circumstance in which we would be forced to reassess our policy."

Sopkin and other company officials probably do not view abandonment as a real danger because they are convinced that company and industry growth provide abundant insulation. Having come through the recession without having to resort to layoffs, or even to any reduction in working hours, Sopkin is convinced that a no-layoff policy is "a good deal" for management, supervisors, and employees. "It's just something that you know is right," he says. Although he concedes that maintaining unnecessary workers on the payroll at the depth of the recession cost the company some money, when asked to list some of the disadvantages for the corporation of the no-layoff policy, he replies: "There are absolutely no disadvantages."

While an accurate evaluation of the success of AMD's no-layoff policy in winning employee loyalty and reducing turnover would require comparison with similar companies and statistics not readily available in the fiercely competitive and secretive semiconductor industry, there is anecdotal evidence that AMD's employees appreciate the policy and respond with improved performance.

One employee, identified only as "Sally," wrote the company thanking it for the policy and reporting that it had enabled her to receive a home mortgage loan. "The bank," she wrote, "told me that at my wage level they would not have given me the loan had it not been for AMD's no-layoff policy."

HEWLETT-PACKARD

Hewlett-Packard, founded in 1939, is both a veteran and a giant in the young electronics and computer industry. It is identified by Frank Williams, manager of Corporate Personnel Administration and Operations, as about ten times "smaller than IBM."[6] It is—depending on who is making the comparisons and when—the third or fourth largest company in the industry worldwide. Sales for 1984 were estimated to be over $6 billion, up from $4.9 billion in 1983. It has 78,000 employees worldwide, with some two-thirds of them in the United States.

The company's desire to avoid layoffs—which it is scrupulously careful to avoid formally labeling as a policy—dates back to its early years when it had an opportunity to obtain a government contract that would have necessitated hiring additional people and increasing its work force by approximately 10 percent. The original and present Board Chairman David Packard asked what would happen to the 12 new employees once the contract was completed and was told that they would have to be let go. "In that case," said Packard, "we won't take the contract."

Since then, of course, the company has taken many similar and far larger contracts but has developed a strategy similar to IBM's of avoiding fluctuations in the work force through the use of subcontracting as a buffer. "Routinely," says Williams, "we subcontract more in boom times, less in tight times."

To outsiders, employees, and even some company supervisors, the company's no-layoff stance is implicit in its management of personnel, even though there is no explicit guarantee. Williams explains the company's approach in these words: "We try to operate the company in a manner that assures that everyone has a job."

It has been remarkably successful in doing so. The largest layoff in the company's history occurred in 1945 following the boom times of World War II. In the mid-1960s there was another layoff in a newly acquired small company, but fewer than 30 people were severed; with those two exceptions, there have been no layoffs due to lack of work.

This record has been achieved in a company of 78,000 employees through the planned use of a variety of strategies. As mentioned, subcontracting is routinely and continuously used, or refrained from, as a method of stabilizing the size of the work force, but other strategies are also employed. Control over hiring is an often-used tool to react to business cycles. In the early 1970s the company experienced a downturn in orders, which meant its productive capacity was about 10 percent in excess of its incoming orders. This problem was dealt with by a hiring freeze and by utilization of what the company called "the nine-day fortnight."

Rather than resort to layoffs, the company reduced production by giving all employees each alternate Friday off without pay, which meant a 10 percent reduction in earnings. The plan was in effect for about six months, until orders rose to match productive capacity.

The nine-day fortnight was, of course, work sharing but no one at Hewlett-Packard called it that. A third of the company's 52,000 U.S. employees work in California's Silicon Valley. Had the nine-day fortnight occurred after the passage in 1978 of California's Shared Work Unemployment Insurance (SWUI) program, these employees could have recouped part of the lost wages through partial unemployment compensation benefits. If it were necessary to institute the nine-day fortnight in the future, Williams says, he would certainly investigate how the SWUI program might be useful to Hewlett-Packard's California employees.

Employee response to the nine-day fortnight in the early 1970s was excellent and there were frequent expressions of gratitude to the company for utilizing that strategy rather than resorting to layoffs. Recalls Williams: "I heard a lot of people say that 90 percent of a paycheck was much better than no paycheck. I think that was the consensus."

Both management and employees seem to agree that the strategy caused minimum damage and provided maximum protection for the interests of both the employees and the corporation. A major advantage was that it preserved the work force intact and left the company the capability of immediately responding to any upturn in demand without the delay and expense of recalling laid-off employees or hiring and training new ones. Williams says that the company would certainly consider using the tactic again should the need arise.

While subcontracting, hiring freezes, and work sharing have all been utilized, and may be utilized again, by Hewlett-Packard to avoid layoff, Williams regards them all as temporary and emergency expedients. The really effective weapon against layoffs for Hewlett-Packard is research and development of new and better products. About 50 percent of the company's sales this year will be accounted for by products which were not invented five years ago. "Of course," Williams points out, "that might not work so well for a company not in high technology."

He believes that the company's employment and other operational practices are evidence of, and are shaped by, its interest in the long haul rather than the short term. He doesn't talk about winning or earning employee loyalty. "If you get the reputation for being a hiring and firing kind of shop," he says, "you don't get good employees in the first place. We like to think that avoiding problems is almost always cheaper and better than solving them."

The company's wage and fringe package, it says, is "above standard" for the industry, and it was put in place as a result of its own philosophy rather than in response to union pressures since the company, like most of the industry, is unorganized. Similarly, the company's employment and compensation practices are designed independent of union concerns.

Hewlett-Packard has manufacturing facilities in about 10 countries, and its foreign plants have tended to follow its markets rather than cheap labor. "Labor costs in this industry," says Williams, "are just not that large a portion of the total cost." Hewlett-Packard also has major manufacturing facilities in the United Kingdom, West Germany, France, Puerto Rico, and Japan.

The company's U.S. labor force is young and well educated with women and minorities well represented. More than 40 percent of the 52,000 U.S. workers are women, and approximately half are professional and managerial. Williams calls the work force as a whole "very highly motivated." Average tenure with the company is four to five years due to the sustained rapid growth.

The company's commitment to avoiding layoff is so long-standing that it seems to have come to be accepted without question or even without much continuing evaluation by top management. "I don't know," said Williams, "what the disadvantages of not having a no-layoff commitment would possibly be unless you're looking at the very short term and we try to avoid that. The advantages of maintaining a stable and well-motivated work force without the bother, expense, and disruption of hiring and firing are pretty obvious. We think it's the right thing to do. And we think it's the smart thing to do."

Supervisory personnel occasionally grumble about not being able to lay off employees. Williams says that periodically management has to explain that "no layoff" does not mean "no firing," and that it is not intended to protect incompetents from discharge. Asked about the comparative number of Hewlett-Packard discharges, Williams said, "We make our share of hiring mistakes."

NUCOR

A visitor to Charlotte, North Carolina, looking for Nucor, the tenth largest steel company in the United States, might have a hard time finding it, particularly if the visitor expected the company to be housed in the kind of imposing, even dramatic surroundings typically associated with the headquarters office of a *Fortune* 500 company. But Nucor, a company with 3,700 employees and expected sales of more than $600 million in 1984, has its headquarters in an unprepossessing four-story office building in a residential area of the city, surrounded by fast-food stores and gas stations, and across the street from a small shopping center. It is the kind of building where one might expect to find the offices of the local real estate agency or the neighborhood orthodontist. Nucor's corporate headquarters, unadvertised except for an alphabetical listing on the lobby directory next to the single elevator, takes up only part of one floor of the building. The entire corporate staff numbers 16 people, and this includes everybody, from Kenneth Iverson, chairman and chief executive officer, to the five-person clerical staff. The typical corporate departments, such as purchasing, research, sales, and so on, are missing from Nucor's corporate structure. Instead, each of Nucor's five main operating divisions performs these functions for itself. Only the personnel, planning, and finance functions are performed at the corporate level.

Nucor is a highly successful specialty steel company which has made a profit every year, despite the recession and competition from imports which have put the U.S. steel industry through the wringer. While other steel companies were closing plants and laying off thousands of workers, Nucor has continued to make good on its boast of never having laid off a single worker due to business conditions, a 14-year record. The company's steel division, with minimills in South Carolina, Utah, Nebraska, and Texas, produces bar and other structural and specialty steel products. All of the mills use the highly efficient electric arc furnaces, for which steel scrap is the primary raw material. The company's six Vulcraft plants make steel joists, girders, and steel decks for building construction. Like all of the company's operations, these plants are located in predominantly rural areas, some near the mills and others in Alabama and Indiana. Other operating divisions of the company produce cold-finished steel products and grinding balls. There is also a small division in Phoenix, Arizona, which produces high-purity, rare earth metals and compounds. This is the only nonsteel operation in the company.

How has Nucor managed to keep its head above water, and even thrive, when every other steel company in the country has been struggling to stay alive? John Savage, manager of Personnel Services for the company, attributes the company's success to two factors: its human-relations system, and its use of the most advanced technology available. The human-relations system is of primary interest here.[7]

Four basic principles underlie the human-relations system at Nucor:

- The company tries to create and implement a compensation system that relates work performance to productivity. As a result, every employee of the company is paid on an incentive bonus system.
- The company believes that job security is essential to productivity—that people will not and cannot be expected to work at the peak of performance if they are concerned that they will be laid off, especially if they feel that increased productivity will result in a need for fewer workers. Although the company has no written job-security guarantee, its no-layoff policy is made known and apparently is well understood by the employees.
- Employees must believe that they are being treated fairly.
- Employees must have an avenue of appeal when they believe they are being treated unfairly.

Since 1966, when Kenneth Iverson took over the company, Nucor has faithfully followed these principles. The compensation system is particularly interesting.

Although everybody works on an bonus incentive plan, from a plant sweeper to the president of the company, actually there are four separate bonus systems. The largest covers the production workers, about 2,800 people. These workers are divided into bonus groups, that is, a natural grouping or work crew whose jobs are linked and who, together, are responsible for a measurable output of a particular product. The groups consist of between 15 and 40 workers and include both the maintenance personnel and the line supervisors. In a steel mill, for example, there will be nine bonus groups, three in each shift. One group is involved in the melting and casting operation and the bonus is based on good billet tons per hour for the week. Another group will work on the rolling line, where the bonus is based on good sheared tons produced. The third is in the straightening section, where the bonus is on good straightened tons produced. A bonus group in one of the plants producing steel joists could include workers involved in cutting, rod bending, rigging, finishing, and painting. Bonuses are paid on a group, and not on an individual, basis. This, of course, can lead to considerable peer pressure for all members of the group to perform efficiently and productively. New employees have a three-month probation period, without bonuses. After that, they are paid on the same basis as the rest of the group and benefit from the same implicit job guarantee.

The bonus is paid on a very simple formula. Performance standards for each of the company's operations have been set at roughly 90 percent of the time it takes to complete a specific job. If the group exceeds the target, a bonus is paid proportionate to the improvement in productivity. For example, if the production target is met in 60 percent of the standardized time, a 60 percent bonus is added to the worker's regular pay. Moreover, there is no waiting for the reward. The bonus is paid immediately, in the worker's weekly paycheck. With the bonus system, Nucor has made remarkable improvements in productivity and, at the same time, Nucor employees have achieved excellent pay. Although the base hourly rate of pay is not as high as that paid to unionized steel workers in the big steel companies, most of Nucor's blue-collar workers earn between $28,000 and $32,000 a year, including their bonuses—about $5,000 more than other steel workers. Of course, when a production line is down and goals are not met, there is no bonus. During the recession, in 1981, and especially 1982, even Nucor was affected by the slowdown in orders. No plants were closed, but the company had to turn to four- and even three-day weeks in order to reduce costs and maintain employment. It was a difficult period for Nucor's employees, whose bonuses had often made up almost half of their total compensation.

Iverson himself was at one time somewhat concerned about the almost one-to-one ratio between base pay and the bonus but, on balance, decided to stick with his policy. His faith in the system has proved justified. Today, Nucor can turn out a ton of steel with only two direct labor hours of work. Even the best of the big steel companies can do no better than four or five labor hours per ton. Nucor's productivity is even better than that of many Japanese firms. Indeed, the productivity factor has enabled the company to cut the Japanese share of the California market for steel rods and bars, reducing it from 50 percent to 10 percent.[8]

One other point needs to be made about the bonus incentive system for Nucor production workers. Making steel is a capital-intensive industry, and this is especially true at Nucor, which has invested—and continues to invest—heavily in the most advanced steel-production technology. Since most of the cost of making steel is represented by the plant and equipment—a fixed cost regardless of output—not must is sacrificed by increasing the wages of workers, even by doubling them. Thus, bonuses are not quite as expensive as they appear.

Making the bonus incentive system work takes both careful planning and a fair degree of trust between management and employees. Insofar as planning is concerned, the managers have to have a pretty good idea of the real capacity of their plant—that is, the amount of product that can be produced on a more or less routine basis above the amount set in the standard—and to accept, or defer, orders accordingly. On the other hand, the workers have to be assured that the system is not just another name for a speed-up. It is for this reason that the standards have not been changed since they were established in 1969. One could legitimately raise the question of whether the bonus is really what it purports to be, a productivity incentive, or whether it is nothing more than a disguised wage increase based on productivity gains over time. There is probably no conclusive answer. What is important is that the system has led to productivity improvement, has enabled the company to compete successfully, and does in fact provide a cushion against the cyclical swings to which the steel industry is so vulnerable.

The three other bonus incentive plans at Nucor cover, respectively, the department managers; the indirect employees who are neither managers nor production workers, such as the accountants, engineers, and clerical personnel; and, finally, the top senior officers. Incentive bonuses for the department heads, that is, the managers of each of the divisions, are based on the performance of their respective divisions and particularly the contribution that the division makes to the company's profits. The bonus is figured on return on assets and can run as high as 51 percent of the individual's base salary. Similarly, the bonus for the indirect employees is based on either the division's return on assets or the corporation's return on assets, depending on where each individual works. Each month all employees covered by this plan are informed of how their division or office is doing. They are kept up-to-date as to exactly what the bonus payout will be. Bonuses to both these groups, however, are paid only once a year, not on a weekly basis as is the case with the production workers. The senior executive officers' incentive program is very much like the others, the difference being that the bonus is a chief source of compensation for this group. Nucor's top executives receive no profit sharing, no retirement plans, or other executive perquisites. If the company does well, the officers' compensation is well above average for a company that size. If not, they receive only their base salaries, which are set at about 70 percent of what an individual in a comparable position with another company would receive. In 1982, a bad year for the company (although it still showed a profit and paid dividends), President Iverson's total compensation was only one-fourth of what he had earned the previous year. Obviously this kind of joint risk taking and sharing of both good and bad fortune builds a solid trust between the management and the workers.

Nucor works hard to encourage this trust. Being fair and being perceived as fair are important elements of the company's basic human-relations philosophy. Management is completely open. The company tries hard to keep all employees fully informed about company affairs and especially about future plans. Iverson and Savage spend much of their time visiting one or another of Nucor's widely dispersed facilities, personally monitoring the progress and problems of each. Communication and the personal touch are the watchwords.

The complete absence of perquisites is one manifestation of Nucor's "fairness doctrine." Not only do the executives work in what, at best, can be described as modest surroundings (some have called them Spartan), but they enjoy none of the perks normally associated with top office in one of the *Fortune* 500s. Nucor has no such thing as reserved parking spaces, executive dining rooms (there is a Hardee's next door for everybody), or hunting lodges and fishing camps. There are not even any company cars. The company has no planes, and everyone flies coach, even the president. At one point, Nucor employees wore different-colored helmets to differentiate between grades in the plants. Managers wore one color, line supervisors another, and production workers still another. But when it was discovered that each group was being referred to by helmet color—the red hats, the green hats, and so on— the company quickly made sure that there would be only one color for everyone.

Further application of the fairness doctrine is seen in the company's grievance procedure. To ensure that anyone who feels that he or she is being treated unfairly has an avenue for the expression of the grievance, the company has an appeal process that is a model of simplicity. There are only five administrative levels at Nucor, and they are organized in a straight line. The organization chart has no staff boxes, no dotted lines. The president is at the top; below him, the vice-president and general manager; below him, the department managers; below them, the supervisory and professional personnel; and below them, other regular employees. Grievances and appeals go straight up the line. If at any point an employee who has a grievance is not satisfied with the decision of the supervisor, he or she can take the case to the next level. No separate appeals boards, no special procedures, no back-and-forth. If you don't like the way you are being treated, you can tell it to the president.

The system seems to work. Nucor employees say they like working for the company, and they stay.

The company tries in other ways to fully involve its employees in the business of the company. There is a profit-sharing plan (in lieu of a pension plan), a monthly stock investment plan in which some 700 workers participate, and an employee stock ownership plan, under which the company sets aside one-half of one percent of each worker's pay to acquire company stock. In addition, longevity of service is rewarded with company stock.

Underlying all of this is the company's commitment to employment security. Nucor has established its plants in rural areas for a variety of reasons, but a primary one was the belief that the work ethic would be stronger there. In general, the people whom Nucor employs are unskilled or semiskilled workers who have already had some work experience and who receive their job-specific training on the job. Most are men, although there are a few women in production jobs and in some supervisory positions. The company is non-union, and although promotion is based to some extent on seniority, it is not the single, or even the overriding factor. In going to the rural areas, the company recognized it would have to provide employment security to its workers in order to capitalize on what it perceived as the advantages a rural area would provide.

To recruit and hold workers who would be responsive to its emphasis on productivity, the company has to offer something in return. That something is money—through the bonus incentive system—and employment security. Indeed, the bonus system may well be the most important element of the employment security commitment at Nucor since it enables the company to compete successfully and to grow. But employment security is provided by a variety of other measures as well.

The company concedes that it staffs lean, at a level just sufficient to meet normal demand. It also relies heavily on overtime to meet surges in demand. It has no specific target as to what a lean staff should be but keeps a wary eye on market trends. Nucor does not have government defense contracts and therefore is spared the vicissitudes and/or the protection of that particular market. The most difficult decision for Nucor production managers is whether to add or subtract a production line, and often they find it is less costly to pay overtime than to add a line.

As indicated earlier, the company has used shortened workweeks occasionally, even going to three-day weeks. But no one has been laid off. Unlike other companies, particularly some of its competitors in the steel industry, Nucor does not use early retirement or subcontracting as a way to protect a core work force.

In a company dedicated to staying ahead in technology, there have been occasions when workers have been displaced by new technology. At the Darlington, South Carolina, steel plant, for example, where there were 530 workers, the introduction of automated equipment meant that about 10 percent of the jobs would eventually be eliminated. In this case, the company relied primarily on attrition to bring the work force down to the appropriate level. In addition, there was some redeployment of workers to other jobs in the company. Whenever this is necessary, however, the company "red circles" the worker's wage for a year; that is, he or she gets the same wage as before, even if the new job pays less than the old one.

For Nucor officials, it is the company's human-relations policy, with its emphasis on open communication, fairness, and employment security that provides the key to success. The record thus far supports that contention.

NOTES

1. Agis Salpukas, "Cutting Airline Costs: Job Shifts Aid Productivity," *The New York Times*, January 25, 1984.

2. Information on the Donnelly Corporation is drawn from an unpublished paper commissioned by Work in America Institute, "Strategies and Tactics Leading to Employment Security," by John F. Donnelly, June 1983, and from an interview with him, June 1984.

3. Robert Levering, Milton Moskowitz, and Michael Katz, *100 Best Companies to Work for in America* (Reading, Mass.: Addison-Wesley, 1984), pp. 84–87.

4. Information on Materials Research Corporation was obtained in an interview with Dr. Sheldon Weinig, chairman of the Material Research Corporation, Orangeburg, New York, May 1984.

5. This case study is based on an interview with Elliott Sopkin, vice-president for Communications, Advanced Micro Devices, May 1984.

6. This case study is based on an interview with Frank Williams, manager of Corporate Personnel Administration and Operations, Hewlett-Packard, May 1984.

7. Information on Nucor is drawn from materials provided by the company and from an interview with John Savage, manager of Personnel Services, Nucor, in Charlotte, North Carolina, May 1984.

8. Levering, Moskowitz, and Katz, *100 Best Companies*, p. 247.

3.
Employment Buffering Strategies

The use of an employment buffering strategy presupposes a desire on the part of the employer to protect employees against fluctuations in the market and to give the work force a high degree of employment stability. As discussed here, employment buffers are preplanned personnel policies that allow for an expansion and/or a contraction of available worker hours while at the same time protecting the employer's core work force. These policies are generally adopted by employers in a deliberate fashion to increase employment stability. Buffering practices which are generally regarded as normal methods of adaptation to changing market conditions include initial "lean staffing," use of overtime, hiring or layoff of temporary workers, changes in production scheduling, shifts in the kind and amount of subcontracted work, rescheduling of deliveries, deferral or acceleration of inventory building, and rearrangement of the kinds of work performed such as maintenance and in-plant improvements. All have the effect of buffering or protecting the permanent work force against the effects of either too many or too few orders.

Employers adopting buffering techniques may or may not guarantee continuous employment to their workers, although clearly the judicious use of buffers can and often does constitute a de facto guarantee. Nor is it always certain that employment security is the employer's chief concern. Employers have different motivations for the adoption of such policies. In some cases motivation may be linked to the employer's perception of employment security as a quid pro quo for employee loyalty and the key to continuous productivity improvement. Or motivation might simply be rooted in a deep-seated paternalistic attitude on the part of top management of the company. Or it might be related to the kind of labor market in which the company is operating, for example, a need to compete for scarce labor skills. But whatever the motivation, employment buffering policies have an important place in the range of employment security strategies that both management and labor make use of. Several examples of buffering policies by U.S. employers are described in this chapter.

Probably the most familiar buffering policies are those of International Business Machines (IBM), which has for many years protected the employment security of its employees with a successful and imaginative application of various buffering strategies. A principal motive behind IBM's employment security policy is its desire to encourage creativity and increased productivity among its employees. Control Data Corporation, another major company in the computer and data processing industry, sees employment security in much the same way as IBM, regarding it as a necessary element in the company's growth strategy. Control Data has experimented—and is continuing to experiment—with several interesting and different approaches to employment buffering. The McCord Corporation, a small company in South Dakota, has managed to ensure employment stability for its employees through buffering, even though the company is part of the automotive industry and as such has had to endure particularly hard times in the past few years. Honeywell, Inc., is another computer giant that has successfully used buffering techniques as well as other layoff-avoidance measures to safeguard its work force. Honeywell's experience is particularly interesting because its management is highly decentralized and because a large proportion—95 percent—of its work force are regular full-time employees.

INTERNATIONAL BUSINESS MACHINES (IBM)

International Business Machines (IBM) is best known to the public as the largest manufacturer and distributor of information handling systems in the world. In addition to computers and other data processing equipment, it is an important manufacturer of office machines such as typewriters, copiers, and dictation equipment. IBM is almost equally well known for its model personnel policies. It is not without reason that data processing instructors everywhere hold up IBM to their students as the nirvana of work environments. While the legend that IBM's employees once in are never out is not strictly true, employees can look forward to a far greater degree of employment security than is the norm in the world of work. Furthermore, employment security is not limited to the professional and technical staff but also reaches the ranks of blue-collar workers in IBM manufacturing plants around the country. The employment security practices, and particularly the employment buffering policies as they were developed in the IBM typewriter plant in Lexington, Kentucky, provide an illustration of how this works.[1]

In the mid-1950s, IBM established the Office Products Division and opened a brand-new plant in Lexington for the manufacture of its typewriters, at first the familiar typebar typewriter, later its Selectric typewriter. Starting fresh in the new location with a new and inexperienced work force in 1956, the plant today has grown to some 6,500 workers, making a variety of electric and electronic office equipment, still including typewriters. When IBM opened its Lexington plant in 1956, it became the largest employer in the area. It still is today.

Responsibility for the management of the plant was given to Clair F. Vough, vice-president of the new Office Products Division. IBM's typewriters had been having a tough time in the market and the division was not performing as well as top management in IBM wanted and expected. The new division was given its marching orders: either show a profit, or face the prospect that the division would be sold. Vough, who had come up through the ranks of IBM, believed that the key to increasing profitability was improving productivity, and that the key to productivity improvement was to be found in the plant's own employees. Not only did he believe that the best ideas come from people, but that the best ideas for work improvements come from the people who know the work best, namely the workers themselves. As far as he was concerned, he had his own experience to prove it. His own initiative, backed by IBM's confidence in him and a relatively free hand, had advanced him from the production line where he had started as an assembler to a top managerial position in the company. So for Vough and his fellow managers at IBM, employment security was seen as a way—indeed, the only way—to encourage workers to take the risks inherent in making suggestions for changes in the way work was performed and thus improving productivity and profitability.

His experience (when he retired from IBM in 1976, he had worked for IBM for more than 40 years) had convinced Vough of two things about workers, managers, and productivity. The first was that people will not voluntarily work better or faster if so doing will jeopardize their jobs or even those of neighbors or co-workers. The second was that "nobody in this world works at top capacity,"[2] and therefore everybody can do more than they are doing and/or do it better. From these convictions came a determination to take the measures necessary to fully protect the employment of his workers and an unshakable faith in the unlimited potential for productivity improvement. It is not intended here to give the impression that Vough was alone in his thinking on this point. Far from it. He was backed by the historical commitment of IBM to employment security or full employment for its employees, a commitment originally made by the company's founder and retired chairman, Thomas J. Watson, Jr., and still held today.

The problem facing Vough and his fellow managers at the Lexington typewriter plant was how to translate that commitment into an improved and profitable operation. The first decision was to concentrate on productivity improvement rather than cost reduction—to look for ways to turn out more typewriters better and faster, rather than to look for ways to cut costs. In the IBM tradition, the Lexington employees were regarded as the operation's most valuable resource—of brain power as well as of needed skills. Vough and his managers reasoned that if the workers were to become the source of new ideas for work improvements, they had to be assured that their jobs were safe, their employment with IBM secure. Every employee had to believe that he or she would not become jobless even if the suggestions made and the ideas offered for work improvement resulted in the elimination of the employee's own job.

This kind of trust is not easy to inculcate. It can be developed only by example and over a sustained period of time. Employment security in the Lexington plant could not be just a slogan, a framed motto on the wall. It had to be practiced consistently, constantly, and in an open manner.

To this end, Vough and his team put into place a carrot-and-stick policy, with somewhat more emphasis on the carrot than on the stick. It was, in fact, a carefully crafted and monitored scheme which linked accountability and pay/promotion practice. Three principles were involved. First, accountability and responsibility were placed where the work was and with the lowest possible rank in the organizational hierarchy. Drawing on Vough's observation that the people who actually performed the work were the ones who knew and understood the problems best, it was thought that putting them in charge and holding them accountable for the results would encourage the kind of ideas necessary to improve efficiency. The second principle, and one that was very hard to adhere to, was that pay and promotion should be tied directly to, and only to, productivity. No one was to be penalized for doing his or her job in a satisfactory manner, but only those whose ideas and work led to more efficient production could expect to advance; there was no other avenue to promotion. Making that system fully operative was not easy, but over a ten-year period, it did produce the desired results. Not only was the time it took to produce a single typewriter cut by more than 65 percent but also costs were reduced 45 percent despite general increases in wage levels. In addition, work quality improved—with service calls under customer warranties declining by as much as 50 percent.

The third element of the program was the commitment to employment security for all IBM employees. This commitment was realized by means of a combination of careful human-resource planning and flexibility in the utilization of those resources, backed by a comprehensive system of training and retraining and imaginative use of various employment buffers. As Vough has stated, "All these motivational methods to increase productivity would be so much wheel-spinning without the foundation of full employment."[3]

The use of employment buffers starts with a decision to staff lean—to keep the initial work force as small as possible. For the IBM Lexington operation, this meant staffing at a level that was about 85 percent of the annual worker-hour requirement deemed necessary to meet normal demand. Actually an 85 percent staffing level is not as lean as that used by many other companies that rely on buffering systems to protect the employment security of their workers. Another large computer company has experimented with a 70 percent initial staffing level, while some companies heavily dependent on government defense contracts reportedly staff at very low levels, relying on subcontractors for as much as 50 percent of the work load.

At IBM however, employment security planning started with the decision to staff at 85 percent of normal demand. At this level, overtime became the first employment security buffering strategy. In fact, willingness to work overtime was a condition of employment for IBM's Lexington employees, who were required to work a "normal" allowance of 10 to 12 overtime Saturdays a year. In addition, it was understood that this so-called "regular overtime" could be expanded to up to 22 Saturdays. Use of overtime permitted the number of available annual worker-days to be altered up or down, thus providing the flexibility needed to deal with cyclical fluctuations in demand. In the Lexington human-resource plan, regular overtime was relied on to add another 10 percent to available worker-hours, bringing the total up to 95 percent of the amount deemed necessary to meet normal demand. The remaining 5 percent was provided by a second buffering strategy, the use of subcontracting.

If demand exceeded the expected normal level, additional buffers were used to shore up the original lean work force. First, by hiring temporary workers, available worker-hours could be increased 5 percent, while overtime beyond the normal 10 or 12 Saturdays for the regular work force could inflate the total worker-hours by as much as an additional 8 to 10 percent. If that did not suffice, consideration could be given to increased use of subcontracting. The plan thus provided for at least a 30 percentage point shift in demand, from 85 percent to 115 percent of normal expectations. Planning, however, was not a once-a-year performance. It was an ongoing process, with review and revision on a monthly basis. As Vough says, "Employment security is not something you just stumble into, or back into. It has to be planned."[4]

Contractions in demand called for the reverse use of buffering strategies. Overtime could be decreased or dropped altogether, temporaries let go, and subcontracted work brought back in-house. If demand continued to drop, a separate series of measures could be brought into play. These included such actions as producing for inventory, a stepped-up program of maintenance and repair, and restocking and reconditioning the demonstration equipment used by the sales force. Delivery schedules could be and were rearranged in order to protect the regular work force. During peak periods delivery schedules were frequently lengthened to more evenly spread the work out over the year. Careful planning of schedules helped add to the general employment stability.

As with implementation of the first layer of buffering strategies, efficient use of the second layer also required considerable advance planning. For example, to be able to produce for inventory, it is necessary to have the warehouse space to which such inventory can be consigned. The Lexington plant layout made provision for such space, and there were times when as many as 50,000 typewriters were on the shelf. Lengthening production schedules requires the cooperation and acquiescence of the customers to such a procedure. Only through the development of good customer relations, the manufacture of consistently high-quality products, and the ready availability of quick efficient service could IBM expect its customers to accept the kinds of adjustments in delivery schedules that might be needed to maintain a stable level of employment. Obviously these are all areas in which IBM has had notable success.

Expansion and contraction of both regular and emergency overtime requires a work force that has a strong sense of loyalty and that identifies its own welfare with the well-being of the company. Development of this sense of community of interest was and still is a principal goal of IBM's personnel policy.

Finally, effective use of all of these buffering strategies, and particularly expansion and contraction of subcontracting, required a flexible work force. As the character of the work changed, management had to be able to reassign workers to different tasks within the plant. This flexibility was and is carefully developed at IBM through a constant process of training and retraining. In Lexington, it was further reinforced by strict adherence to the policy of basing pay and promotion on productivity rather than on the typical seniority system, in which workers can progress only by an undeviating ascent of a rigidly prescribed ladder of explicitly described jobs.

IBM's ability to plan and implement its buffering strategies, as well as its position in a growth industry, are important elements in the success of its employment security program. In addition, there apparently has also been a bit of luck involved. Thomas J. Watson, Jr., talking about the company's commitment to full employment, tells the story: "There have been times when we might have taken the easy way out to save payroll. During the Great Depression for example, when nearly one-quarter of the civilian labor force was unemployed, IBM embarked on a program of expansion. Rather than resort to factory layoffs, IBM produced parts for inventory and stored them. It was a gamble that took nerve, especially for a company doing less than $17 million worth of business a year. Happily, the risk paid off in 1935 when Congress passed the Social Security Act and IBM, in competitive bidding, was selected to undertake one of the greatest bookkeeping operations of all time. Thanks to our stockpiling of parts, we were able to build the machines and begin delivery almost at once."[5]

The use of subcontracting for employment buffering purposes raises other interesting issues. However, any discussion of these issues must recognize that there is a difference between preplanned subcontracting for employment buffering purposes and subcontracting as a normal mode of doing business. Most manufacturing companies, as well as many service companies, routinely subcontract some part of their output to other producers. Under normal circumstances, the subcontracting route is chosen because it is more efficient, and particularly because the part or service can be provided at a cost that is lower than if the work were done in-house. On the other hand, since the use of subcontracting as a buffer requires that the work done by the subcontractors be brought back in-house in periods when demand falls off, buffering subcontracting clearly implies a willingness on the part of the principal employer to forgo the efficiency gain and/or the cost advantage in order to protect employment. It is not a decision to be taken lightly and, in fact, it was not at the Lexington plant. Vough emphasized that the subcontracting buffer was only one of several, and certainly not the most important. However the process involved in the manufacture of typewriters did increase the potential for successful use of the subcontracting buffer.

Making a typewriter is a complicated business, involving the manufacture and assembly of 35,000 to 40,000 parts. Both operations took place at the Lexington plant. There was a machine shop to make the parts, and many assembly operations to put them together. The existence of such a large number of subassembly operations offered a good opportunity for implementation of a subcontracting buffer. In addition, some of the machine-shop work could be subcontracted out to job shops, particularly machining of parts made by standard equipment. Machining that required skills relating only to that firm's products clearly would not be appropriate for subcontracting, nor would those operations dependent on workers who had been trained in these skills. Efficient operation will always demand that such capital, whether in the form of physical plant or a uniquely skilled work force, be fully and continuously utilized to the maximum extent possible.

One of the problems with the use of subcontracting as a buffer concerns the necessity to maintain good working relationships with the buffer subcontractors. No manufacturer can afford to be known to subcontractors as simply a fair-weather friend, providing business when things are going well, but recalling it the minute things go badly. The IBM managers at Lexington tried to meet this problem in several ways. First, to the maximum extent possible, their own buffers were also used to buffer the subcontractors. Such buffering mechanisms as the stretch-out of orders, rearrangement of delivery schedules, and production for inventory obviously provided a degree of employment stability for the subcontractors as well as for IBM's own employees. Vough reported that in the 17 years that he was in charge at Lexington, although there were some very big swings in demand, these swings had very little effect on his regular subcontractors.

Second, the subcontracting was widely spread out and dispersed geographically, rather than being concentrated in the Lexington area. This could be particularly helpful to the job shops which performed machine operations for IBM. Job shops are of course set up to cater to a broad array of customers and are, in a sense, designed to be able to offset the temporary downturns in orders from one customer with substitute orders from another. Geographic dispersion of the subcontracts can help to soften the impact of cyclical economic swings which frequently are concentrated in one locality or region. In all fairness, however, it must be said that at IBM the dispersion was more the result of accident than design since the subcontracts, even those that were planned specifically with buffering in mind, were let on a competitive bid basis.

Finally, Vough and his associates tried their best to inculcate their subcontractors with their own philosophy of human-resource management, holding seminars and meetings for whomever would come, to encourage acceptance of a full-employment policy among the subcontractors. In Vough's view, employment security or full employment is not something that is reserved only for a few big companies, but it is a style of management that works and that can and should be practiced by everyone. As he says, "If everybody had a full employment policy, there would be no recession."[6] This may sound like the obverse of President Coolidge's memorable remark that when people are out of work unemployment results, but in both cases the logic is unassailable.

Did the IBM buffering policies lead to a widening of the chasm between a primary and secondary labor market in Lexington, with some workers on the inside protected from the vicissitudes of the market and changes in the economy, at the expense of others on the outside, who had to bear the brunt of any downturns? It can be argued that this is indeed one of the effects of buffering policies such as lean staffing, overtime, the hiring of temporary workers, and the use of subcontracting buffers. Whether that happened in Lexington is not known. Asked whether his program might not create a secondary labor pool, Vough commented, "Perhaps so, but you have to start somewhere." He could, of course, also point to the record. The IBM Lexington plant had no layoffs during some 20 years that Vough was in charge of the Office Products Division, despite the fact that there were four major recessions during that period. And this record still holds good today. In addition, in a period when imports—for the most part produced by U.S. manufacturers who moved abroad—took over the U.S. market, only IBM continued to make its typewriters in the United States. In Lexington, IBM is still regarded as a good employer, its reputation is still high. Although the plant now makes other office equipment in addition to typewriters, and although there have been some changes in the management in the past few years, the commitment to full employment remains—bringing the same positive results as before.

CONTROL DATA CORPORATION

Like IBM, Control Data Corporation (CDC) puts a high priority on employment security for its employees. This goal is not pursued for its own sake, but rather is seen as an integral part of the company's growth strategy, a necessary accompaniment to its ability to grow and prosper in the highly competitive industry in which it operates. There is no such thing as a guarantee of lifetime employment at Control Data, however. Instead, the operating principle is clearly stated by the company in these terms: "Control Data will pursue a policy which provides an increasing level of job security to the greatest number of its employees."[7]

Control Data is one of the largest firms in the data processing and information services industry. In 1981 it was second only to IBM in sales of computer software products and services. A relative newcomer to the field compared to IBM, the company was founded by William C. Norris in 1957 when he left another computer firm, Sperry Rand, to try his luck with a new venture. Norris is still chairman of the board and chief executive officer. Although it was started as a high-technology computer hardware company, by the late 1960s the company had moved to the production of computer peripherals— the products that accompany a computer, such as disk packs, punch cards, computer forms, magnetic tape, and so on. Ten years later the company was well into the development and sales of data processing services. An antitrust suit brought and won by Control Data against IBM in the mid-1970s permitted the company to acquire IBM's data services division along with some of its 1,700 highly skilled staff, thus giving it a substantial leg up in the data services field. The settlement of the suit also stipulated that IBM stay out of the data services market for the next seven years, from 1974 to 1981, giving Control Data an additional advantage.

Growth is what it is all about at Control Data, which by the end of 1983 had over 51,000 employees and over $4 billion in sales. More than half of Control Data's employees are engaged in manufacturing, most of which is done in the United States in about a dozen different locations. Of the number involved in manufacturing, many work in plants in the Minneapolis-St. Paul area, where the company's headquarters are also located. Although there are at least two manufacturing plants overseas, the provision of data services is the principal activity of the foreign operations of Control Data. Control Data, however, is not just a computer company. It is a diversified company with significant activity in finance (through its subsidiary, the Commercial Credit Company), education, and the provision of services to small business.

It has not always been smooth sailing, however. In the 1974 recession, brought about by the first OPEC oil crisis, Control Data was forced to lay off some of its personnel. It was a painful experience for the company and one that has not been forgotten. The company's concern is typified by remarks made by Chairman Norris at a meeting of the company's executive management in 1980. "In this day and age, a clearer and more meaningful commitment to the maintenance of employment must be made by business if anywhere near the present operating freedoms enjoyed by business, especially big business, are to be preserved. Immediate layoffs in response to a decline in business are becoming increasingly unacceptable in our society. Nor is it acceptable to abruptly close plants as soon as there is a lack of need, without reviewing the reasons and possible alternatives with the affected community."

With this sentiment in mind, the company began to look for ways to avoid layoffs, or at least cushion them with alternative avenues for affected employees. Certainly the concern with the acceptance or nonacceptance by society of the personnel decisions of big business—as a sort of quid pro quo for continuation of a degree of management freedom—was one element in the search for employment stability. Another and perhaps more important element was a perceived need to link employment security with the economic growth and well-being of the company. Just as the IBM managers linked employment security with productivity improvement, Control Data saw employment security as an important element in its growth strategy.

To develop this strategy, a Job Security Task Force was formed during the summer of 1980. Its challenge was to develop and implement an employment security strategy that would help to achieve the company's basic longtime human-resource policy goals of planned growth and the maintenance and encouragement of an entrepreneurial spirit among its employees. The task force, as is typical in many companies, was made up of very senior staff and given a limited lifetime to complete its work. Its most important products were a so-called "rings of defense" strategy for fostering growth, and its obverse, a strategy for protecting the employment of a core staff in times of serious economic decline. As developed by the Task Force, the "rings of defense" strategy provides a means of expanding the work force available to the corporation without jeopardizing the future employment security of its core staff. While there are some obvious similarities between the Control Data approach and that of IBM, there are also interesting differences.

As with IBM, the basis of the Control Data strategy is initial lean staffing, with its goal a full-time regular work force that is only 70 percent of the level needed to fulfill demand. These full-time regulars are visualized as being at the center of a series of concentric rings. Moving outward, the next two rings are made up of regular part-time workers and the work forces of small CDC-sponsored vendors. The relatively sheltered, even favorable position of the personnel described in these two rings is directly linked to the philosophy of CDC regarding flexibility in its utilization of personnel within the organization and to the company's well-known efforts to encourage a spirit of entrepreneurship. As regards the first group, CDC seeks and hires part-time workers on a permanent basis in order to take advantage of the pool of skills and talent which the company is convinced exists on a part-time basis. Control Data has now begun to offer these part-timers prorated benefits.

The concept behind the development of CDC-sponsored vendors is somewhat different. With companies, as with individuals, it is well known that with age and maturity comes a certain stiffness and lack of enthusiasm for new ideas and new methods of doing things. But in the computer and data processing industry, growth and even survival depend on a continuing ability to develop and exploit new ideas. Therefore, in a conscious effort to stay ahead, CDC has followed a practice of sponsoring small entrepreneurial operations, setting them up as affiliates, and requiring them to bid in competition with other entrepreneurs for the parent company's business but permitting them to sell their services or products wherever they can. Most of these affiliated firms are highly dependent on CDC for business and therefore vulnerable to changes in the company's fortunes. For this reason, they are accorded a favorable position in the ring strategy.

Moving farther out from the core of the circle, the next ring includes what CDC calls supplemental employees. These are temporary, part-time workers, who have the same prorated benefits as other part-time employees at CDC, but who, obviously, are not considered to have the same attachment to the company. Company spokespersons stress that in hiring supplementals a great effort is made to recruit workers who are "specifically looking for a nonpermanent supplement to their income." The problem is, of course, that workers will take nonpermanent jobs in preference to no jobs, and they are more apt to do this when the competition for jobs is tough.

The outer rings of defense consist of small and then of large independent vendors or subcontractors. The last ring is the use of overtime, a very common practice. All of these rings are visualized as a kind of priority ranking of the strategies CDC uses to expand its work force and, if things go poorly, to contract it. The strategy is designed to encourage a climate in which new ideas will flourish and be given a chance to be tried out because the full-time regular work force feels secure.

The Task Force recognized that the strategies envisioned by the rings of defense might not suffice in cases of a severe downturn and that further programs might be needed to protect the inner rings, the full-time and part-time regular employees. There might be times when it was not enough to reduce overtime, cut back on subcontracts or bring them in-house, let the temporaries go, and rearrange contracts with the sponsored vendors. Therefore, the Task Force devised a second ring of strategies, again establishing a priority order of actions that should be taken with reference to the core employees in preference to layoff. Starting from the outside and working inward, the steps to be taken, considered, or included are, first, a hiring freeze and a program of managed attrition, followed by voluntary layoffs, involuntary layoffs based on performance factors, the development of alternate products, a reduction in work hours and, the next to last step, the redeployment of personnel. The final step, layoff or involuntary termination of qualified permanent staff, was not to be considered until all else had been tried. In the words of Dr. Claire Kolmodin, principal consultant of Control Data Business Advisors, "Layoffs are not taken lightly here."

Control Data's employment security plan is much more than a simple enumeration and ranking of various means for expanding and contracting the work force. The "rings of defense" strategy is only the beginning, a framework for carrying out a corporate commitment to employment security. An underlying concept is to provide a means for the conversion of future permanent jobs to other forms of work association with the company, forms that can be given up or brought back inside the company during downswings in the economy but used to expand the company when things are going well. This process of conversion is an integral part of the employment security strategy and an ongoing activity.

Management at Control Data is fairly centralized, certainly insofar as personnel planning and administration are concerned. No one can be laid off without central office approval. In case of a cutback, the operating divisions must prepare a social impact statement identifying all of the actions being taken to avoid a layoff and the outcome planned for each worker. The social impact statement is in addition to the divisions' five-year human-resource plans, which are revised and updated each year and coordinated by the central office.

The Task Force had hardly finished its work, and the process of implementing the new employment security strategy had barely begun, when the recession of 1982–83 forced the company to deal immediately with a threat to the "inner rings," a proposed cutback of full-time and part-time regulars. To deal with the situation, CDC established what they call SWAT, or the Special Workforce Action Team, to operate in the Minneapolis-St. Paul area. Its assignment was to find ways to provide continuous employment for employees in the Twin Cities for whom no work was available in their regular jobs. An Employee Placement Center was also set up to work with the affected employees. As a starter, employees in the affected facilities were encouraged to take time off without pay, while overall work hours were reduced by closing some plants on a short-term basis during holiday periods. It is estimated that this effort alone saved the company over $20 million. SWAT then focused its efforts on finding temporary assignments in other parts of the corporation for the displaced workers. To make it easy for the other divisions to accept them, the corporation itself paid their salaries. In addition, some individuals were helped to move into new careers, with the corporation providing support for career counseling, outplacement services, and some retraining. Although SWAT is technically still in operation, its work is mostly finished and the majority of the workers on temporary assignment have been placed in permanent jobs. All in all, the company counts its employment security program a success—at least in terms of its ability to protect permanent employees during a severe recession. Control Data points with some satisfaction to its record during the 1982–83 economic slump, when less than 1.5 percent of its domestic work force was laid off.

Employment security is not a static program at Control Data, but a dynamic process. One example of this is found in the company's evolving policy regarding use of its vendors or subcontractors as employment buffers.

Remember, as part of its "rings of defense" employment security plan, CDC divided its vendors into three groups: small independent vendors, large independent vendors, and the affiliated vendors in which the parent company has minority ownership. Theoretically, all of these groups might be considered potential employment buffers, but clearly some are more so than others. CDC practice takes this into account.

CDC-sponsored vendors, usually established for the purpose of encouraging entrepreneurship and often dependent on the company for much of their business, are not normally considered or treated as employment buffers. Without a diversified customer base, they would not be able to withstand the sudden withdrawal of company contracts and, in any case, assigning them a buffer status would be counterproductive. Moreover, the contracts let to vendors producing parts and materials which involve very little labor content are not considered appropriate for buffering purposes because they cannot provide enough substitute work for the idled permanent employees if brought in-house during a downturn. Similarly, work subcontracted to outside vendors because Control Data had at some point made a deliberate choice *not* to make the initial capital or skill investments required to do the work in-house would be unsuitable for buffering purposes. Geographic considerations are also taken into account because CDC is sensitive to the impact on the community of using vendors as employment buffers. Finally, vendors holding long-term contracts of, say, five years or more could hardly be considered to be in a buffering position.

Reviewing its subcontractors in light of all of these factors, the Job Security Task Force determined that too low a percentage of the existing work contracted out could be pulled back in an economic downturn to be considered an employment buffer. Therefore, an important element of the present CDC program is to try to increase the buffer subcontract percentage, apparently with some degree of success. A company spokesperson reports that "One division which compiles ratings for radio and television stations," a business which is somewhat seasonal in nature, "not only subcontracts administrative and computer-related work, but also uses a large proportion of temporary workers." Another CDC organization which is designed to service small business is reported to have subcontracted for a significant amount of software and courseware development. In addition, other divisions of CDC regularly use contract employees and consultants. Since all of this work can be performed in-house if it were necessary to do so, it all qualifies as buffer subcontracting. In effect, by avoiding taking on additional permanent staff and substituting outside vendors, the existing core staff of the company is protected.

Control Data has wrestled with the question of exactly how far to go in its use of employment buffers, both in subcontracting and in hiring temporary workers. When the company initially launched its employment security strategy, a specific percentage goal was set for future growth through the use of temporaries or supplementals. It is important to note, however, that the company regards this goal as a benchmark and not fixed in concrete. As it explains, the purpose is to raise the level of attention paid by company managers to the long-term commitment to increasing employment security for the greatest number of company workers and to try to get managers thinking about ways of accomplishing this objective.

Percentage goals were also used in regard to buffer subcontracts. Each operating division has been asked to develop a plan for moving some future work into subcontracts by 1988. It is recognized, however, that the different kinds of operations performed by different divisions make it unlikely and impractical for all parts of the company to achieve the same goal.

Control Data has also experimented with the idea of establishing buffer plants—a difficult task, both conceptually and as a practical matter. "Buffer" is probably the wrong word to describe the role of these plants since it connotes abandonment of the plant by the CDC in adversity. And that was certainly not the original intention nor the whole story. Concentrated as it is in the midwestern part of the country, CDC is not insensitive to its environment, nor to its impact on the communities in which it operates. The company has a well-deserved reputation for having a social conscience. There was always a dual objective behind the idea of buffer plants: the first, to produce a viable product or service with a buffer, or temporary work force; the second, to place these facilities in situations where the need for such temporary employment exceeded the risk of its temporary nature.

The locations planned for the establishment of buffer plants were in inner cities, where there were a number of people unemployed, often minority workers, without the skills necessary to compete successfully in the job market. The idea was to take advantage of the kinds of incentives provided in some of these areas, hire chronically unemployed people on a part-time or supplemental basis, use Control Data's own products to give the workers the necessary job skills, and then help "bridge" the workers into full-time, permanent non-CDC jobs. It was hoped that everybody would gain from the operation. Unemployed workers trapped by lack of education, skills, and opportunity would be enabled to break into the primary labor market where they could have good, well-paid, permanent jobs, and CDC would be able to meet its expansion goals without risk to the employment security of its permanent regular staff. There would even be a bonus in that CDC could test and improve its own products in the process, especially its education-and-training materials and services.

Unfortunately, in a recession, the idea of painless temporary employment just doesn't wash very well. Not only is it almost impossible to limit recruitment to those who, by some unknown measure, "sincerely" prefer temporary or part-time work, but with unemployment reaching record peaks in 1982–83, especially in the inner areas of large industrial cities, there was nowhere for CDC supplementals moving out of the buffer plants to go. No other employers in the area at that time could or would hire these employees on a full-time permanent basis. In CDC's view, perhaps the most successful buffer plants would be those in which both the work and the work force are seasonal—students, for example, who are in the job market for only a limited part of the year. CDC is not ready, however, to give up on the idea of buffer plants. In its words, "The jury is not yet in."

Nor is the company unconcerned about the possible unemployment of part-time and supplemental employees that may result from its policy of protecting the employment of the permanent staff. Chairman Norris's policy statement cited at the beginning of this section, pledging CDC to work to increase employment security for "the greatest number" of its employees, recognizes that not all its employees, nor all of those associated with the company, will be or can be protected. CDC's goal is to expand employment security as far as possible. And that is what the company is working on.

McCORD CORPORATION

The McCord Corporation is a small metal-working manufacturing company with two plants, one in Canton, South Dakota, and one in Plymouth, Indiana. The company is a division of the Ex-Cell-O Corporation of Detroit—a diversified manufacturer in the automotive and aerospace industries. It is the Canton plant that is discussed here.

McCord is a supplier of heat-exchanging equipment, such as automotive condensers, oil coolers, and radiators. Its customers are the largest agricultural equipment manufacturers (John Deere, Caterpillar, International Harvester), the heavy truck industry, and the military. McCord supplies the heat exchangers for armored personnel carriers, jeeps, and other military vehicles. Obviously, the company operates in a highly volatile market. Being dependent on such a combination—the agricultural economy and government contracts—could hardly be described as anything else. Yet, the company operates on a no-layoff, job-guarantee policy and has succeeded in maintaining that policy despite the nature of its market, even during the 1982–83 recession. How does it do it?

First, it must be noted that the Canton plant is headed by Gary Lemon, a dedicated follower of the personnel-management system developed and implemented by Clair Vough at IBM's typewriter plant in Lexington, Kentucky. Under Lemon's direction, the Vough system—with some adaptations—has been the modus operandi at McCord since the plant opened in 1976. It should also be noted that Ex-Cell-O, the parent company, is itself fully committed to a program of employee participation and employee involvement. Therefore, although no other divisions of the company have adopted the same no-layoff job guarantee, the application of the Vough system at the McCord Canton plant is fully consistent with the company's general policies. Finally, the guarantee is not a written commitment, included in every worker's job contract. It is a policy that is "understood." Employees know when they are hired that if they meet the company's performance standard, they are hired for good; they will not be let go for economic reasons.

Two basic elements characterize the employee-relations program at McCord. One is its pay-for-performance system. All employees of the company are salaried, production workers as well as the administrative, clerical, and managerial staff. All are paid on a biweekly basis and, for everyone, pay is adjusted to recognize performance. Standards have been established for every job, and performance is reviewed for each worker every six weeks. Each worker is judged on his or her own merit and not on the basis of the performance of an entire group. Whenever an employee is found to have exceeded the standard, pay is adjusted upward. For example, if a worker has been producing at a rate that is 125 percent of the standard for the six-week period, he or she receives a salary that is 125 percent of the standard rate. The worker continues at this rate unless or until another adjustment is made at a later date. Adjustments can also be made downward—but in this case, the review period is eighteen weeks.

The company also follows a strictly enforced policy of promotion from within; 80 percent of the job vacancies are filled from the existing work force. This promotion policy is backed by a training program, in which the company supports and pays for additional off-the-job education and training so that its employees can qualify for advancement within the company. A prime example is Rita Stockberger, currently director of Employee Relations at the Canton plant. She started at the company's Indiana plant as a receptionist-typist, but on the basis of her performance, she moved steadily into progressively more responsible jobs as openings occurred. To help herself qualify for these jobs she enrolled in college-level courses at night, at company expense. When the opening for an employee relations director occurred at the Canton plant, she was picked for the job.

The second basic element of the employee-relations program is the use of employment buffers to protect the work force in periods of slack demand. The years 1982–83 were especially difficult for the company, but no one was let go. In early 1984, the company employed 143 people, 115 of whom were blue-collar production workers; the rest were in administration and management. This was 13 fewer than the company employed at the end of 1981, before the full impact of the recession. The shrinkage that occurred during those two years was entirely due to attrition.

As is the case in other companies which use employment buffers, McCord starts with an initial lean staff, something less than the number of workers necessary to meet normal demand. There is no set percentage limitation on the permanent staff at McCord as there is at IBM, but there is an acknowledged caution in hiring so as to lessen the pressure for staff reductions in an uncertain future. The gap between the regular permanent employees and the number necessary to meet current demand is filled first by the use of overtime and then, if necessary, by hiring temporary workers. It is made clear to the temporaries at the time they are hired exactly what their status is, although it is also possible for them to move into the permanent staff if and as vacancies occur. McCord uses subcontracting as a buffer to expand its capacity only as a last resort.

All of these buffering strategies are applicable, of course, when times are good and the company has plenty of orders to fill. In downturns, the buffers are used in reverse to contract capacity. First, work done by subcontractors is called back in-house, then the temporary employees are let go, and finally, overtime is eliminated. If at that point there is still not enough work to keep everybody working a full 40 hours a week—the promise implicit in the company's job-guarantee policy—the company turns to a variety of other strategies. One strategy is to produce for inventory. Another is to initiate projects. In the last recession, company projects included repainting and refurbishing the plant and a series of other environmental improvements and cost-saving projects, such as building picnic tables for workers' use on the plant grounds and landscaping. In addition, the company used the idle time to bring workers together in groups to elicit new ideas for improved management and production methods.

Obviously, it is not possible to keep more than 100 people busy for over a year in such projects and discussions and, fortunately for McCord, the company did not have to. Throughout this period there were always some orders coming in, and the plant was never completely shut down. Neither did the company resort to short time, shortened work weeks or other forms of work sharing. Indeed, to do so would not have been consistent with the company's guarantee of full employment.

As might be expected, the slowdown in orders and the conversion to projects instead of regular production work played havoc with the pay-for-performance system. In fact, during an 18-month period in the recession, performance increases were not awarded to anyone, not even to managers. The workers were lucky if they had enough work to meet the performance standard, let alone to exceed it. This was hard on everybody and, in time, there was some grumbling, some complaints. But McCord is the biggest employer in Canton, and Canton is a very small town, with a population of about 3,000. Everybody knows everybody at the company. Everybody knows everybody in town. The entire community was bearing the hardship of the recession together. People accepted the idea that it was better for everybody to continue working, even with no increase in pay, than for some in the community to work and others not to work at all. The feeling of community is such that when business finally picked up, the company awarded what they called a "community wage adjustment"—a pay increase for all employees, in recognition of the sacrifices all had made together.

That a company operating in the farm-equipment industry was able to weather one of the worst recessions this country has had without a single layoff is a remarkable achievement. That the company's employment security policy was responsible for this record cannot be absolutely proven, but it certainly must have been an important factor.

HONEYWELL, INC.

Honeywell, Inc., like such competitors as IBM and Control Data Corporation, is a high-technology company where employment security is becoming increasingly important. At Honeywell, employment security, or employment stability as it is called there, has always been considered an important goal. But in recent years, the increased competition for employees with the requisite technical skills, and the resulting need for the high-tech companies to retain such employees, plus the demand for ever greater productivity gains and concern for employees, has given employment stability policies added significance. Honeywell has looked at its approach to employment stability and that of other comparable companies and is considering available alternatives that could serve to improve employment stability.[8]

Honeywell is a large multinational corporation employing approximately 100,000 people, some 70,000 of them located in the United States. As might be expected, the majority of Honeywell employees are not in the factory but rather are involved in administrative, engineering, technical, scientific, sales, installation, service, and managerial functions. About 20,000 employees are in blue-collar occupations, such as production and maintenance. About half of this group is represented by trade unions. The International Brotherhood of Teamsters has several locals representing employees in several facilities in Minnesota and other states. Other unions with which Honeywell conducts collective bargaining in the United States and Canada are the International Union of Electrical Workers (IUE), the International Association of Machinists and Aerospace Workers (IAM), the International Brotherhood of Electrical Workers (IBEW), the United Automobile Workers (UAW), the United Electrical Workers (UE), and the United Association of Plumbers and Pipe Fitters (UA).

Although the company traces its history as far back as 1885, it only began using the Honeywell name in 1927 when the Minneapolis Heat Regulator Company merged with Honeywell Heating Specialties Company. The company soon began branching out from heating-control regulators into other kinds of control instruments, and by the end of World War II it was involved in the development and production of a broad variety of sophisticated instruments and systems. The company also provided related engineering services.

Today Honeywell has divided its operations into four main businesses. The Control Products business is the outgrowth of the company's early activity and is still involved in the manufacture of products to regulate heating and cooling systems. It is also, however, a significant producer of semiconductors and microswitches. The Control Systems business produces electrical, electronic, and pneumatic control systems, which include computers used in automated manufacturing processes and building controls. It also makes fire-detection and alarm systems, medical instrumentation, and in addition, sells a range of services related to the products which it produces. The activities of the Aerospace and Defense business are defined by its name. The divisions in this group produce guidance and control systems primarily for military applications. Finally, the Information Systems business produces and services a wide range of data processing and computer systems.

The management approach within Honeywell is decentralized; each business unit operates quite independently and autonomously. However, seven overall "Honeywell Principles" have been established and communicated to all employees. Every business unit is expected to reflect these principles in their policies, practices, management style, and approach. One of these principles states that "People are key to Honeywell's success." This statement is supported by the company's view of employees as a critical and valuable resource—one to be treated well, fully utilized and developed, without engaging, as may have been the case 20 or 30 years ago, in an overly paternalistic approach which tends to reduce rather than encourage individual innovation and initiative.

Historically, layoffs were used by Honeywell to address surplus-employee situations or to reduce costs as necessitated by business fluctuations. But the company found the 1981–82 layoff process particularly difficult. Overall, approximately 2,000 employees were directly affected by the business downturn in the form of transfers, new assignments, outplacements, or layoffs. This situation, together with the company's concern with productivity and its keen awareness of certain skill shortages, highlighted the need to examine alternatives to the "traditional" layoff and recall process and to improve human resource planning and its linkages to business planning.

To help facilitate this undertaking, among others, the company utilized its Organizational Development Advisory Board. Composed of top-level staff and line management, the Advisory Board is chartered to assess Honeywell's cultural and human resource environment and to suggest effective areas and means of change. The Advisory Board meets regularly three to four times a year, with each session lasting two full days. One of its first activities was "to define, evaluate, and recommend policies for improving employment stability at Honeywell" in order to determine better means to help reduce or eliminate undesirable fluctuations in employment. It was not an attempt to find ways to provide a lifetime guarantee of employment. Stability, not stagnation, was the idea.

Employment stability had been a goal of the company for many years. A 1975 company policy statement from the Employee Relations Guidelines for salaried employees states that "It is a Honeywell objective to provide continuing employment and job opportunities for all employees." Recognizing that business fluctuations are inevitable, the guideline further states that the company will do its best to minimize surplus work force conditions and to avoid layoffs. If the layoff cannot be avoided, Honeywell policies call for advance notice to both hourly and salaried employees of impending layoffs. In this regard, business units are strongly encouraged to keep their employees informed of the state of the business—both good and bad news. The amount of notice (or pay in lieu of notice) actually provided is specified by the policies of the individual business units. Particularly in the case of salaried employees, the exact amount of notice or pay is dependent upon the individual employee's length of company service.

In cases of significant reductions in the work force, the layoff plan and its impact are normally reviewed by higher levels of management and the corporate human-resources staff, who can help examine alternatives, coordinate outplacement, reorganize activities, and so on. Finally, the company policy requires that certain precepts be followed. These are that layoffs shall be handled in a nondiscriminatory fashion; that layoffs of older workers with long company service shall be reviewed; and that in no case shall layoffs be used as an excuse to shed poor or, in Honeywell terms, "marginal" performers. This last precept deserves a word of explanation. There are two reasons for prohibiting the layoff of poor performers under these circumstances. One reason is that to do so would, in the words of a company spokesperson, "taint the whole group" being laid off due to lack of work. The other reason is that laid-off employees are often eligible for recall to "comparable work" at the Honeywell facility from which they were laid off. Poor performers require specific help or attention in order to improve their performance, or the situation may have to be resolved via termination, transfer, demotion, or other means. Therefore, layoff with recall rights is not appropriate for either poor performers or the company.

Aside from these general constraints on layoffs, the Advisory Board's study showed that, as might be expected in such a diversified and decentralized company, the kinds and combinations of employment stability measures used may vary considerably between divisions due to differences in business and work-force composition and demographics. For example, in some parts of Honeywell, voluntary early-retirement programs have been used as an effective way of encouraging or facilitating retirements, which have the effect of reducing the size of the work force.

Approximately 95 percent of all Honeywell employees are regular full-time employees. This proportion is beginning to decline via normal attrition as the company experiments with other forms of employment status. For example, the Micro Switch Division in Freeport, Illinois, has introduced a "supplemental" work force in an effort to tap into a hitherto unused source of labor in the community and provide more flexibility in meeting peak work-load demands without hiring additional "regular" employees. In this division, supplemental employees are scheduled to work part time if work is available.

The Micro Switch Division had experimented with flexible employment policies before. A division facility in Marlborough, Massachusetts, introduced a so-called "mothershift," a special 9:00 a.m. to 2:30 p.m. work shift designed to accommodate, and appeal to, mothers of school-age children. In another instance involving the Marlborough plant, Honeywell demonstrated its commitment to employment security. When the division moved its product line to Illinois, another Honeywell division in the Boston area—in the process of expansion—took over the Micro Switch plant and hired most of Micro Switch's former employees who did not transfer to Illinois.

At the present time, Honeywell is gradually working its way toward more effective employment stability policies and practices. As part of this process, divisions are doing more effective human-resource planning, including giving consideration to work-force stability issues. Under Honeywell's decentralized system of management, there is no hard and fast rule requiring the divisions to undertake such planning, but interest in this is sufficiently strong that, in this case, the end result is the same—they are all doing it, albeit with different approaches and different degrees of effectiveness. Some, of course, have always involved themselves in detailed human-resource planning; others are becoming more sophisticated in their approaches. With employment stability and maximum utilization of the available work force as the goals of the various business units, divisions are looking at future hiring practices, the relation of current job classifications to the ability of the company to make flexible assignments of staff as economic or other demand conditions dictate, opportunities for individual initiative and advancement, and opportunities for improved communication at all levels of the company. Although Honeywell does not have a specific policy of consciously fixing the hiring level at something less than 100 percent of the staff needed to meet normal demand, as is the practice with some of its competitors, with careful human-resource planning, the end result may be the same.

Management is considering alternative ways to avert layoffs by experimenting with new ways to provide flexibility in the work force, reduce costs, and improve productivity. Achievement of this objective is, of course, linked to planning and, as might be expected, some divisions of Honeywell already have a high degree of employment stability.

Layoff prevention in Honeywell business units often starts with controlled-hiring practices and moves from there to the use of preplanned employment stability buffers. As indicated earlier, Honeywell managers can and do consider the use of temporary employees hired when demand is high and let go when demand slackens. Unpaid shutdowns, voluntary layoffs, personal leaves of absence and a temporarily shortened workweek or work hours are other buffering strategies that have been used. These approaches, however, are not highly utilized in union locations, which generally tend to focus on strict application of contractual seniority rules as the preferred method to handle a layoff situation. A number of Honeywell locations use subcontracting as a means of buffering their regular employees.

Managers *may* involve employees in identifying and developing alternatives to layoffs. In one case involving the Medical Electronics Division where a reduction of staff was contemplated, the managers brought together groups of employees and asked for their recommendations on how to handle the proposed reduction. The groups' suggestion—which was followed—was that shutting down the facility entirely during a holiday period was preferable to significant work-force reductions.

Honeywell's experience has shown that employees are willing to endorse or identify additional or different approaches and may prefer alternatives to layoff when given a choice.

Retraining, solely as an alternative to layoff, is not an option that as yet has been given much consideration by Honeywell, although some examples can be found. In one case, the company retrained a group of drafters in computer-aided design rather than hiring qualified people outside of the company and then possibly having to lay off the drafters. Honeywell, of course, continuously conducts training programs for its employees as a normal, routine matter, particularly in relation to the constant need to keep abreast of changing technology in the fields in which the company operates. In that sense, it could be said that the training and retraining program is an integral part of the employment stability program, although Honeywell management usually does not tend to think of it in those terms.

The Honeywell experience is interesting because it demonstrates how one company is trying to meet the challenges to its internal human-resource management system posed, in part, by external developments. Honeywell has identified these external forces as (1) current and future shortages of highly qualified technical personnel in a world where technology itself is changing so rapidly; (2) competition from other companies such as IBM, Control Data, and Hewlett-Packard, which have developed their own policies to attract and hold staff; and (3) the need for continuous productivity growth which, in turn, is dependent on the company's internal environment. Finally, Honeywell is well aware of the social and economic implications of structural unemployment on the country's communities and on those individuals directly affected. For Honeywell, with its strong, traditional sense of obligation and responsibility to its employees and the communities in which it operates, this is not an insignificant matter.

Honeywell had decided that one way to meet these challenges and needs is to improve employment stability for its employees, and that is what it is trying to do.

NOTES

1. This case study is based on an interview with Clair F. Vough in Lexington, Kentucky, April 1983 and materials provided by him.

2. Clair F. Vough, with Bernard Asbell, *Tapping the Human Resource: A Strategy for Productivity* (New York: AMACOM, a division of American Management Associations, 1975), p. 7.

3. Vough, with Asbell, *Tapping the Human Resource*, p. 37.

4. Interview with Clair F. Vough, April 1983.

5. Fred K. Foulkes and Anne Whitman, "Full Employment, Product/Marketing Strategies, and Other Considerations," an unpublished paper commissioned by Work in America Institute, April 1984.

6. Interview with Clair F. Vough, April 1983.

7. This case study is based on an unpublished paper by Dr. Claire Kolmodin, principal consultant, Control Data Business Advisers, "Employment Security at Control Data Corporation," commissioned by Work in America Institute, June 1983. Information was also drawn from an interview with Dr. Kolmodin on December 7, 1983.

8. This case study is based on interviews with Kenneth Kostial, corporate director, Industrial Relations, and with Kristine Lindholm, manager, Human Resources Practices, Honeywell, Inc., Minneapolis, Minnesota, December 1983.

4.
Voluntary Work-Force Reductions

In the previous chapter several different kinds of buffering strategies used by employers to protect the employment security of their employees were described. A different approach to employment security is taken with the use of voluntary reductions of the work force to accommodate economic downturns. These voluntary reductions—several of which are described in this chapter—are layoff-avoidance measures and can be either temporary or permanent in nature.

The first is "short-time compensation," in which employees temporarily work fewer than normal hours per week and are partially compensated for the loss of time through the unemployment insurance system. Widely used in Europe, especially in West Germany and France, the utilization of this strategy has only recently begun in the United States and on a very limited basis. Although a federal statute encouraging the use of short-time compensation has been enacted, implementation requires legislation by each of the states wishing to adopt such a program. The problem arises because under normal circumstances a person who is working, even though for fewer than the normal hours, is not eligible to collect unemployment compensation. The idea under short time is to permit an employer to temporarily reduce the total number of worker hours, without layoffs and without undue economic hardship for the workers. Until recently most unions have not expressed much enthusiasm for the program because it is contrary to the cherished seniority-based principle of "last in, first out" in dismissal procedures. These objections are being overcome, however, and several states (see page 6) have now enacted legislation making it possible for employers to use the program if they wish. Two cases describing employers' use of the short-time compensation option are presented here. Motorola, the electronics and computer industry manufacturer was instrumental in persuading the state of Arizona to put a short-time compensation program into effect and was one of the first to take advantage of the new law when it was enacted. A second case describes the experience of a California company, Signetics, a manufacturer of integrated circuits located in Silicon Valley. Even in that much-envied environment, market stability is far from assured, competition is tough, and the ability to provide employment security for one's employees is recognized as a valuable asset.

Another kind of work-force reduction is through the reassignment of personnel to other areas of the company on a temporary basis. The West German automotive company Daimler-Benz has developed a systematic program to shift its workers to other plants and other shops where business is good when there is not enough work for everyone at the home plant. Although other companies, both in West Germany and elsewhere, follow similar procedures, Daimler-Benz probably relies on this technique more than most.

One additional method to reduce the work force for a short period is the lending of employees to outside ventures, in either the public or private sector. Although this is not a strategy that is widely used, several examples can be cited.

In the fall of 1982 when the Prudential Insurance Company decided that it would have to reduce staff at one of its large branch offices, some 300 workers faced the prospect of layoff. Instead, Prudential undertook a series of measures to protect the employment of those workers. A hiring freeze was put into effect, with the thought that attrition would help to ameliorate the problem. In addition, Prudential lent some of the employees to other departments and offices of the company and transferred processing work from other Prudential branches to the affected office. In a major departure from the ordinary job-protection techniques, Prudential also lent some of the surplus workers to outside civic and charitable organizations for a limited period of time.[1] In a similar case, when the Porter Paint Company in Louisville, Kentucky, experienced a fall-off in orders, it lent 17 of its temporarily surplus employees to the local Boy Scouts organization, to help clean up and prepare the site of a prospective scout summer camp. The loan was only for a short time, when the plant had a temporary fall-off in orders. When orders picked up, the workers returned to their regular jobs. The company management believes that the cost of retaining the workers on the payroll while they worked on the Boy Scout project was about equal to what it would have cost the firm if they had continued to work at the paint factory and the company had been forced to maintain an excessive inventory.[2] In another instance, when the UAW workers in a General Motors plant in Mansfield, Ohio, accepted a change in work rules that would eliminate 145 jobs, the company was not permitted under its agreement with the union to lay off anyone. Various measures were taken to protect the jobs of the affected workers. Most were assigned to other jobs in the plant, but 52 workers, for whom no other suitable work could be found, were "donated" by the company for a limited period of time to local social service agencies.[3]

Voluntary work-force reduction can also take place on a permanent basis. In many European countries, voluntary early retirement is perceived as being the best means of achieving employment security, enabling the employer to protect the jobs of a core work force by encouraging older workers to retire. Such schemes are usually intended to be temporary measures, that is, in effect for a limited period of time. Those who retire are supposed to be retired for good, although there have been instances where the employer made the wrong decision and then had to rehire some of his retirees on a contract basis at considerable expense. Examples of several European early-retirement experiences are described in this chapter.

Finally, a word needs to be said concerning the concept of "flexibility" in personnel management, particularly as it is being discussed by European employers. For many Europeans, especially in West Germany, flexibility in the utilization of the company's employees is seen as an answer not only to the need to increase productivity, but also to the concern of both companies and unions to strengthen employment security. One of the strongest proponents of increased flexibility in personnel management is Siemens, the multinational engineering and electronics conglomerate.[4] Siemens, like other West German companies, has had to shrink its work force in the past three years, but implementation of early-retirement schemes has made the task fairly easy. Operating as it does in high-technology areas, the problem for Siemens is to remain competitive. Providing its workers with increased employment security is seen as one way to contribute in a positive way to the company's ability to compete. In fact, Siemens has a reputation for being an employer with a social conscience (it is sometimes referred to as "Mother Siemens") and for providing "wonderful things" for its employees and the communities in which its facilities are located.[5] Dr. Walter Schusser, personnel director for the company, states that, in addition, the company believes that it has an obligation to help reduce unemployment in West Germany. The way to do this, he says, is by introducing more flexibility into the company's personnel practices—increasing the opportunities for part-time work on a daily or weekly basis, and part-year work. He believes that this will allow the company to better cope with, and even to take advantage of, shifting life styles and changing expectations, particularly among women and young people. He also hopes to develop more cross-training so that workers can take on a different task as the need arises. Greater use of reassignment or redeployment is another aspect of the flexibility doctrine. At the present time, Siemens is experimenting with all of these approaches to increased flexibility. It will be interesting to see how far it can be taken.

MOTOROLA

Motorola, which claims first place in U.S. sales of semiconductors, has a carefully structured plan designed to deal with economic downturns without the necessity of layoffs. "Since about 1975," says C. F. Koziol, corporate director of Personnel Administration, "we have formalized a system of buffers—most of which we had used before but not in such a structured fashion. We now have established these buffers as levers to be pulled in a defined sequence to deal with economic downturns and to minimize the necessity of layoffs."[6]

The corporation, with headquarters in Schaumburg, Illinois, had sales of $3.78 billion in 1982, increasing to $4.3 billion in 1983. It has approximately 65,000 U.S. employees and more than half that number abroad. The bulk of its U.S. manufacturing is concentrated in Arizona, Illinois, Florida, and Texas, but it also has plants in Arcade, New York; Mansfield, Massachusetts; and Cupertino, California.

Abroad, there are Motorola plants in West Germany, France, the United Kingdom, Korea, Malaysia, Hong Kong, Taiwan, Australia, Japan, Canada, Puerto Rico, and Israel. Its work force, at home and abroad, is said to be young, well-educated, and highly motivated. Turnover is described as "not significant."

Semiconductor production is concentrated in the greater Phoenix, Arizona, area, which is also the headquarters of its semiconductor and communications sectors. It has over 20,000 employees in the Greater Phoenix area and it was there that the company suffered through the most massive layoff in its history during the 1974–75 recession. That painful and costly experience provided an immediate impetus for the development of the company's present employment security system.

During the recession, many companies started cutting back and laying off in the spring of 1974, but Motorola did not start to do so in Phoenix until the latter part of that year. Partly because of the delay, layoffs were more concentrated. At the peak of the layoff, 9,000 Motorola workers had been let go; it was nine months before the company was able to begin calling them back. Explains Koziol, "We miscalculated the business."

The layoff was costly to Motorola in dollars, in talent, and in its ability to return to normal operations. While the high-tech industry subsequently mushroomed in the Phoenix area, at that time Motorola was the only large high-tech employer in the area. Consequently, those on layoff had no option but to seek work elsewhere. By the time the recall started, many had moved out of the area and Motorola was forced to recruit and train replacements.

While the dollar cost of the layoff was high, Koziol insists: "Of greater concern to us was the reputation of the Motorola culture. We were really letting our people down by not providing the job security that we felt we had an obligation to provide."

The company immediately began research to determine what steps could be taken to prevent a repeat of the traumatic 1974–75 Phoenix experience. Motorola visited Hewlett-Packard and IBM, among others, "because those companies have the reputation of being able to survive recessions without the necessity of layoffs."

Motorola Chairman of the Board Robert Galvin, son of founder Paul Galvin, had asked: "Is there some way that we can combine unemployment insurance with a reduced workweek?" Partly because of Galvin's question and partly because of favorable reports on work sharing with unemployment compensation at some of its European plants (primarily in West Germany), Koziol went to New York to meet with the proponents of work-sharing (with unemployment compensation) legislation that had been introduced but not passed in that state. "The more we learned," Koziol recalls, "the more interested we became in the idea and the more convinced of its potential."

"What we learned from our research of other company practices," says Koziol, "was that contract workers—not subcontractors but contract workers working alongside your regular employees in your own plant—could serve as a buffer in lean times." Motorola learned that some companies routinely understaffed their plants to leave room for such contract workers—people hired on six-month, nonrenewable contracts. The contract workers were paid the prevailing wage scale, but without benefits and without conversion privileges to regular-employee status.

Motorola adopted the concept, but with modifications. Using a six-month contract period, Motorola pays contract workers the same as regular employees, including fringes, and provides both for the renewal of a contract and the conversion of a contract worker to a regular employee. "It just didn't seem to make economic sense not to capitalize on the experience and training of a contract worker," says Koziol.

Motorola has found the contract-worker concept to be a viable buffer. Its general policy is to staff at 80 percent to 85 percent of requirements and fill the 15 percent to 20 percent gap with contract workers.

Following its investigation of the New York work-sharing proposals, Motorola began to push in Arizona for the passage of legislation to permit work sharing with unemployment compensation. As the largest private employer in the state, it wielded considerable influence, and Koziol held out to state officials and lawmakers the possibility that Arizona might become the first state in the nation to adopt the plan.

State officials seemed reluctant to be pioneers in the venture and Motorola was, at various times, urged to: (1) utilize the existing unemployment compensation structure through the rotation of full weeks off; (2) pay unemployment benefits directly without funneling the money through the unemployment fund; and (3) explore the idea in some other state since Motorola operated all over the country, indeed, all over the world.

Motorola persisted, however, and a survey made at its instigation revealed widespread support for the plan from unions, employers, and trade associations, with no focused opposition. However, the critical boost may have come, Koziol feels, from passage of similar legislation in California. Psychologically, Arizona seemed far more comfortable in following California's lead. Koziol is clearly still somewhat disappointed that the state did not capitalize on the opportunity to be first.

The formalized structure of buffers that Motorola has made standard operating procedure in all its operations begins with a hiring freeze, lever number one. "The hiring freeze," says Koziol, "is the easiest, the quickest, the least painful, and the least disruptive."

Lever number two is the elimination of all possible overtime. "Even in cases where it may be required," says Koziol, "it is particularly important to eliminate as much overtime as possible. Nothing can be more devastating to morale than to have some people working overtime while others are on layoff or threatened by layoff."

The third lever in the system is to reexamine work that has been sent elsewhere to see if it could be done in-house. In Motorola's case this is probably not as significant a buffer as for IBM since Motorola tends to subcontract mostly work that it does not have the capability of doing itself. This lever also includes the investigation of transferring work between divisions and between facilities.

Only after all of these buffers have failed to accommodate the problem is work sharing to be considered. That was precisely the situation in which Motorola's Phoenix-area semiconductor operation found itself when Arizona's work-sharing law became effective in January 1982. When the law became effective, Motorola was almost literally waiting in line to use it; throughout that first year, Motorola was by far the heaviest user of the plan.

Initially, Motorola had stressed that work sharing was not appropriate for permanent cutbacks but only for temporary downturns of no longer than three to six months. The company had concerns about possible resentment from senior and highly skilled employees and was not certain that they would be willing to subsidize, in effect, junior and lesser-skilled employees for longer than three months—or six months at the very most.

Koziol and other Motorola officials witnessed the program succeed in Phoenix even beyond the rather rosy expectation that they had painted when lobbying for the law. For the whole of 1982 there was a reduction in working hours of approximately 10 percent. While some of the 10 percent loss in wages was recouped by employees in unemployment benefits, there was still a very real sharing of the burden among the 9,000 employees who participated in the program.

The company made a concerted effort to sell the program to the employees before it was started, emphasizing that it was temporary and that it applied uniformly across the board, from top management to junior production workers. Employees who wanted to go on full-time voluntary layoff were given that option—and the company did not challenge their unemployment compensation claims—but the number choosing voluntary layoff was not significant.

The company had been particularly worried that some of the very highly skilled employees, who would have little difficulty in finding jobs elsewhere—including, by then, the Phoenix area—might rebel against the reduction in working hours by seeking another job. This fear turned out to be totally groundless. The company lost no skilled employees and there was little negative reaction to the reduction in hours, even though it continued longer than expected. There were many positive reactions, particularly from the veterans of the massive layoffs of 1974–75.

The company learned that people were willing, in Koziol's words, "to share the burden for much longer than we had expected." The experience convinced Koziol that "The social responsibility of people, their willingness to help others, is far greater today than it was 10 or 15 years ago."

Since the passage and successful utilization of the Arizona legislation, Motorola has been active in successful campaigns to enact similar plans in Florida and Illinois, and it expects legislation to be passed in Texas in 1985. It will then have, thanks in large part to its own political efforts, the benefit of work sharing with unemployment compensation in the four states where it has the majority of its manufacturing operations. Koziol has testified twice before Congressional committees in favor of a federal work-sharing law introduced by Representative Patricia Schroeder (D-Colo), which was incorporated in the Tax Equity and Fiscal Responsibility Act of 1982. Under that act, the Department of Labor is to conduct an evaluation of work sharing and develop model language for state work-sharing legislation.

Motorola is not unionized and the company attempts to set competitive wages and benefits. Its benefit package and stock ownership plan are described as "pretty standard," but it did pioneer, both in the industry and in the nation, a profit-sharing plan that dates back to 1947. Under the basic plan, employees contribute up to 3 percent of their wages to the plan and the company contributes approximately 20 percent of its profits, based on worldwide performance. The company contribution is divided among participants according to a formula that takes into account both the amount of each individual's contribution and points earned through years of service.

Labor costs are intensive in the semiconductor industry, and Koziol insists that "labor is still a significant, a sizeable part of our business." He concedes, however, that with automation, the labor content will be reduced and employees will need to be retrained to acquire new skills. "The Japanese challenge is forcing us to achieve extraordinary production efficiencies," says Koziol.

SIGNETICS

"This industry is like a light switch—it's either on or it's off, boom or bust," says Judith Williams, corporate manager of Employee Relations for Signetics, a large manufacturer of integrated circuits.[7] "Business conditions in the electronics industry can change fast and change dramatically. One day you may come to work and it's all gloom and the next day, everything will be turning up roses."

The suddenness with which its sales may pick up after, or even during, a recession is one of the reasons that Signetics searched for a way to adjust to downturns in business without having to resort to layoffs.

Another and related reason is the fierce competition for experienced workers among the high-tech companies located in California's Silicon Valley.
Signetics' headquarters and principal plant, employing some 4,000 people,
almost half of the corporation's U.S. work force, is located in Sunnyvale
within easy commuting distance of scores of other companies with similar
labor requirements. These firms compete for employees in a labor market
that, certainly in good times, is too small; even in bad times, competition for
the very highly skilled continues.

Signetics employees are a "diverse and eclectic" group, according to Williams. More than half of them are women, just under half are members of
minority groups, and ages range from 18 to 80. About 60 percent of the
employees are production workers. The educational level of the Signetics
work force as a whole is better than average, and the wages and benefits they
receive are described by the company as "competitive in the area and in the
industry."

Like other employees in Silicon Valley, Signetics employees are highly
skilled—in many cases due to company training programs. The company
describes itself as a place where an untrained worker can come in "off the
street" and, with hard work, acquire the skills and knowledge to win advancement. Many of them do just that—but such training is expensive in direct and
indirect costs. It may take a production worker three to nine months to reach
peak production and during that period the worker's training has not only
meant lost production but, more important, has required the time of other
employees.

Even when the newly trained worker has reached peak production, he or
she is probably not the equal of a real veteran. Explains Williams: "Some of
our more highly skilled workers can not only turn out maximum production,
but when something goes wrong, they can troubleshoot their own machines
and repair them. That kind of skill and knowledge comes with years of
experience, not months."

Understandably then, the company is reluctant to lay off employees. "Nobody likes to lay off people," says Williams, "but what we found was that we
can't afford to do so. Not in this business. It costs too much for many reasons.
When you lay off, you may never get your trained people back. In addition,
the company has to pay all of the costs associated with recruiting, interviewing, training, and waiting for the new people to come up to peak production.

"Those costs we could probably live with. What really hurts is when the
orders start coming in—and that can happen in an instant—and you are not
prepared to meet the demand. Even if you're very lucky and find most of your
folks, the lag time in getting back to work can be critical.

"You also run the risk that the business of one of your competitors will pick
up before yours does and that it will siphon off the best workers," she adds.

The problem with layoffs is exacerbated by the fact that Signetics' goal is a
full, permanent staff in good times and bad. Some companies operate with a

lean work force during periods of prosperity, using subcontractors, overtime, and temporary workers to absorb the large volume of work so that they can quickly shrink to a core work force during economic downturns. Signetics, however, does not ordinarily use subcontractors and relies on overtime only for temporary surges in demand. Temporary workers at the moment represent no more than 1 percent of the Signetics work force, with that number seldom going as high as 5 percent. Thus, it needs to find some other means of avoiding layoffs when business slows down.

Because the integrated circuit business is cyclical, Signetics has had periodic layoffs since the company was founded in 1961, but the worst layoff came during the prolonged recession of 1974–75. It was mostly the memory of that recession that prompted company officials to search for an alternative when business slowed down again in early 1981. That alternative turned out to be California's Shared Work Unemployment Insurance (SWUI) program.

Passage of the SWUI law had made California the first state in the union to encourage work sharing by enabling employees to receive unemployment insurance benefits for a short workweek. This kind of program, more generally known as short-time compensation, had been talked about and indeed advocated by a number of individuals and groups in the United States over a period of years, but California became the first to actually try it.

California's program offers partial benefits for up to 20 weeks a year to workers whose companies put them on short time in order to avoid a layoff. Benefits are proportional to regular unemployment insurance benefits. For example, a worker who would be entitled to $100 for a full week of unemployment would receive $20 for being unemployed one day a week. Since unemployment insurance benefits are tax-free and the worker is freed of job-related costs, such as transportation and lunch, most work sharers in California end up with about 90 percent of take-home pay. Both the firm and the employees have to meet regular California unemployment insurance eligibility requirements. Employers must declare in writing that a reduction of hours is necessary to avoid a layoff, and normal hours must be reduced at least 10 percent a week for at least 10 percent of the normal work force. If there is a union, it must agree to the plan.

Williams had read about the SWUI program, so when business began to decline, it was one of the options considered. A comparison of the advantages and disadvantages of reducing hours and using the SWUI program versus closing the entire Sunnyvale plant for two-week periods was prepared. Though both plans were viable options, it was felt that the SWUI program would be less of a hardship for the employees.

One of the early decisions—and one that undoubtedly enhanced the ultimate popularity of the program with employees—was to alternate Monday and Friday closings every other week and thus give everyone a four-day weekend (some came to call these "extended weekends" or "minivacations").

Closing the plant for four consecutive days also resulted in savings in maintenance and utility costs.

In addition to the reduced workweek, employees were also given the option of taking renewable 30-day leaves of absence during which time all their regular benefits were paid. All employees were sent advance copies of the SWUI enrollment forms and instructions, together with a booklet describing the SWUI program, which the company had prepared.

Arrangements were also made for officials from four different Employment Development Department (EDD) offices to come into the plant so that employees could avoid the traditional lines at the EDD offices near their homes. Careful advance planning made it possible for groups of workers to sign up without waiting longer than ten minutes. One employee, thanking the company for its sensitivity and efficiency, wrote: "It cost me seven minutes of my time and none of my dignity."

To give employees some idea of what they could do with their leisure time, the company prepared a special edition of the company newspaper giving information on amusement parks, museums, fairs, concerts, swimming pools, and other recreational and cultural facilities and events. In some cases, it was able to arrange group discounts for Signetics employees.

The SWUI program, when in full use, gave the company a 20 percent reduction in working hours. It was in use for most of 1981 and 1982, but only in the first summer were all employees affected. Its flexibility allowed individual departments to use the program at other times, however, depending on work requirements.

For the nonexempt employees who used the work-sharing program, the 20 percent reduction in working time amounted to approximately a 10 percent to 15 percent reduction in take-home pay. Some of the lost earnings may have been offset by savings in commuting and other work-related expenses, but exact figures are not available. Benefits remained the same for work-sharing employees, with the company continuing to pay full benefits during the periods of work reduction, even though that meant some increase in the hourly cost of its benefit program.

Early on in its efforts to calculate and compare the costs and benefits of work sharing, the company became convinced that the exercise was mostly academic because the actual costs of the program are almost impossible to quantify. Explained Williams: "There may be an increase in our unemployment tax, for instance; however, its impact may be spread over several years. In addition, we have always tried to avoid layoffs, so our experience rating has been good and our unemployment taxes have been low."

Signetics employees had few problems in adapting to the unorthodox SWUI schedule because they are accustomed to a diversity of work schedules even when they work full time. At least four such schedules are available: three 12-hour days; four 10-hour days; five 8-hour days; or a fourth variation that provides for three days of work, one day off, four days of work and seven days off. It was not as easy to adjust to reduced take-home pay. Despite the loss of earnings, however, the program was popular with employees. More than half of the 4,000 Signetics employees are women and they, in particular, seemed to welcome the opportunity to spend more time at home and with their children, especially during the summers when the program was in full swing. Said one woman: "When work sharing first started, I sat down and made a list of all the things I wanted to do and normally don't have the time to do. For the first time in years I caught up." "I wish we were on work sharing again" has become a frequent refrain in the plant since the upturn in business and the end of the program.

The company was as pleased with the program as employees were, and Williams describes the work-sharing experience as "one of those rare and happy occasions when a bureaucratic program really works." For the company, the two most important benefits were the ability to respond instantly to any sudden, even temporary increase in orders and the retention of a trained work force. One of the earliest large users of SWUI in California, Signetics would not hesitate to use the program again should the need arise, says Judith Williams.

DAIMLER-BENZ (WEST GERMANY)

When there is a slump in demand and a consequent surplus of workers, two ways to spread the work—and thus provide an element of employment security for the employer's work force—can be considered. One is by reducing total work time, principally by curtailing the weekly hours worked by each employee. The other is to reduce the work force itself, usually on a temporary basis, but sometimes permanently. West German companies use both methods, often with the support and financial assistance of government programs designed for this purpose.

The reduction of weekly work time has provoked different responses in West Germany. When the reduction is done on a temporary basis, as in the implementation of the German short-time compensation program, there seems to be full and complete acceptance by all parties concerned—the unions, the employers, and the government. Under this program, which served as a model for the U.S. short-time compensation programs, an employer faced with a drop-off in business can reduce the workweek, apply to the government for short-time compensation, and be reimbursed in part by the government for the time not worked by employees. For example, if a company using the short-time scheme put its employees on a four-day week, they would be paid for up to 68 percent of the amount that would have been paid for the fifth day, in addition to being paid for time actually worked. Workers receive their pay from the employer, who in turn submits his claim for reimbursement from the government unemployment insurance system.

The program is strictly temporary, limited to six months, although under certain circumstances it can be extended to a year. Many West German employers have taken advantage of "short time," particularly during the recessions of the mid-1970s, when the drop in demand was recognized as being temporary. Today, although still popular, the program is not an appropriate remedy for the more permanent structural dislocations that are presently taking place. To cope with the structural problem, the West German unions proposed a permanent reduction of the workweek to 35 hours as a means of spreading the work and ensuring employment security for workers in the future. The demand was strongly rejected by employers. A long, drawn-out strike/lockout situation was finally resolved in a compromise agreement in June 1984, reducing the workweek to 38½ hours, starting in 1985.

Work-force reduction—as opposed to work-*time* reduction—is still another story. The government-assisted early-retirement schemes described in the following section are an example of a permanent work-force reduction. So is the West German government's program of providing financial inducements to its foreign guest workers to encourage them to return to their native countries. A temporary work-force reduction that takes place in some of the larger companies shifts workers from plants and factories with temporary unused capacity to other plants unaffected by the drop-off in demand and still operating at full production. The Daimler-Benz Company provides a good example of this strategy.[8]

Daimler-Benz is one of the largest German automotive companies, producing trucks, buses, and other commercial and industrial vehicles in addition to the well-known Mercedes cars. A multinational corporation with production plants on every continent, the company has earned a worldwide reputation for the superior quality, excellent workmanship, and consistently reliable performance of the vehicles it produces. Daimler-Benz has also earned an equally admired reputation for its employment policies. Just as the company prides itself on its superb engineering, so does it pride itself on its personnel management. Employing almost 150,000 workers in 11 factories and more than 40 subsidiaries and workshops throughout West Germany, Daimler-Benz works hard to apply a well-planned, consistent personnel program that will provide maximum employment security for its workers. Although there is no specific job guarantee, as a practical matter jobs are secure, and the company's written policy states: "Our aim is the security of continuous employment."[9] To achieve that goal, the company has dedicated itself to a carefully developed system of personnel planning, including the preplanning of redeployment or, as they call it, the "delegation" of personnel as needed to assure continuity of work for all workers.

Although Daimler-Benz makes use of both buffering and other employment security strategies, such as controlled overtime, special shifts, and the use of temporary employees, the company has probably made more use of intracompany shifts than most other West German companies, and certainly more than most companies in the United States. In 1982, a total of 1,380 workers were shifted to other Daimler-Benz factories when there was not enough work in their home plants to keep them busy. For the most part this meant shifting workers from the truck and commercial-vehicle factories, which are usually the first to feel the effects of a recession, to the factories producing autos, which in the case of Daimler-Benz appear to be immune to recessions, certainly to the recent recessions. In carrying out the shift, Daimler-Benz pays the worker's transportation to the new locations, and guarantees his or her normal rate of pay plus an additional 750 Deutsche marks per month to compensate for the inconvenience of working away from home. Lodging is also provided free of charge, and in addition, each worker is allowed a company-paid trip back to visit his family every two weeks.

In 1982 Daimler-Benz estimated that the cost of the program was about 1,500 Deutsche marks per worker per month, or about $750, over and above normal rates of pay. A company spokesperson agreed that it is expensive, but examined that it is well worth it. As Rolf Weller, director of Personnel Planning for the company in Stuttgart, said, "Our experience shows that it works well for short periods. The worker's know-how is increased by the exchange, which is valuable to us; for example, a worker from Mannheim who usually assembles buses learns to assemble a passenger car. And there are other factors to consider too. We set great store on quality and, therefore, on maintaining the know-how of our workers. Also hiring and firing is expensive. We try to get volunteers for the delegation and give first precedence to single employees." The company limits to one year the time any one worker will spend in such a redeployment situation because, as Weller says, "Delegation of a longer period of time creates problems of reintegration."

In the years 1983–84, Daimler-Benz became more interested in using part time workers as a means of introducing more flexibility into the work force which, in turn, company planners feel will enhance its employment security policies. Weller explained, "We see part time as one possibility of improving the labor market because it's a means of distributing work to more people. However only certain types of work lend themselves to part time. . . . It is not the same in every workplace and much will depend on how this is viewed by the works councils. . . . We used to be against part time because additional social benefits made two part-timers more expensive than one full-time employee. Today we're a bit more generous, both because of the labor market and because the efficiency of two part-timers, we have found, is greater than [that of] one full-timer."

Insofar as employment security is concerned, nothing is left to chance at Daimler-Benz. Planning starts at the top and includes not only the personnel planners but the company's strategic, production, and market planners. Daimler-Benz readily admits that it sets its market and production sights a bit low in order to assure both a stable market for the company and stable employment for the workers. The company's market strategy is to stop short of producing for maximum demand, holding back on capacity expansion until it is sure of a stable and continuous market for its products. Of course this can give the competition an advantage, but over time it has proved to be a profitable route for Daimler-Benz. Certainly it has been beneficial for the company's employees. Summing up the company's employment security program Weller says, "When we see a weak market approaching, we try to deal with it step by step, trying always to avoid the ultimate step, dismissal. . . . The decisive point in our employment policy—I believe it's specific to Daimler-Benz, although other companies are moving in this direction—is that we try in *good* times to follow a cautious policy in hiring. We ask ourselves whether we can afford to hire an individual on a long-term basis. We want our employees to have a feeling of security. This has proved to be a good policy for us."

EUROPEAN EARLY-RETIREMENT SCHEMES

For many European companies, early retirement of older workers is an accepted and, it would appear, favorite buffering strategy to protect the employment security of the remaining work force. In most Western European countries, laying off workers is not easy. Employers cannot adjust their work force to changing economic conditions by laying off surplus workers at will either temporarily or permanently. They must go through a series of mandatory, restrictive, and often time-consuming steps, which can include negotiations with the government as well as the union. Usually the restraints on using a layoff are in the form of advance-notice requirements, together with procedures involving the state employment service agency plus specified mandatory separation payments for the laid-off workers. French law requires that no one can be laid off for economic reasons without the specific permission of the state employment service. In West Germany, employers who wish to lay off personnel must prepare a "social plan," in cooperation with the union, which details the expected outcome for every worker affected by the layoff and which must be submitted to the employment service agency for approval. The British government is not as directly involved with layoffs as that of France or West Germany, but even there, advance notice of proposed layoffs is required and specific separation payments are mandated.

During the 1960s and early 1970s employment security was no problem for Europeans, and the legal restraints on layoffs were easy to live with. The OPEC oil crises in the mid-1970s and the subsequent worldwide recessions changed all that. European employers, like those in the United States, have had to find an acceptable way to adjust their work forces to changing conditions. Voluntary early retirement, even at the relatively early age of 50, has been their overwhelming answer. For Americans, this reliance on early retirement may be hard to understand. The present trend in this country is to extend the work life of the individual, not to shorten it. We are concerned with removing employment barriers for older workers, certainly not with encouraging them to leave the labor force. Why are European employers so enthusiastic about early retirement as an employment security strategy? Several reasons have been suggested.

First, the European reconstruction effort after World War II, the ensuing industrial expansion, and rapid economic growth required a concomitant expansion of the labor force. This was done by hiring very young workers (at least by U.S. standards), by importing non-native "guest" workers, and by requiring that everybody work long hours and long days. It should be noted that until recently, the legal school-leaving age in most Western European countries was 14 or 15, compared to 16 to 18 in the United States. (Moreover, in contrast to the pattern that prevails in Western Europe, a majority of U.S. youths continue their formal education beyond high school, thus deferring entrance into the full-time labor force until their early 20s.) All that is now changing, of course. But at the present time, many European workers have already worked for more years than their American counterparts and are ready for retirement at age 50 or 55.

Second, the European culture encourages—or at least does not inhibit—early retirement. There is no stigma attached to an older person not working, as is often the case in this country, where not working is perceived as not having social value. In Western Europe, retirement is viewed as a perfectly reasonable, respectable estate, particularly in the smaller towns and communities. In addition, there appears to be a certain fatalistic acceptance among many Europeans that current economic and technological developments require a change in life-styles. They believe that there will not be enough work for everyone in the future and, therefore, that they and their children cannot expect to be able to work 40 hours a week all their lives. In effect, they believe that there must be a willingness to share the work and to accept the consequences.

Third, the governments of the three countries whose programs are included in this study—West Germany, France, and Great Britain—provide financial support to early-retirement programs, both directly and indirectly. The financial burden of putting people on early retirement is not borne entirely by the employer as it would be in the United States. Indirect support comes from the extensive network of social programs for older people (e.g., health care, housing, and recreation), which are typically provided by Western European governments. With these programs, the annuities paid to early retirees, or to any retirees for that matter, can be lower than might otherwise to be the case.

Direct support is provided in various ways, often by linking financial aid to companies using early retirement to schemes for the employment of the currently unemployed. For a period in the early 1980s, the French government had a program in which employers were subsidized if they hired unemployed youth to replace those who left employment through voluntary early retirement. It was a relatively popular program with French employers, but it was dropped when it became too expensive. The British also subsidize a program which exchanges older workers for the currently unemployed. Under their job-release scheme, the replacement does not have to be a young worker, only someone who is unemployed. If an employer recruits a replacement for a voluntary retiree from the unemployment register, the government then helps to pay the pension costs of the retiree. The cost per job thus "created" has been estimated at from £6,000 to £9,000 per job.[10] This British exchange program is in addition to the regular program of financial aid initiated by the present conservative government to help companies meet the gap between early retirement at 50 or 55 and eligibility for normal social security benefits and/or regular earnings-related pensions.

In West Germany, the government normally pays up to 50 percent of the cost of the pension that an early retiree receives until he or she reaches the normal retirement age and is eligible for social security. This payment is made from the state unemployment insurance fund, which is supported by a payroll tax. With the present high rate of unemployment, this fund has come under increasing strain, and some benefits have had to be reduced. In 1984, the government enacted legislation under which the state would guarantee 65 percent of the former salary level to workers who opted for early retirement; additionally, if the employer rehired a replacement worker from the unemployment register, he would be reimbursed for 40 percent of the wages of the replacement worker. Although this proposal was clearly designed to take some of the steam out of the union demand for a shortening of the workweek to 35 hours, it did not have the desired effect. One reason, no doubt, is that most unionized workers were already guaranteed maintenance of income at a higher level under their collective-bargaining agreements.

Finally, early retirement is supported by the trade unions in all three countries. William Daniel of the Policy Studies Institute in London describes the current situation this way: "Yes, of course early retirement puts a heavy strain on the community. But the unions have accepted it. In fact they support it. The unions used to fight for no layoffs, but now they are torn. Their own members like voluntary early retirement, although often it is not really voluntary. The employers 'make them an offer they can't refuse.' £10,000 looks very good. This is a lump-sum payment, plus they get a guaranteed annual income. The unions used to fight for recognition of seniority. Last in, first out. But now it's the other way around."[11]

A good example of the change in union attitudes toward early retirement is seen in the employment security agreement between the Post Office Engineering Union and the British Post Office. Under this agreement, voluntary early retirement is listed as one of a number of strategies that should be used to protect the employment security of postal workers. The agreement provides that when there is a surplus of workers, anyone voluntarily retiring below the normal retirement age (60 for women; 65 for men) would receive not only the regular Post Office redundancy compensation (separation pay), but also normal retirement benefits. However, voluntary retirement is to be considered as an option *only* after other strategies, such as a hiring freeze, redeployment of surplus personnel, and reduction of overtime, have been considered. A spokesperson for the union felt that eligible workers would readily accept early retirement under these conditions. "If the situation can be resolved by voluntary redundancy, that will happen," she said. "Morale is pretty low right now; the terms are good. They will be tempted to go."[12]

Similarly, when British Steel was forced to cut its work force by approximately 160,000 workers, almost 75,000 left on either early or normal retirement, an outcome that was generally regarded by the union as the best alternative under the circumstances.

West German trade unions are divided on the issue of early retirement as a solution to the problem of employment security. Some unions, particularly the weaker unions, which have been less successful at the bargaining table and therefore more apt to look to government for solutions to employment-related problems, lean toward a state-subsidized early-retirement program. The stronger unions, like I. G. Metall, the metalworkers union, whose gains have come through the collective bargaining process, have made a reduction of the workweek to 35 hours instead of the present 40-hour level a major negotiating goal. (After a prolonged strike/lockout in 1984, the union settled at a compromise level of 38½ hours to commence in 1985.) The position of both groups, however, is fully consistent with the general trade-union thinking in Western Europe that employment security in the future can only be achieved by means of a reduction in the time each worker spends at work during a lifetime.

The French trade unions too face a dilemma with regard to early retirement. They recognize the need to restructure many of the older industries, particularly coal and steel, and they know that this will mean fewer jobs in those industries. "We can't put a bandage over our eyes."[13] Although there is concern with what appears to be a wholesale movement toward early retirement—indeed some trade unionists claim that the employers are practically pushing workers out at ages 55—in general the unions accept what they believe is inevitable and are trying to do the best they can for both the remaining workers and the retirees.

The age at which early-retirement is offered differs from country to country and from one industry to another. When British Airways offered early retirement in order to trim its work force, flight-crew members were declared to be eligible at age 50, other employees at ages 55 to 58. Both groups were offered an indexed pension and were also credited with an additional five years of service, thereby qualifying for a larger separation payment. Excepting only the pilots—who would be less likely to find other jobs in the same occupation at the same high rate of pay—about 25 percent of those eligible accepted

British Airways' early-retirement offer, and they did so very quickly. The offer was to be open for six weeks, but most of those who accepted had made their move within three days.

In France, where the normal retirement age has been lowered from age 65 to 60, the typical early-retirement age is now 55. Rhone-Poulenc, the big chemical company, routinely offers early retirement to its workers at age 55; so many accept that by the end of 1983, only 2.6 percent of the work force was over 55.[14] The company is very proud of its record of never having laid off anyone for economic reasons, and early retirement is the principal means of maintaining that record. When Rhone-Poulenc first began its early-retirement program, almost 90 percent of the workers who were eligible accepted the offer to retire.[15]

By 1984 that figure had dropped to about 60 percent, the chief reason being the decline in pension benefits resulting from the general downturn in French economic activity since 1981. (The French earnings-related pension system is supported on a pay-as-you-go basis, with employers contributing an annual assessment toward an independently managed pension fund. Thus, during a recession, the assessment is adjusted, payments into the fund decrease, and there is a concomitant decline in pension benefits.)

Early retirement is a major element in the restructuring of the French coal and steel industries, both of which have been nationalized. In the coal industry, retirement is offered, and at times required, at age 50. In the steel industry, the retirement age is 55. However, both miners and steel workers who retire at this age are prohibited from working again, or at least from working in a job which is covered by the social security system. No doubt there are many who find jobs in the underground economy.

The age factor can present a problem for employers. British Airways reports that its early-retirement program left the company with certain skill shortages when the company lost many people whom it had hoped would continue working. As a result they have tried to restrict eligibility, but that of course can cause dissatisfaction and create other problems for management. When the Ford Motor Company used early retirement to reduce the work force in its West German operations, 7,000 workers accepted the offer. Their departure caused the average age of Ford workers in those plants to drop from 43 to 38.[16] I. G. Metall, the largest of the West German industrial unions, is reported to have hardly any members left over 60.

The experience of the West German auto company, Adam Opel, a subsidiary of General Motors, provides an interesting illustration of some of the problems in using early retirement. Like Rhone-Poulenc, Opel claims to have been able to avoid any layoffs for economic reasons. The company is proud of its employment security program, and given the vicissitudes of the auto industry in recent years, with good reason. But there has been a cost.

Opel faced the first real challenge to its employment security policy with the OPEC oil crisis and world recession of 1974. A decline in orders required that Opel slim its big Russelsheim plant down from 38,000 workers to about

27,000. To accomplish this objective without layoffs, Opel's management offered two programs: an early-retirement offer to workers between 59 and 63 (63 being the normal retirement age for men in West Germany) and a greatly increased separation bonus to any other workers who could be persuaded to take it. Approximately 2,500 workers accepted the early-retirement offer. Among them were many who had been soldiers in World War II, and often prisoners of war. They had worked long and hard, and apparently were ready to retire. In the management's view, it was a fair deal for both sides.[17] About 3,500 younger workers and foreign guest workers took advantage of the generous separation inducement, the so-called "golden handshake" offer. Evidently they felt confident that they could readily get other jobs. By 1975 business had picked up and Opel had to rehire many of the younger workers who had been encouraged to leave.

In the fall of 1979, the company faced its second major crunch. Business slumped and once again it became necessary to shrink the labor force, which at that time totaled 43,500. The goal was to reduce staff to 34,000 by 1984, relying primarily on attrition and early retirement. But this time the union was not completely comfortable with the early-retirement solution. "That is not the right way to go," said Richard Heller, chairman of Opel's Russelsheim Works Council. "It is a difficult decision for a worker to have to make." Opel's management confirms that the process has not been easy. As a result of union pressure, the separation bonus was increased and the program cost the company more than it had in 1974. In addition, there was a loss of skills that affected the plant's efficiency. "We did indeed lose a lot of skilled, experienced workers. It was hard on some shops; the toolmaking departments especially had their difficulties." The union now would like to make retirement at age 59 a permanent feature of Opel's employment policy, but the company is reluctant to do so, precisely because of the buffering nature of the early-retirement program. "If we adopted retirement at 59 as a permanent thing," said Scholl, assistant personnel director at Opel, "we would lose our cushion [against cyclical downturns]."

Another West German firm, Siemens, the multinational electrical, electronics, and data processing conglomerate, has an early-retirement program with a twist. As a successful competitor in a high-tech industry with a growing market, Siemens' chief concern with employment security has been to assure the loyalty of its employees. The company has a reputation as a good employer, even as being somewhat paternalistic in its dealings with employees. As we have seen, even the high-tech industries have come under pressure to balance their work forces in order to cope with the world recession. Siemens has met this challenge with a variety of measures, early retirement being one of the most important. It was the Siemens' legal staff which found a way to use the West German unemployment compensation system to ease the burden of early-retirement schemes for employers, a procedure now followed by many German companies. Under West German law, it is possible for a worker to collect unemployment compensation for the year between his 59th and 60th birthdays, when the worker qualifies for the government-supported, early-retirement social security pension. Thus, if Siemens retires a worker at 55, the company need only pay a pension until the worker reaches 59, when the government programs become operative. Even so, the company has found the program very expensive. To reduce the costs, Siemens has developed another approach, a gliding-retirement program. Under this arrangement, older workers who have 20 years of service are given the opportunity to work half time, starting at age 55. They can continue on this basis for a maximum of four years, receiving 75 percent of their regular salary. A worker who enters this program at age 55 must, however, retire at age 59. If he or she enters later, the worker can still stay with the program for four years, but not beyond age 63, since that is when the regular West German social security system begins. In an industry where the pace of technological change is so rapid, early retirement and gliding retirement offer distinct advantages to employers since they permit the company to retain younger workers who, in this case, will be more likely to have up-to-date knowledge than the older group.[18]

Clearly, early retirement is costly, both to the companies which offer such programs and to society as a whole. In France, 25 percent of all 1982 public expenditures for employment-related programs—including unemployment compensation at a time when unemployment averaged more than 9 percent—went to support the early-retirement program, a substantial increase from the 17 percent used for early retirement in 1980. This amounted to one-third of the resources of the unemployment fund. It has been estimated that the average annual cost to the state of an early retiree in France is about 65,000 French francs, or about $8,125. With from 600,000 to 700,000 early retirees already on the rolls, the drain on the French budget has to be significant.[19]

NOTES

1. "Layoff Alternative," *Industrial Relations News*, November 20, 1982, p. 3.

2. "Loans vs. Layoffs," Bureau of National Affairs *Bulletin to Management*, June 12, 1980, p. 1.

3. "A Work Revolution in U.S. Industry," *Business Week*, May 16, 1983, p. 103.

4. Information on Siemens is drawn from material provided by the company and from interviews with Dr. Walter H. Schusser, senior director, Corporate Division Personnel and Industrial Relations, Siemens, AG in Muncih, May 1983 and Dusseldorf, January 1984.

5. Conversation with Fritz Hauser, labor counselor, Embassy of the Federal Republic of Germany, Washington, D.C., November 1983.

6. This case study is based on an interview with C. F. Koziol, director of Personnel Administration, Motorola Corporation, Schaumburg, Illinois, May 1984.

7. This case study is based on an interview with Judith Williams, corporate director of Employee Relations, Signetics, June 1984.

8. This case study is based on interviews with Rolf Weller, manager of Personnel Planning, May 1983, and Manfred Knigge, assistant manager of Personnel Planning, January 1984, both of Daimler-Benz, Stuttgart, West Germany. Information was also drawn from additional materials provided by the company.

9. *Daten und Schaubilder zur Personalarbeit bei Daimler-Benz, Marz 1983.*

10. Estimates provided by John Cahill, economic policy advisor, Confederation of British Industry, in an interview, January 9, 1984.

11. Interview with William Daniels, Policy Studies Institute, London, October 1983.

12. Conversation with Vicky Kidd, assistant secretary, Post Office Engineering Union, London, January 1984.

13. Conversation with Genevieve Rendu, Confédération Francaise Democratique du Travail (CFDT), Paris, January 1984.

14. "Rhone-Poulenc: Better Red than Dead," *The Economist*, May 26, 1984, p. 85.

15. Interview with Philippe Lecerf, SOPRAN, Rhone-Poulenc, Courbevoie, Paris, January 1984.

16. Conversation with Fritz Hauser, labor counselor, Embassy of the Federal Republic of Germany, Washington, D.C., November 1983.

17. Information on employment security practices at the Adam Opel Company was obtained in interviews with Dr. Horst Dieter Scholl, assistant director, Personnel and Labor Relations, Adam Opel Company, and Richard Heller, chairman of the Works Council, Russelsheim plant, Adam Opel Company, January 1984.

18. Information on the Siemens retirement programs was provided by Dr. Walter H. Schusser, senior director, Corporate Division Personnel and Industrial Relations, Siemens AG in interviews in Munich, May 1983, and Dusseldorf, January 1984.

19. Christophe Boulay, "Quelle Politique d'Emploie," *Social*, March 1984.

5.
Worker-Oriented Adjustment Strategies

In one sense, all employment security strategies could be said to be oriented toward the worker, since their ultimate aim is to make it possible for workers to keep working, if that is what they want to do. However, some strategies are designed to accomplish this objective by changing the conditions under which people work; others are designed to change the worker, or at least to help him or her adapt to changing circumstances. This chapter describes various kinds of strategies aimed at helping the worker make whatever adjustment is required, especially those adjustments necessary to adapt to economic fluctuations. It covers a wide spectrum of approaches.

Labeling is always imprecise, and as with the cases described in other chapters, the policies and practices carried out by both the companies and unions described here are not as definitively categorized as might be wished. Nevertheless, the cases included do demonstrate the variety of adjustment strategies that are being used successfully both in the United States and in Europe to promote employment security.

One of the oldest examples of the use of *retraining* as a way to foster worker adjustment to change is found in the program adopted by AT&T when the introduction of automatic dialing equipment drastically reduced the need for local manual telephone operators.[1] Fortunately the engineering processes involved in changing the switching equipment required a long lead time—two years or more—which gave the company time to plan work-force solutions. Company policy was to retain as many employees as possible, avoiding both downgrading and dismissals. The union representing AT&T employees, the Communications Workers of America (CWA), was informed early on of the coming changes and, throughout the period of change, management and union personnel worked closely together. The first step was to estimate the number of people who would be needed after the conversion took place. Using seniority as a guide, the planners then determined exactly who would be affected and began to devise solutions for each worker on an individual basis. Attrition, controlled hiring, transfer, and reassignment were all utilized to help smooth the transition. But retraining played an especially important role.

Probably in no other industry is change so much a way of life as in the telecommunications industry, where technological advances continue to have a major impact on jobs and on the workers who hold them. For this reason, the CWA has always had a particular concern for retraining its members. In fact, in recent years the union had established its own retraining centers, funded by joint contributions from the union and several employers. At these centers (which have since been disbanded with the breakup of AT&T) union members could, at their own volition and on their own time, take the necessary courses to upgrade their skills and thus keep up with changing technology. As could be expected, AT&T too has traditionally supported a substantial in-house training program for its employees. The break-up of the company may have changed the way training programs are administered, but it has not changed the priority that is given to the retraining issue by both the union and the company. One of the provisions in the collective-bargaining agreement reached by the CWA and AT&T late in the summer of 1983— before the breakup but with a carry-over provision to the new regional companies—continues the companies' commitment to retraining.

Such adjustment measures may be traditional in the telecommunications industry, but it has not always been so in many other industries, particularly the auto industry where, until the last decade, retraining was not a priority for either the companies or the union. Today, however, the picture has changed. Two case studies of retraining efforts are described in this chapter: the United Automobile Workers (UAW) and Ford Motor Company Employe Development and Training Program, and the new State of California Employment Training Program. (Another retraining program, this one at General Motors, is described in chapter 6.)

Redeployment (i.e., reassignment) of surplus workers to other jobs within a company is another means of preserving jobs discussed in this chapter. Redeployment may appear to be a logical and easy solution to work-force adjustment needs, but that is not always the case. There are many barriers to redeployment—among them the nontransferability of skills, inflexible job classifications, craft demarcations (usually formalized in collective-bargaining agreements), pay differentials, geographical considerations, and the negative attitudes of some managers and supervisors. Nevertheless, in Great Britain, British Airways has conducted an extensive program of redeployment and retraining as it has struggled to trim its work force in order to retain its competitive position. This successful program is described in some detail in this chapter.

Two examples of *multipurpose adjustment programs* are included here. One is the Canadian Manpower Consultative Service, a government-sponsored program which provides the stimulus, and half the money, to effect a range of adjustment measures to cope with employment changes. The second is the

Swedish Employment Security Council, an innovative institutional arrangement to protect the employment security of white-collar workers. In both cases, the emphasis is on developing a comprehensive package of adjustment services, using whatever resources are available, or creating new ones to deal with each problem on an individual basis. Flexibility is the rule. Individual tailoring is the method. Employment security is the hoped-for outcome.

A fourth worker-oriented adjustment strategy that has become popular in recent years is *outplacement*, the efforts made by companies to find jobs for their employees with another employer when dismissals are unavoidable. The experiences of the Dana Corporation when it had to shut down one of its plants demonstrates how outplacement efforts can provide employment security to workers in such a situation. A description of how Dana went about developing such a program and putting it into operation is included in this chapter.

UAW-FORD EMPLOYE DEVELOPMENT AND TRAINING PROGRAM

Tucked among the functional buildings of the Henry Ford Community College in Dearborn, Michigan is the UAW-Ford National Development and Training Center (NDTC). The surroundings are hardly evocative of a revolutionary spirit, but in fact the National Center is the outward manifestation of an entirely new, and one might even say, revolutionary commitment, jointly undertaken by the United Automobile Workers (UAW) and the Ford Motor Company to improve employment security for Ford workers. The National Center, with its relatively small staff, serves as administrative headquarters for the pacesetting UAW-Ford Employe Development and Training Program (EDTP), established as a result of contract negotiations between the union and the company in February 1982.[2] As described by Thomas J. Pasco, the executive director of the National Center, it is "the flesh-and-blood, bricks-and-mortar embodiment of the Employe Development and Training Program."[3]

It is important to remember that the 1982 agreement was forged at a time when the auto industry was facing its most severe test; the bottom had dropped out of the U.S. auto market, plants were being idled or closed, and tens of thousands of auto workers had been placed on layoff, many of them permanently. The Ford Motor Company's hourly employment dropped from a peak of just over 200,000 workers in 1978 to around 100,000 at the lowest point of the recession in early 1983. By April 1984, hourly employment had increased slightly to 110,000, with another 27,000 on layoff who still had recall rights.

The ultimate and mutually supportive goals of the UAW-Ford Employe Development and Training Program are two-fold: to enable Ford employees to more fully realize their personal growth and career development potential, and to improve the company's ability to compete successfully in the market. Its more immediate principal objectives are to:

- Provide training, retraining, and developmental opportunities for both active and displaced employees.
- Support local and national UAW-Ford Employe Involvement efforts and other joint activities.
- Provide opportunities for the exchange of ideas and innovations with respect to employee development and training needs.

These rather formally worded phrases camouflage to some extent the unique and innovative nature of the program. At least four significant elements make the UAW-Ford program stand out.

First, the EDTP is designed for both active and laid-off workers, even those who may have been laid off permanently. This is a break from normal practice. Most companies do not as a matter of course provide training and other development services for nonemployees. In this instance, not only are laid-off employees eligible for the program, but they were the principal focus of attention during the program's first year of operation.

Second, the program is called a "development" program with good reason. The purpose is to make it possible for UAW-represented Ford employees to fully develop their skills, aptitudes, and interests and thus enhance their personal growth and career opportunities. These goals flow from, and are fully consistent with, the ongoing, successful UAW-Ford Employe Involvement process, which was established by the 1979 Collective Bargaining Agreement well before the inception of the Employe Development and Training Program. Employe Involvement, or EI, as it is called at Ford, is not really a program but a process through which workers and management can work constructively together to solve work-related problems, improve the work environment, and enhance work relationships. The company and the union are full partners in the EI process which, with its local joint steering committees and voluntary employee problem-solving teams, paved the way for successful implementation of the EDTP.

Third, in line with the commitment of both UAW and the Ford Motor Company to recognize and, indeed, to make use of the individuality of its employees, the EDTP offers a wide range of options to Ford workers so that each can choose the personal growth and career development path most appropriate to his or her needs. The focus is entirely on individual development.

Fourth, the program is not intended to be, and in fact does not operate as, a national plan imposed from the top down on every Ford facility. Rather, it is an articulated effort to encourage and develop local employee development projects from the bottom up. The National Center in Dearborn is not a national academy, but a resource which local joint management-union committees can call upon to meet their needs.

How does the National Center operate? Under the 1982 Agreement, a Joint Governing Body (JGB) was established, to be comprised of an equal number of representatives of the company and the union. The JGB provides general direction to the program, establishing policy, providing overall guidance, and authorizing expenditures by the National Center. It is co-chaired by Peter J. Pestillo, Ford's vice-president of Labor Relations, and Stephen P. Yokich, UAW vice-president and director of the union's National Ford Department. These two also co-chair the National Joint Committee on Employe Involvement, further strengthening the tie between EDTP and EI. The Joint Governing Body includes six other members, three from each side. It also has responsibility for selecting the National Center staff, which is headed by Executive Director Thomas J. Pasco and Associate Director Richard J. Collins. A small professional staff includes specialists experienced in vocational education, career counseling, and job development. As Executive Director Tom Pasco points out, "No attempt was made to set out the details of all of what we wanted to do or how to do it. . . . We knew we could work together to fashion specific programs and allocate funds and staff intelligently for these purposes. We wanted to encourage local union and plant management autonomy and local ownership so that those closest to the situation would be intimately involved. . . . That is why we established a Center concept. . . . We wanted to serve the needs and desires of individual employees and not impose our own preconceptions."[4]

Financial support for the EDTP and the National Center is provided by a fund set up as part of the 1982 Collective Bargaining Agreement. At that time the company agreed to pay five cents per employee hour worked into this special EDTP fund. By the spring of 1984, this formula was generating about $10 million annually. With improvement in the economy and particularly in the automotive market, it seemed likely that this amount would be increased, thus permitting further expansion of the program.

The enabling documents for the EDTP and the National Center reflect a recognition by both the union and the company that the program, in order to be certain to meet the varying needs of individuals and groups within the company, would evolve over a period of time and would not—should not— spring forth as a fully detailed, elaborate panacea for employment security.[5] A phased operation was envisaged that would include, first, identification of training and education needs and resources and, second, a gradual development and implementation of specific programs designed to meet those needs. This would be followed later by the institution of the means to further the exchange of ideas and information and by evaluation studies of current efforts.

Assistance to Displaced Workers

When the program began, it was clear that the first problem was to do something about the thousands of displaced workers. Within a year and a half, six distinct but not mutually exclusive program approaches have been developed. They include career days, vocational-interest surveys, career counseling and assessment, job-search skills training, prepaid tuition assistance for self-selected education or retraining, full-time group-sized retraining in skills for which there has been a forecast of job growth, and special comprehensive assistance programs for workers involved in necessary plant closings.

All of the elements of EDTP come together to create a variety of paths to accommodate what laid-off employees feel will best meet their needs. As indicated in the program design, many options are available to laid-off employees, and they are free to select the path they feel is best suited to their interests, abilities, and goals. The available options follow:

Career Day Conferences. The first step in the EDTP is the organization of Career Day Conferences to inform groups of laid-off employees of program options and available community resources. Typically, these conferences are coordinated by the local EDTP committee, with assistance from the National Center representatives, and bring together local community and public-service agency representatives to explain appropriate social programs. For example, in a limited period, from January through March 1984, 14 Career Day Conferences were conducted—11 at local union halls and 3 on community college campuses—attended by over 5,800 laid-off employees from 22 company locations.

Vocational Plans and Interest Surveys. Upon local request, and usually in conjunction with a Career Day Conference, the National Center assists the local EDTP committee in designing and administering a survey instrument to gather information on employee career plans and interests. Such surveys assist individuals in beginning the process of self-evaluation and exploration of alternatives and are essential to facilitate and focus the planning of specific local activities. From October 1982 through March 1984, 23 separate surveys of over 7,300 laid-off employees were conducted.

Career Counseling and Guidance. Career Counseling and Guidance (CCG) programs and projects assist employees in their self-evaluation process by helping them formulate specific career goals and plans to attain them. These programs may vary from location to location but generally consist of four main components: self-awareness, career awareness, career decision making, and career planning. With the help of the Macomb Community College in

Michigan, the National Center developed general specifications and guidelines for potential vocational CCG applications. Using these model guidelines, the National Center helps local unions and plant management obtain the delivery of specific programs from qualified local institutions. Local committees review the proposed content, length, time, and place; solicit attendance; and evaluate results with professional help. A consultant has been retained to assess local efforts, identify the most promising aspects of a number of local programs, and recommend changes as warranted. From December 1982 through March 1984, 10 local joint committees, with National Center assistance, initiated Career Counseling and Guidance projects covering more than 2,000 participants.

Prepaid Tuition Assistance. The National Vocational Retraining Assistance Plan, launched in August 1982, is a prepaid tuition plan for laid-off employees, to help them better equip themselves for new and perhaps different jobs; even for jobs outside the auto industry. Coverage was broadened in early 1983, and there have been over 4,800 enrollments through March 1984. Briefly, the plan pays tuition and certain fees—up to $1,000 per year for up to four years, depending on seniority—for self-selected education and retraining. In order to participate in the program, the worker must apply to the National Center, where a check is made to determine his or her seniority status and the validity of the educational or training program in which he or she plans to enroll. The participant must also present certification of enrollment. Payment is then made directly to the training facility by the National Center on behalf of the worker. An important difference between this program and the regular tuition assistance program, which for many years has been available for employed Ford workers, is that tuition for laid-off workers is prepaid, while, until recently, employed workers have had their tuition payments reimbursed.[6] This is in recognition that laid-off workers will probably be less able to pay the cost of their retraining programs in advance.

There are some restrictions on eligibility. Participants must be a UAW–Ford-represented employee on layoff and must have recall rights under the Collective Bargaining Agreement but have no immediate prospect of recall. Courses covered under the plan include high school completion or general equivalency courses, as well as college, business, trade or vocational school courses, or other courses approved by the National Center.

Targeted Vocational Retraining Projects. Another retraining strategy, called Targeted Vocational Retraining (TVR) projects, differs from the National Vocational Retraining Assistance Plan in that it is designed to serve groups of permanently laid-off Ford employees on a project basis, rather than on an individual basis. The retraining projects, approved on a one-by-one basis by the Joint Governing Body, consist of specially designed, full-time, technical or skills-oriented retraining programs focusing on areas identified as having job prospects or representing future job-growth markets. In other words, TVR is not a "fishing license" to upgrade skills and thus enhance general ability to compete in the labor market. It is a training program for specific occupations for which a need has been identified. It is expected that the training will be long, involving full or half days, and lasting from 15 to as many as 50 weeks. Further, to ensure a direct link with the local labor market, the projects are closely coordinated with the activities of community agencies as well as with local unions and management.

The initial pilot project was established in September 1982 at the Henry Ford Community College. It consisted of two training programs: a welding certification program and a course for tool-and-die detailers. Seventy-two individuals benefited from the programs, including both laid-off Ford workers from 15 southeastern Michigan locations and 18 individuals from other companies. It was funded through joint EDTP and other funding arrangements, principally the state-operated Trade Readjustment Assistance programs. Successful completers were helped by the Michigan Employment Security Commission (MESC) in finding jobs. MESC also assisted in the recruitment and selection process, as did the Downriver Community Conference, a local cooperative community agency.

Job-Search Skills Training. For various reasons, many individuals neither need nor want retraining and are interested principally in job-search assistance for employment consistent with their background and experience. Job-Search Skills (JSS) workshops provide laid-off employees with professional job-search assistance that supplements the basic state employment service and employment search orientation sessions. The workshops help laid-off employees with labor-market information, job-seeking support systems, resumés, and interviewing skills. JSS training may vary from about a week to more extended programs that include "job club" support techniques. From December 1982 through March 1984, special Job-Search Skills workshops were attended by over 900 laid-off employees at eight locations.

In addition to these six general program approaches, EDTP has been particularly effective in implementing action plans to assist workers displaced by plant closings in San Jose, California, and Sheffield, Alabama, as well as those laid off from Ford facilities in southeastern Michigan.

Special National Center Assistance for Plant Closings. Assistance for employees displaced by plant closings in terms of income support, other benefits, and placement in other jobs at Ford traditionally has been a provision of the UAW-Ford Collective Bargaining Agreement. Now, the EDTP and the

National Center provide special assistance to the local parties with respect to career guidance, outside job search, and retraining matters. The UAW-Ford National Center, through on-site consultation and liaison with governmental and community agencies, has assisted the San Jose[7] and Sheffield plants in the design of their approaches.

In addition to directly funding particular features of local action plans, the EDTP has facilitated the use of outside resources. The program and the National Center have helped local unions and management obtain assistance under the Job Training Partnership Act and other federal and state dislocated employee and training assistance provisions. External commitments for monetary and in-kind service contributions of over $7.8 million have been received either through action of the center directly or through local parties with center assistance.

The local EDTP Committee at San Jose has aggressively pursued a full range of assistance programs for laid-off employees. By early 1984, every employee at San Jose had had the opportunity of participating in at least one education, retraining, or counseling activity—and many had participated in more. At the Sheffield plant, a Career Services and Reemployment Assistance Center has been established at the local UAW union hall. A number of employee development actions and training programs are currently operating, and others are in the planning stage.

National Center Assistance for Employees Laid Off in Southeastern Michigan. In March 1984, the UAW and the company, in a further effort to assist laid-off workers, expanded their joint training and retraining efforts with the dedication of three Southeastern Michigan Career Services and Reemployment Assistance Centers. There were approximately 12,000 employees in the area who had recall rights and thousands more who had lost recall rights. Experience indicates that approximately 20 percent to 40 percent of laid-off employees are interested in job-search assistance and in training for new jobs. Based on the successful experiences of EDTP in Sheffield, Alabama, and San Jose, California, the centers offer such services as vocational and educational counseling, selectively targeted and accelerated retraining programs, and prepaid tuition assistance. They also refer individuals to other community-service agencies and programs, as appropriate. The participation of dislocated workers is voluntary.

The centers are locally operated by selected consortiums representing educational institutions and service-providing agencies under the direction of the UAW-Ford Center. These one-stop service centers have an advisory committee comprised of local company and union representatives and are funded by an initial $1.6 million from the UAW-Ford National Development and Training Center and a $1.7 million grant from the state of Michigan.

Specific local training and development projects are established through joint local committees and, to the extent practical, rely on a network of existing educational institutions and local community resources to provide counseling, education, and retraining. Whenever possible, such projects are coordinated and integrated with government and community assistance programs.

A Summing Up. "The basic goal of the dislocated worker is reemployment, but not just any employment," says National Center Associate Director Dick Collins. "Dislocated workers, especially, may feel that the system has let them down. They want a quality job—one with dignity and one that will last." The EDTP tries to help them achieve these goals but also tries to be realistic about what programs can achieve in time and in places of high unemployment.

The rate at which laid-off workers use the EDTP is high compared to similar programs—largely attributable to the joint company and union commitment to the program; the dedication of national and local management, union representatives and professional staff; and support from local community resources. Utilization is generally higher in counseling and job-search assistance programs as well as in plant closings, where employees recognize clearly that there is no prospect of reemployment at their former plant. It is obviously dependent on the number of employment opportunities available and the level and type of unemployment in a particular labor market, but it is also influenced by skill levels; by personal mobility, family obligations, and income availability; by individual characteristics; by the time and effort necessary to upgrade skills; by an individual's perception of the short-term versus the long-term gains in areas of great uncertainty; and by a host of other factors.

In the future, the Joint Governing Body (JGB) plans to make the program more readily available in all the communities in which the company operates resulting, perhaps, in a doubling of the number of people using some part of the program. The JGB will also strive to improve the quality of the various approaches, develop new ones where needed, enlarge the network of community and educational interactions, and arrange for an evaluation of the total effort by outside observers.

"The success of the EDTP will ultimately be measured by a number of indicators: jobs secured, the quality of jobs, duration in new employment, speed of reentry, training entered and completed, participant testimony, and independent evaluation," said Ernest J. Savoie of the UAW-Ford Joint Governing Body in a presentation to the Joint Economic Committee of Congress on September 23, 1983. "But perhaps the key measure of success should be expressed in less statistical and more human qualities—the sense of accomplishment in attaining new skills and reemployment, and the confidence of individuals and families restored in themselves, in their society, and in their institutions."

Assistance for Active Workers

With the programs for dislocated workers well under way in December 1983 the National Center announced that it was ready to move into the second phase and give increased attention to programs for active UAW–Ford-represented workers. While making it clear that programs for displaced workers would continue to be promoted vigorously and supported fully, the new program, called "New Avenues for Employe Growth," offered six new initiatives for continued education and further training for active employees:

- prepaid tuition assistance for formal education and training
- career and educational counseling and guidance
- basic skills education and enhancement
- specially tailored college-level associate degree programs
- preretirement counseling
- other special education and training projects

These six programs are to be offered to active employees on a voluntary basis—consistent with their individual interests—to enhance their career potential and personal growth. Some can be initiated directly by employees, but most will depend on actions and programs shaped by joint local Employe Development and Training Program committees, assisted by the UAW-Ford Center. All programs must be approved by the Joint Governing Body. They include the following:

Education and Training Assistance Plan. This plan incorporates the Tuition Refund Program previously in place and improves on it. Employee tuition is prepaid, as it is for dislocated workers; the former limit of $500 on some courses has been raised to a maximum of $1,500; and the range of courses has been expanded to include courses which may lead to a new career or support individual employee personal growth. This program, which is now administered by the UAW-Ford National Center, has provided assistance for over 2,500 employees since the beginning of 1984.

The second provision of the Educational and Training Assistance Plan is Personal Development Assistance. It covers noncredit, nondegree courses such as communications skills, self-motivation, and computer literacy.

Career and Educational Counseling and Guidance. In the past, few employees in the hourly work force have received encouragement to think about—let alone do something about—upward mobility within the work force. Career and Educational Counseling and Guidance is designed to assist employees in achieving personal and career goals. As with other such programs, the joint local EDTP committees initiate and administer this program.

Basic Skills Education. The third major program for active employees is Basic Skills Education. Launched in one plant as a pilot in August 1983, this program has since enrolled over 475 employees, forming the basis for further expansion as a national program. Basic Skills Education has four fundamental components: adult basic education for those functioning at the elementary school level; general educational development, or GED, for those desiring a certificate; and high school completion for those who need to acquire a few credits to get a high school diploma. A fourth element is "English as a Second Language" for those whose native language is not English.

This program has resulted in some innovative approaches to basic education. At the Dearborn Engine Plant, a computer-assisted program determines the grade or school level at which an employee is functioning. The computer produces a printout which specifies where an employee has or does not have mastery of math and language skills. A second printout lists what math, reading, and writing courses the employee should start with. Additional features are the convenient on-site, in-plant learning center, which is available to employees before or after work; voluntary participation; and self-paced learning programs, which permit each employee to progress on a separate track and at his or her own rate. Teachers are experienced in adult education techniques and are provided by local public schools.

Special Associate Degree Programs. Intended to address employees' personal and career development needs and to provide advanced credit for life and work experiences, these programs better prepare employees for promotional opportunities. They are administered by local colleges, with most courses being offered at the work or plant site. Counseling experiences at pilot plants suggest that skilled trades workers, in particular, may find this program especially attractive. For this program, as well as for the other "New Avenues" programs, the joint local EDTP committees oversee development and implementation.

Preretirement Counseling. This program assists senior employees in making the transition to retirement. Information on insurance and pension benefits is offered at local union halls, in-plant facilities, or other facilities that may be selected by joint local EDTP committees. Additional information on legal, financial, and estate planning; time utilization; travel; and other relevant topics are presented by representatives of outside organizations.

Targeted Education, Training, or Counseling Projects. The sixth program is intended to supplement other program offerings and to cover specific needs of a particular location or segment of the work force. In addition, it provides opportunities for locations to initiate special Employe Development Research pilots. By March 1984, pilots had been launched at seven locations for 35 employees.

Worker dislocation hurts the United States' competitive position. It also diminishes the domestic market's buying power, increases the costs of social service programs, extracts high psychological costs from its victims, and diverts attention, energy, and resources from the search for technological innovation.

In regard to active workers, their underutilization is a serious drag on the country's industrial competitiveness. Initiative, motivation, and innovation are all inhibited if individual workers are not encouraged to develop their capabilities.

Many of the features of the UAW-Ford approach to assisting the dislocated worker with respect to retraining and reemployment services, and the active work force with respect to various education and training options, are not unique or unusual. "What is new and dynamic," says Tom Pasco, "is the spirit, care, and cooperation with which UAW and Ford have approached these problems and the solutions which they have developed."

Anyone visiting the National Center must be struck with the upbeat atmosphere of the place. No doubt the program will have its failures as well as its successes, since it cannot be expected to resolve everyone's employment security problems. It seems clear, however, that both the union and the company are committed to increase employment security. The UAW-Ford Employe Development and Training Program, in which more than 12,000 employees from Ford locations throughout the country have already participated, is an experiment well worth watching.

CALIFORNIA'S EMPLOYMENT TRAINING PANEL

In full operation for less than two years, California's novel experiment, which diverts a portion of unemployment insurance (UI) funds for retraining purposes, has already made a difference in the state. Over 1,000 businesses, in industries as varied as construction, telecommunications, auto, computers, electronics, food processing, aerospace, and agriculture are participating in the program, retraining many who are unemployed or who would have otherwise been laid off. To date, a total of $67.8 million has been committed to train more than 20,000 people.

Although the program is being directed under the aegis of a state government agency, the seven-member Employment Training Panel which administers the fund is entirely drawn from the private sector. Appointed by the governor and leaders of the legislature, the panel includes representatives of business, labor, and the general public. In addition to taking people off the unemployment rolls by retraining and putting them back to work, the panel has adopted a twin goal to stimulate the state's economic development. Training support provided by the panel has helped troubled industries to retool and survive and has convinced other healthy businesses that might have moved out of the state to stay and expand in California. In this respect the program can be called a layoff prevention program. Certainly it qualifies as an unemployment prevention program and, as such, it contributes to the employment security of all of California's workers.

The program differs from traditional vocational training programs in two major respects. First, training is financed by diverting $55 million a year that otherwise would have gone into the UI system. The financing will last for a period of four years, until January 1, 1987, when the program expires (unless extended). California is the first, and so far the only, state to use UI funds in this manner. Second, all training is directed toward specific jobs, and there must be a commitment on the part of the employer to hire the trainees. Furthermore, the panel only pays employers or other trainers if the trainees go to work.

The Employment Training Panel was created in 1983 "out of a recognition that the economic transformation California faces today is as profound as that in the 1930s and that the unemployment insurance system must change as well," according to an April 1984 report published by the panel.[8] Steve Duscha, the panel's executive director, elaborates: "During the last recession, California suffered as greatly as any other state. There had been feelings of insulation, but these quickly dissipated. It became clear to business and labor that the changes in the economy were so great that they had to take another look at training for people already in the labor market who were being pushed out by technology, foreign trade, and other deep-seated structural changes."

At first, there was enormous skepticism on the part of both business and labor toward "another government program." But as unemployment and plant closings continued to mount, both sides became convinced of the program's potential and actively supported the legislation creating the panel and the retraining fund. (The bill establishing the Employment Training Panel was authored by California Assemblyman Pat Johnston, while the legislation that funded the program was introduced by Assemblyman Alister McAlister.) Because of federal restrictions on the use of unemployment insurance funds for training, the state legislation first reduced the UI tax paid by positive-reserve employers (those who have experienced little or no unemployment and have therefore underutilized their UI account) and then imposed a new state tax, to be collected with the UI tax, on the same employers.[9] There was little concern about eroding the UI fund in California since at the time the legislation was enacted there was a surplus in the fund. Nor did employers object, since the program did not involve any additional taxes for them. In effect, a portion of the tax that private-sector employers pay to support the federal/state unemployment insurance system was set aside in a separate fund for training and retraining.

From the very start, the policy was to avoid burdensome paperwork. Staff members were instructed to work directly with business and labor and with public and private training agencies in developing training programs in high-demand and expanding fields. In large measure, input from employers and labor unions determines the structure and operation of specific training projects. Employers—and unions, when appropriate—have the opportunity to determine who will be trained, what the training will consist of, and what the standards are for completion.

Because the money comes from the unemployment insurance system, it must be spent to retrain (1) unemployment insurance recipients, (2) unemployed workers who have exhausted their UI benefits within the last 12 months, or (3) workers who, in the judgment of the panel, are likely to be laid off and claim unemployment insurance.[10] In many cases, the full cost of training is shared between the state and the employer or other groups involved in training. However, the financing arrangements—depending on the number of trainees, the complexity of skills to be taught, and other factors—vary widely.

In seeking out businesses that need assistance in training, the panel meets regularly with employers, labor unions, schools, and vocational training agencies in an attempt to establish programs that serve businesses and workers. In addition, the panel has initiated several special projects with other entities that have particular experience in retraining and economic development. For example, a major cooperative effort is under way with the California Department of Economic and Business Development to train workers for new and expanding firms and to encourage reconversion of older plants through training assistance and grants to cover business feasibility studies. A $3 million contract with the California Manufacturers Association will train 1,000 people for the association's member firms. The panel has also developed joint programs with administrators of the federal Job Training Partnership Act (JTPA). To avoid duplication, a notification system has been worked out in which the Employment Training Panel and the local Private Industry Councils (PICs) which administer the JTPA programs keep each other informed about their local projects. According to the panel's April 1984 report, training assistance is provided "when business is unable to find an adequate number of appropriately trained workers." Director Steve Duscha looks upon the state's training assistance as a valuable government incentive to increase investment in human capital, not as a "tax break" for a service which business might have performed without the state's help. "We make no apologies for serving business. The only way to put somebody to work is to satisfy a real business need," states Duscha.

Accordingly, the panel itself operates in a business-like manner and demands results. "Performance-based contracts" with employers or other groups designate the number of people to be trained, the types of jobs to be filled, and the company or companies that will hire these trainees. Contracts can last up to two years or be as short as six months. As of May 1984, the Employment

Training Panel had negotiated 152 separate training contracts. In order to be paid for training costs, employers must certify that the trainees have been hired and have remained on the job for at least 90 days. The panel does not pay any of the wages of hired trainees. Another requirement of the program is that training be for "good, steady jobs that pay a decent wage and keep people from cycling back onto the unemployment rolls. Only in that way can the panel fulfill its responsibility to reduce unemployment insurance costs," according to the panel report. Temporary, make-work jobs that pay minimum wage are avoided.

A program to retrain 100 machine operators at ITT Cannon, a company that designs, manufactures, and markets electrical connectors, operates under a typical contract. Employees are being trained to work on advanced automated equipment. They had been hired as low-skilled assemblers and progressed to machine operators, but their skills were not sufficient to run the technologically advanced machinery their jobs now demanded. A local school in the Rancho Santiago Community College District is providing the classroom instruction. The Technology Exchange Center, a broker for job training involving business, labor, and the public schools in Orange County, marketed and helped develop the program.

"We're seeing a tremendous diversity in training needs," states Duscha, "and we are going to train for whatever positions business tells us there is a demand." Many of the positions are in high-technology businesses, but there are even more in traditional manufacturing industries where there are frequent high-tech applications. Blue-collar workers are learning new technologies in their changing industries instead of facing unemployment. Projects include training in the use of computerized numerical controls for machine tools, computer-assisted manufacturing systems, automated manufacturing equipment, and high-technology specialties for electrical and sheet-metal contractors. In other instances, training has been provided for businesses that have undergone extensive modernization and need additional workers, such as a recently reopened portion of a lumber mill in Siskiyou County that is hiring workers and training them on the job in plywood manufacturing skills. White-collar workers are also learning new skills to adapt to changing technologies. Among the projects supported by the panel are those that teach computer-assisted drafting, automated bookkeeping, and word processing to office workers, and electronics to business-machine repair people who fix computerized equipment.

Several retraining projects have been targeted to the needs of special groups, including farm workers, construction workers, women, minorities, and veterans. A special pre-apprenticeship program in welding and blueprint reading for women and minorities new to the sheet-metal trades is being offered, since contractors report more demand for workers skilled in these areas. In order to reduce their cyclical periods of unemployment and the significant drain this represents on the unemployment insurance system, building-trades workers and farmworkers are involved in a variety of projects that will upgrade their skills and strengthen their position in the labor market. Carpenters, for example, are being taught how to install prefabricated modular systems, which are replacing traditional carpentry methods in modern office-building interiors. Fifteen California growers are participating in a project that will retrain farmworkers to become farm equipment maintenance mechanics and supervisors.

The Employment Training Panel is convinced that retraining and economic development in the State of California go hand in hand. It defines its economic development responsibility as follows: to ensure that California has smarter and better-trained workers than any other state or foreign nation. While many factors affect a business decision to locate or expand in any given area—proximity to markets, cost of land, availability of financing, natural surroundings, housing—the availability of a trained work force plays a crucial role. Larry Borgman, a site selector for Intel, a California electronics firm, told members of the panel that when his firm makes a decision to open a facility, the most important factors to consider are "the availability of labor, the type and quality of labor—everything else absolutely pales in comparison to that item."

According to the panel's report, until the Employment Training Panel was created, California had no statewide program that could effectively compete with other states that lured businesses away from California, partly by promising tailor-made training that prepared workers to perform specific jobs for specific companies. Although training is only one part of California's economic development strategy, it already has had a direct impact on the decision by some companies to locate or expand in California. Integrated Device Technology, an electronics firm in Silicon Valley, had been planning to build a new plant that would employ approximately 400 workers. Two sites were under consideration: one in Boise, Idaho, and the other in Salinas, California, an area hit hard by recent plant closures. The company chose Salinas. Says Duscha, "Management told us that the training assistance they received from the panel was a major factor in their decision to expand in California." The panel negotiated an $825,000 contract to train 275 people in high-tech fields.

Some projects have helped new or recently reopened companies survive the first critical months of operation. Training support was crucial in the conversion of Poppy Foods, a turkey-processing operation in Central Valley. The company had closed its turkey-killing plant in February 1983 and later reopened as a producer of cooked and processed turkey specialties. The panel worked with the Tulare County Economic Development Corporation and the California Department of Economic and Business Development to retrain the laid-off workers for new jobs in the converted plant. Other economic development projects include training assistance for an expanding recreational vehicle service and sales company, a plastic bag manufacturer, a lumber company, several expanding electronics firms, and a bank credit card accounting and billing system.

Based on his experience and involvement in the California program, Steve Duscha believes that training is one area where the interests of both labor and management clearly coincide and where there need not be conflict. "A lot of the talk about labor and management working together on economic problems is unfortunately mostly talk. But that's not what we're seeing here," he says. The benefits to both sides are clear: Quality training results in a highly skilled work force and improves productivity, wages, and profits—all factors that ensure the long-term prosperity of industry and increase employment security for workers. Many of the training projects have kept union members working and have reemployed others who had lost their jobs. Organized labor has taken an active interest in the California program, serving as the catalyst for developing about one-third of the panel's training projects.

Projects have also been jointly developed by labor and management. The International Brotherhood of Electrical Workers and the National Electrical Contractors Association are retraining 60 electricians in San Mateo County in high-technology specialties, including programmable controllers, semiconductor devices and security systems, and instrumentation. One of the first contracts signed by the panel involved the retraining of laid-off auto workers from Ford's San Jose assembly plant. The panel has worked closely with Ford, the United Auto Workers, and the Santa Clara County Manufacturing Group to develop four separate training projects which will retrain one-fourth of the 2,000 workers laid off when the plant closed in May 1983. Auto workers are being retrained in a variety of occupations—as microwave technicians, welders, machinists, and others—for nearby small- and medium-sized firms. Another joint project, developed by Blue Shield and Local 3 of the Office and Professional Employees International Union will retrain 60 claims processors as microcomputer operations specialists. The workers were laid off when Blue Shield closed its branch in San Francisco. The retrained workers, mostly minority women, including many older workers and heads of households, will work in automated offices at Bank of America, Levi Strauss, Lanier, ITT World Communications Division, Clorox, and Diebold.

Clearly, the response to California's retraining and economic development project has been overwhelmingly positive. The fact that jobs have been saved and new jobs developed, and that plants on the verge of closing are today in operation testifies to the effectiveness of the program. Since most of the projects are still under way, it is too early to evaluate the program objectively on such data as the number of trainees back at work or the reduction in unemployment insurance costs. However, statistics on these items are currently being developed. Meanwhile, Executive Director Steve Duscha is optimistic about the results: "I believe we'll see some clear reductions in unemployment insurance costs. In a large number of projects, trainees are employed from the first day of their training, so we are immediately taking them off the unemployment rolls and putting them back to work. Even if workers remain on unemployment insurance while training, they will have a better chance of staying off UI in the future."

Are other states likely to emulate California's innovative approach to preventing unemployment? Some, including New York and Massachusetts, have already shown an interest. "I have received a number of calls about our program," reports Duscha, "and I believe we'll have more. My impression is that a lot of states are looking at this kind of approach. It's a very logical way to do business."

BRITISH AIRWAYS

The experience of British Airways is particularly interesting because it shows how a company faced with the need to retrench has managed to trade off employment security for its workers with flexibility in assignment for the management, apparently to the benefit of both parties. Two important ingredients in the success of this effort were the role of the British Air Trade Union Council (BATUC) and the ability of management to develop and adapt training programs that allowed the flexible assignment policy to work.

Actually there are two British Airways stories to tell. The first concerns an event that took place about two years ago. The company, acting through the BATUC, informed the unions that it had decided to shut down a part of its "highland and island" service in the north and west of Scotland since the route was losing money and, in the company's view, there was not enough traffic to justify its continuation. The unions were given about five weeks' notice of the decision. Immediately two committees were established by the unions: one to look at the issue from the point of view of preserving the jobs, and the other to investigate how to continue service to the area. The committees' suggestions for a more efficient operation included reducing the number of jobs by half, and using a different kind of aircraft. The key to the plan's success was in union acceptance of a more flexible approach to job assignment. For example, the flight personnel—pilots, flight attendants, and others—also handled the baggage, served as passenger agents, and performed duties not normally associated with their job. The committees argued that they could continue the service and break even within a year and, in fact, they did just that. Obviously the plan did not result in gaining employment security for all, but 108 jobs were saved out of the total of 400 that were originally scheduled for elimination.

The second British Airways story involves the company-wide effort to reduce costs and maintain a competitive position.[11] At the beginning of the 1980s, British Airways found itself facing a falling market and tough new competition. In addition, the new planes which the company had ordered in more prosperous times began to arrive, and these had to be paid for. A complete review of all costs was undertaken, including routes, equipment, fuel, and labor—the largest operating cost item. As a result of this review certain targets were set, among them the reduction of personnel from a high of almost 60,000 to a final target of 35,000 over a period of four to five years. The level at the end of 1983 was about 36,500.

While predecessors had encountered the problem (British Airways was formed in 1976), British Airways had never had to cut its personnel before, at least not its domestic personnel. It was a mammoth undertaking. The first steps, typically, were a hiring freeze and the institution of an early-retirement plan. For flight crews the early retirement age was 50. For other personnel, it was originally set at 55 and then reduced to 50. The result was something less than successful: The company lost valuable technical personnel and specialists and, in addition, an age problem was created. So many people in the middle and upper echelons—the group most apt to be eligible—accepted the fairly generous offer of early retirement that there were large gaps on the progression ladder. Not enough people were left with sufficient experience to move into the higher grades when those too became vacant.

For British Airways, the initial answer was redeployment, but this was not an easy task. Suggestions for redeployment of a person or group of employees were met with much resistance and a great deal of internal pulling and tugging. Managers and supervisors tended to think of their staff as "their" personal staff and felt threatened by what they regarded as a loss of effective influence over their team. The issue was almost one of "ownership" of particular people. The redeployment effort creaked along.

Organizational change then offered other solutions. The number of operating divisions, each with its own personnel management, was reduced from twelve to three, and responsibility for recruitment and deployment of staff was placed firmly in each of the three divisions. The reorganization helped, as did the strong role played by the corporation's personnel office, but still there were problems. The next step was the publication of a corporate employment strategy. This stated that the objective of corporate personnel policy was to offer employment protection to employees, and this would be accomplished in two ways. The first was the redeployment of personnel, with great flexibility in the way the goal was pursued. Second, to the extent that the target ceiling could not be met through attrition and redeployment, the company would offer a voluntary severance scheme to further reduce the number of employees. The severance scheme offered was a one-time cash payment of between 70 percent and 130 percent of annual salary based on length of service. The program was aimed primarily at workers between the ages of 28 and 40. There was no expectation that they would cease working, but only that they would be induced to leave British Airways and seek work elsewhere.

Meanwhile the company persisted in its efforts to redeploy personnel, but always assuming complete flexibility. What was added was a strong commitment to the training and retraining necessary to make the redeployment work.

Initially, some trade-union officials were opposed to redeployment, and indeed there was considerable unease among all levels of workers. The problem was not usually with the person being moved, but with the group to which he or she was reassigned. One issue, of course, was the seniority question. This issue, however, was worked out with the unions through the National Joint Council. The second problem was one of jealousy, since the transferees carried their grade and salary with them to the new assignment, even if their new co-workers had lower grades and wages. Moreover, the transferees were allowed to keep their grade and salary forever, or until they left the company— something that clearly could cause trouble. Although the existence of such disparities in pay for the same work clearly can affect employee morale and perhaps lead to lower productivity, the company was willing to take this risk for several reasons. First, it was fully committed to making every effort to offer other positions to those employees who chose to stay. Second, there was the concern that certain skills be retained within the corporation in the eventuality that business improved. Finally, the move was an important element in gaining union acceptance for the deployment program. As it has turned out, the transferees themselves have worked hard to gain acceptance by their fellow workers in their new assignments—with a certain degree of success.

In the beginning, there was a genuine disbelief among both managers and workers that British Airways actually meant business, and that it could make redeployment happen. But this disbelief has given way to gradual acceptance. British Airways has successfully moved people to assignments that would previously have been considered at the very least inappropriate and, at the most, impossible. Reservation clerks, engineers, maintenance personnel, and even administrative staff have all been successfully reassigned as cabin crew. Some of the former flight-crew personnel were opposed to the idea, and one group even threatened to strike; however, when another group indicated its acceptance of the reassigned workers, the threat was withdrawn. Motor transport drivers and security personnel have transferred successfully into administrative work. They have also been trained as reservation clerks and passenger agents, an idea which initially raised some eyebrows among some of the more tradition-oriented employees.

To help in the retraining and reassignment process, the company introduced a broad-scale counseling program and, in so doing, discovered "skills that we didn't know were there." But even this wasn't easy. One problem was simply to find enough counselors to handle the load. This was solved by drawing on the managerial staff, giving them quick training in counseling, and sending them out on a temporary basis to work in teams with regular professional counselors. As time went on, the British Airways spokesperson admitted, "We got better at it."

Training, of course, also played an important role. Again British Airways had to feel its way in establishing the kinds of training programs that made sense for its particular situation. British Airways worked closely with the unions in shortening the time it takes to receive a basic trade certificate—in one case the time was reduced to twelve weeks from three years—and in eliminating some of the previous jurisdictional demarcation that existed between the trades. Training has had to be especially tailored to British Airways' needs. Older workers, British Airways found, had to be given more time to learn new trades and generally did better learning from experience than from textbook situations. For this reason the company has often shunned the regular classroom training available in colleges and technical schools and has relied heavily on the skills centers of a government agency, the Manpower Services Commission.

British Airways has not yet reached its staffing target. And it will face an uncertain future when it becomes a private rather than nationalized company in 1985. But the corporation is very much aware of the need to protect employment. Like other service industries, and particularly other airlines, British Airways is highly dependent on the efficiency and skills of its workers for its success. British Airways is determined to build a personnel policy that will enable the company to count on a high level of performance from its employees.

CANADA'S MANPOWER CONSULTATIVE SERVICE

The immediate focus of Canada's Manpower Consultative Service (MCS), a small division within the government Department of Employment and Immigration, is on worker adjustment—making it possible for workers whose jobs are affected by economic and technological changes to adjust in a positive way. However, the long-term result of the division's activities may well be increased employment security for the work force as a whole. What the Manpower Consultative Service has to sell is a program designed to stimulate, encourage, and support private-sector solutions to work-force adjustment problems. How well they have been able to do the job is shown in its longevity and in the high repute in which the program is held both in Canada and among employment-policy practitioners in other industrialized countries. Operating with a small staff and relatively low budget, the MCS stands ready to move into situations where some form of adjustment is necessary. The agency's role is to act as a catalyst in bringing together the parties involved and to lend support to whatever joint solutions are reached. The chief mechanism is a tripartite committee, composed of representatives of both labor and management and chaired by an outside party, selected jointly by the other members of the committee.

Key to the program's success is MCS's ability to gain the confidence of the parties involved and the committee's commitment to follow through on the solutions chosen. An additional factor that is perhaps equally important to success is the availability to the MCS of a range of government support programs, although it is the ability and ingenuity of the MCS staff in using these programs that make the real difference.

The program works in this way: When the Manpower Consultative Service hears that an employer is having or expects to have some sort of adjustment problem, the agency sends one of its officers to offer its services to the company. (In Canada, most employers are required by law to provide their employees with advance notice of proposed cutbacks or plant shutdowns; at the same time they must also notify the Canadian employment service. It is this notification that frequently triggers the initial MCS visit.) Participation in the MCS program is voluntary and not all of those visited by an MCS officer are interested in taking part in the program. One MCS official estimated that no more than one in ten of the initial visits resulted in the establishment of an MCS program; others reported that the proportion may be somewhat higher, especially in areas where the MCS program is well known.[12] From years of experience, the MCS has learned that the initial contact with the company should be made with the company's top decision maker, since only that person can make the commitment necessary to the program's success. The same principle applies to the agency's dealings with the unions. In companies in which one or more unions are involved, the top officials of those unions are brought in. If no union is involved, the MCS officer arranges with the work force for suitable representation.

Once both the company and the union have expressed an interest in taking advantage of the MCS program, a formal agreement, called a Manpower Assessment Incentive Agreement, is drawn up and signed by the company, the union, and the government, represented by the Minister of Employment and Immigration. Sometimes the agreement also includes the provincial government. The agreement is a relatively simple document in which the parties agree to set up a tripartite committee called a Manpower Adjustment Committee with responsibility for assessing the adjustment problems and suggesting appropriate solutions. The agreement also sets the termination date of the committee and establishes the roles of the participating parties in meeting the administrative costs associated with the committee's business. This includes the salary of the chairperson as well as the costs of necessary research, professional, and clerical staff. The Manpower Consultative Service will pay 50 percent of these costs, but only on a reimbursement basis. Generally the company assumes full responsibility for the remaining 50 percent, although there have been some instances where the union or the provincial government has borne a share of the expenses. It is thought that requiring the parties involved, primarily the companies, to initially be responsible for paying all expenses, half of which are reimbursed later, helps to ensure the necessary commitment from the company to make the program a success. Most agreements last from about six months to a year. If necessary, they can be extended. The agreements follow a fairly standardized format, except for the section in which the parties set forth their own objectives and responsibilities.

Once the agreement is signed, the two principal parties, with the help of the Manpower Consultative Service officer, who sits in an ex-officio capacity on the committee, select a chairperson. This person must be someone from the private sector and must be approved by the MCS. Chairpersons are often selected from the ranks of retired business or labor leaders, from university staffs, or from nongovernment organizations whose function is to assist small businesses. There have been several cases where the chairperson is the former head of a company which itself experienced a serious adjustment problem. Often the same people have chaired a committee previously. A good chairperson will probably find it necessary to spend almost full time working at the job, certainly during the first part of the committee's life, and often throughout the entire period.

The Manpower Consultative Service program began in 1963 when the most important employment issue was automation and its potential effect on employment. Then, as now, government officials were concerned about the problems of worker adjustment and were looking for a way to help smooth the process. The basic design of the MCS program has not changed in 20 years. From the beginning, the program was based on a reliance on private-sector implementation through the establishment of tripartite committees, backed with technical and monetary support from a highly skilled and dedicated cadre of government personnel. That is still the way it operates today.

The only significant change that has taken place over the past 20 years is that the program has grown. In 1963, three staff members were located in the department's headquarters in Ottawa; by 1969, when the program was regionalized, the staff had increased to 12. MCS had a staff of 50 located in five regional offices in 1974; this number, including clerical as well as professional personnel, increased to 66 in 1983. During the fiscal year ending March 31, 1983, the staff concluded some 428 agreements, a record high. The government's expenditures for this effort in 1982–1983 amounted to C$4.6 million, more than double the amount spent in the previous year.

Approximately two-thirds of the cases handled by the MCS are located in small population centers of 50,000 or fewer. Of the companies which use the MCS, approximately twice as many are in manufacturing than are in service industries, and in most cases fewer than 100 workers are involved in the adjustment process.

The adjustment program is not the only program handled by the Manpower Consultative Service. In recent years it has also had responsibility for the administration of a mobility program, a temporary work-sharing program, and a program providing assistance to communities facing serious employment adjustment problems. Moreover, the adjustment program itself is not limited to cases of layoff or reduction or a particular work force. In 1974, the concept of the program was broadened to include adjustment problems related to plant or company expansion and to changes in employment resulting from technological change.

Since every labor adjustment situation is in some ways unique, the MCS adjustment program is designed to permit the greatest possible flexibility of approach. In cases of technological or economic change forcing layoffs or closures, the committees' work generally focuses on finding acceptable outcomes for the individual workers affected. This can include such activities as establishing a counseling service, setting up an outplacement program to help find new jobs for the displaced workers, investigating alternate assignments within the company structure, or arranging for necessary training or retraining. The committees can also make use of the MCS mobility program in which the MCS can provide up to 50 percent of the cost of moving an individual to a similar job in another town or city. In one such situation, the MCS provided over C$1 million to move some 600 Saskatchewan displaced miners to other mining jobs.

In situations where expansion, high turnover, or low productivity are the principal problems, and where there is no significant layoff, committee activities tend to concentrate on the development of human-resource planning, improvement of work-force utilization, the design of training courses, and project monitoring. The committees can, and sometimes do, also involve themselves in feasibility, managerial, and operational studies. Probably the biggest single activity of most committees, however, has been the placement of employees who are displaced because of economic changes, and it is in this area that the MCS has built up its best known record of success—placing from 65 percent to 85 percent of those asking for placement help, at an average cost of approximately C$120 per worker.

The Manpower Consultative Service has worked with companies in all of Canada's ten provinces, although by far the largest majority of the cases are concentrated in the two provinces of Quebec and Ontario, the center of industrial activity. Over the years the service has found it easier to get into plant-closing and layoff situations than into situations where expansion or job restructuring is the problem. However, MCS officials indicate that this situation has changed somewhat in recent years and that the research activity of the committees is taking on increasing importance. Instead of simply making a list of the workers who are being laid off and then helping them find new employment, the committees are increasingly following a preventive strategy and looking for alternatives to layoffs. In effect, they are prospecting for new and different ways to keep people employed. To be sure, this trend can involve the committees in activities that might previously have been thought to be the sole prerogative of management. But as MCS staff point out, the committees do not, for example, actually make the decision to update equipment, change product mix, or develop new markets; they simply research such ideas, giving management the opportunity to try an alternative to layoff. Increasingly the committees are looking at the adjustment problem as a whole—the underlying causes necessitating the adjustment, as well as the immediate problem—and trying to help management decide how the problem should be handled. In this respect, the MCS program is following much the same path as the Swedish program described in the next section.

One might well ask how a government agency, and a small one at that, can successfully fill the role described here. How can a group of government employees pretend to have the answers to so many difficult managerial problems? In fact, MCS does not pretend to be able to solve every problem. It is, however, a unique group of exceptionally talented and dedicated public servants. Generally speaking, officers are recruited especially for the Manpower Consultative Service from the private sector and from both management and labor. For the most part, they come to MCS with a depth of experience and a particular sensitivity to their role in the program. As one officer notes, "We have to be able to put ourselves into the situation." Several are former business owners or managers who themselves have been through the MCS process. One official described the staff in this way, "We need people who have no qualms about talking to the top people, so we try to recruit either from top management or top union people." The MCS officers have to be able "to sense the little tidal waves" of interaction between management and labor. They have to have a "lot of union-type savvy."[13] They also must have a detailed knowledge of the kinds of government support that can be made available to the committees if and as they require it. They need to know, for example, the procedures necessary to take advantage of government mobility programs, of training and retraining assistance, how the early-retirement system works, how to go about utilizing the government employment service and other agencies in running an outplacement program, and where the committees can go for technical advice and assistance on such matters as the introduction of new technology or computer-assisted design and computer-assisted manufacture (CAD-CAM).

The MCS staff hold senior-grade positions in the civil service and are relatively well paid by Canadian government standards, about C$35,000–$45,000 per year. They are given a great deal of freedom to conduct their activities on their own, and many work from their own homes. The hours are terrible, with many night and weekend meetings, long drives between cases, plus the time spent in preparing the inevitable forms and reports. During the early period of a committee's work, they often find themselves more or less on call, to answer individual questions and deal with emergency situations. It is not an easy job but it is, apparently, a rewarding one. Here are some examples of the kinds of cases in which the Manpower Consultative Service has been involved.

When Canada General Electric (CGE) decided to shut down its hydro-generator plant in Scarborough, Ontario, an industrial community just out-side of Toronto, 420 employees—120 white-collar and 300 blue-collar workers—faced the prospect of losing their jobs. Because of the plant's age and the declining market for hydrogenerators, the company had reluctantly decided that shutdown was the only solution. As soon as the closing an-nouncement was made, the MCS offered its services. This was immediately accepted by the management and the white-collar work force, but not by the United Electrical Workers (UE), the union representing blue-collar employees. The committee that was established to help white-collar employees promptly went to work, distributed a questionnaire to determine the skills, aptitudes, and preferences of the affected workers and, on the basis of that inventory, began a systematic canvass of other employers in the area to find new jobs for those being displaced. Within three months, almost all of the white-collar workers had been given assistance and helped either to find new jobs or to take some other route, such as early retirement or retraining.

The UE, however, remained adamant in its refusal to accept the MCS program, feeling that to do so was tantamount to surrender to plant closure. Instead, the union focused its energy and attention on keeping the plant open, by whatever means possible, appealing both to the public and to the political process. The closing was given much publicity. Hearings were held; the mayor and the city council were involved. But all to no avail. Planning for eventual closure continued, and in November 1983 the first group of approximately 50 blue-collar workers were laid off. Further layoffs were planned for December, with the last group scheduled to leave the following March. At that point the workers, realizing that the closing was inevitable, belatedly accepted the MCS offer. A committee was quickly established and began its work. But the task was not easy. The average age of the work force was 45, and many had skills which had become obsolete. The chairperson selected for this committee had served in that capacity on at least three previous occasions and had also worked with the MCS officer handling the Canada General Electric closing. They knew what was required. After conducting a work-force assessment, one of the first tasks of the committee was to explore with the local education system the possibility of establishing a counseling and job-search skill devel-opment program tailored specifically to the needs of the CGE workers. To-gether the MCS officer and the chairperson approached the local community college, fortuitously located only a few blocks from the plant, to arrange such a course. Costs of the program were to be borne by the provincial govern-ment. Although skeptical at first of the value of the course, which included a week of individual career counseling and a week devoted to development of job-search skills, the union representatives finally agreed that it might be worthwhile, particularly since many of the workers had never had to look for a job before.

There was some concern that unemployment benefits would be cut off during the time that a worker was attending the course, but this fear was quickly allayed by the MCS officer who immediately interceded with the local UI benefit office to make certain that the CGE workers' benefits would continue. For those workers near retirement age—and quite a number were in this category—the committee made the necessary arrangements for them to take advantage of Canada's preretirement program. A few workers expressed an interest in starting up their own businesses; the committee, with the help of the MCS officer, put them in touch with the appropriate government units offering technical assistance and support for new small business. For those interested in leaving the community and taking new jobs elsewhere, the committee was the vehicle through which these individuals could make use of MCS mobility grants. Obviously the adjustment committee could not find the perfect solution for everybody—but it went a long way toward smoothing the adjustment process for this particular group of workers.

In the case of a company manufacturing structural steel products, the problem was not one of plant closure, but of productivity and maintenance of the ability to compete. Because the company was losing money, it decided that it had to cut back on its work force. Layoffs were announced, the MCS came in, a committee was established, and the assessment process begun. After carefully researching the situation, the committee concluded that the main problem was quality control. Subsequently, with the committee's help, the company's personnel management was changed by the introduction of quality circles, and its production methods were changed by the utilization of new technology—computer-assisted design and computer-assisted manufacture (CAD-CAM). The company began to recoup its market position and to show a profit. The proposed layoffs never took place. The costs of the program were minimal, although it must be noted that the introduction of the CAD-CAM technology came about as a result of the government-supported system of CAD-CAM centers, where businesses can get the technical assistance and training they need to take advantage of new technology. In this case the role of the MCS officer was to provide the liaison between the company and the CAD-CAM center, arranging for a specialist from the government center to work directly with the company.

Another instance where layoffs were largely prevented involved the Ontario Paper Company, a large newsprint manufacturing company in Thorold, Ontario. In 1981, the company announced that it planned to shut down the plant and lay off its personnel, preparatory to reequipping the plant with new technologically advanced machinery. Of the approximately 1,300 workers originally employed at the plant, the company planned to retrain some 800 and to lay off about 350. The problem of who to retrain and who to lay off was complicated by the fact that the work force was represented by nine separate unions, each of which bargained separately and each of which had its own seniority line. The adjustment committee that was established included representatives of all nine unions—something of an accomplishment—as it was the first time all of the unions had worked together. Although each union wanted its members to have access to jobs on the new machinery, these new jobs were not necessarily within the jurisdiction of any one union. The committee wrestled with this problem and others for more than three years, but in the end there were some notable accomplishments. First, early retirement was offered to those workers who were eligible, and more than 100 accepted this option. Normal attrition also reduced staff. To help those actually laid off find new jobs, a subcommittee canvassed local employers within the region, going door-to-door to locate potential openings. And to make it easier for this group, their old job descriptions were rewritten by the committee so that their transferable and marketable skills were made more obvious to prospective employers. For those who remained, a large-scale retraining program was carried out, for which all workers were eligible, with selection on a seniority basis. Consultants were brought in and the training was conducted at the plant. The cost of the training was shared equally by the government and the employer. New job descriptions acceptable to both the unions and management were written for the jobs on the new machinery. And, finally, a system of plant-wide seniority was installed. The company is maintaining its market and has even hired some additional people.

Two final cases illustrate the diversity of the MCS approach. A farm implement manufacturer in Brantford, Ontario, which was forced to shut down its operations for a period of months, felt that its principal problems were in quality control and poor supervision. The adjustment committee suggested training to upgrade the supervision and arranged for a government training grant to keep the supervisors on the payroll and train them during a part of the shutdown. And in Hamilton, Ontario, a small food-processing company developed a new way to package fresh food. With MCS help the company was given assistance in marketing its products and in training its employees. The happy result was that employment grew from 3 people to 135 people.

Given the long life and deserved good reputation of Canada's Manpower Consultative Service adjustment program, it might be expected that other countries would have tried to replicate it, but apparently such is not the case. A state program that is similar to, but does not replicate, the MCS has been established in Ohio. It consists of a Community Economic Assistance Team operating out of the governor's office, which coordinates state services to assist workers who have lost their jobs as a result of plant closings in the state. The team is comprised of representatives of all of the state agencies capable of providing some kind of assistance. As in Canada, the method utilized is the establishment of a tripartite committee consisting of representatives of the company, the union or other worker representatives, and the community. This committee's function is to plan for a long-term response to a plant closing. This, of course, is not quite the same as the Canadian approach, which tries to avert layoffs and to provide assistance in all kinds of labor-adjustment situations, but there are similarities in the two programs.

No other national government has tried to adopt or even adapt the Canadian formula. One reason may be the difficulty in recruiting the right kind of staff. The Canadian approach requires a flexibility in the management of personnel—a flexibility which may not exist in the civil-service systems of other countries. Another reason relates to the interface between employers, workers and their unions, and the government in other nations. These relationships, established both by law and by custom, are the principal determinants of the kinds of employment security policies and programs that are carried out in each country. Thus far they have not been conducive to export of the Canadian model.

THE SWEDISH EMPLOYMENT SECURITY COUNCIL

Whenever Hans Ursing, the managing director of Sweden's joint Employment Security Council, the Trygghetsradet SAF-PTK, talks about his program, he takes care to point out the "special" nature of Sweden's economy. Sweden is a small country of only eight million people and a labor force of about four million, of whom one and a half million are in private industry. There is a very high degree of unionization, about 90 percent among blue-collar workers and 80 percent among white-collar workers. Unemployment has never been as high in Sweden as in other industrialized countries, one reason being that the Swedes have used a variety of measures to keep unemployment low, such as state-subsidized training programs for unemployed workers and early-retirement schemes. Although a few industries, such as steel and shipbuilding, have been nationalized in order to speed up a restructuring and rationalization process, about 90 percent of Swedish industry is in private hands. Collective bargaining takes place on a truly collective basis, with private employers as a group—the Confederation of Swedish Employers—bargaining with either the federation of blue-collar unions or the federation of white-collar unions. The agreements that are concluded are applicable to all employers and to all unions. Acknowledging these differences—and they are not unimportant—there are still enough similarities between the U.S. and the Swedish social and economic structures to make the experience of the Swedish Employment Security Council of interest to Americans.[14]

The Employment Security Council was established in 1974 by collective agreement between the Confederation of Swedish Employers (SAF) and the Federation of Salaried Employees in Industry and Services (PTK). The PTK itself is the joint negotiating body for the Swedish Union of Clerical and Technical Employees in Industry, the Union of Commercial Employees, the

Swedish Association of Graduate Engineers, the Swedish Foremen and Su-perivsors Association, and about 20 other smaller white-collar unions. With only a few exceptions, all white-collar workers, about 500,000 in all, are covered by the agreement.

The initiative for the establishment of the Employment Security Council came from the unions, which were concerned about what appeared to be a trend toward reducing surplus personnel and more frequent dismissals for their members. During the 1960s, the PTK had negotiated an agreement that provided advance notice and generous severance pay for those white-collar workers who lost their jobs for economic reasons. By the 1970s, however, the unions' concern was not only to provide compensation for workers who were displaced, but also to find ways to enable employers and workers to adjust to change without dismissals. The unions, therefore, proposed a joint coopera-tive effort: (1) avoid layoffs if possible, and (2) if dismissal could not be avoided, help the individuals affected find new jobs. The Employment Secu-rity Council is a mechanism to do just that.

The council is a joint body, with five members representing the employers and four representing the unions. There is a staff of about 80 people, headed by Hans Ursing. The central headquarters are in Stockholm, but most of the staff are located in three regional and four branch offices. Activities of the council are financed by a fund which was established as part of the agreement. This fund is supported by a mandatory contribution from each employer of an amount equal to 0.65 percent of his annual payroll. Nonmember compan-ies may also participate in the program, but they must pay a higher levy to the fund, about 0.95 percent of the payroll. By the end of 1983, the fund stood at over 700 million Swedish crowns, or about $87 million.

The council's current objectives, Ursing says, is "to repair old jobs and to develop new ones." The description is apt. By "repair," Ursing means making the kind of adjustments within the particular work situation that are neces-sary to keep people working despite cyclical ups and downs and despite structural change. The development of new jobs, while outside the work situation, sometimes can be an integral part of the repair operation.

Insurance Programs

To accomplish these objectives, the council operates in five different areas. The first area is the administration of the various basic insurance programs which have been negotiated between the employers and the unions. The severance-pay agreement is one of these. Under this program individuals who are laid off can receive 70 percent of their gross salary, including unemploy-ment benefits, for up to 12 months. Another is the early-retirement program. In those cases where a company chooses to institute an early-retirement scheme for older workers nearing retirement age, the council can help the employer bear the cost. In addition, in cases of bankruptcy, the council can, if necessary, take over the obligation to cover full payment throughout the period of notice of termination. All this is done because of the strongly held presumption that the first requirement for workers affected by a layoff is to be made to feel secure financially. Unless they have such security, it is felt, other measures to help them, no matter how positive or ingenious, cannot succeed.

Personnel Clearing

The second area in which the council is involved concerns "personnel clearing." Basically this is a program to help people find jobs. It involves extensive employment counseling, the identification of appropriate jobs, discussion and negotiation with prospective employers on behalf of the displaced workers, and outplacement. The goal is to find a new job for each individual, and then to do whatever is necessary to put him or her in that job. The counseling staff numbers about 50 and is located in the regional offices. Counselors have at their disposal funds to use at their discretion to provide assistance to individuals. Sometimes it is money to pay for travel to an interview. Another time, it might be necessary to pay for training or further education to improve the person's qualifications for a particular job. Another person might need only books or other literature to upgrade technical or professional skills. Or the individual might want to try working at a new job for a limited period of time. If so, the costs associated with such a trial could be subsidized. There is no limitation on what can be spent to help any one individual, since different cases require different amounts of money. Flexibility and the provision of individually tailored assistance are the guiding principles. Apparently the system works: In 1982, about 8,000 individuals received assistance under this program, and there were no complaints.

Dismissal Prevention

A third activity that has received increased attention in recent years is dismissal prevention. The focus of this activity is to help companies with surplus personnel reduce their staffs without dismissal. This has become an increasingly important activity as Swedish industry has tried to restructure itself in order to increase productivity and thus maintain an ability to compete successfully in international trade. For Sweden, which must trade in order to maintain its high standard of living, rationalization (the reduction of surplus personnel) is an imperative. For the Employment Security Council, dismissal prevention also became an imperative when the crisis in the steel industry in 1976–77 threatened to swamp the council's personnel-clearing programs. There were simply too many people for too few new jobs. Both to reduce that work load and to try to alleviate the long-term damage that dismissal does to an individual's self-assurance and self-confidence, and thus to his or her ability to work productively and creatively, the council decided to try a dismissal-prevention program.

The way it works is this: Whenever the council hears about an impending reduction of staff—and it does hear about it, either through employers or through unions affiliated with the PTK—it sends in professional staff to work with both the management and the union to plan a prevention program. Essentially, the plan is the result of a cooperative effort on the part of both the employer and the union, with the council in a supportive role.

Typically, a plan will include a full range of employment security measures. It will probably start with a carefully calculated program of reduction by attrition. This will be backed up with an early-retirement program. It will always include provisions for retraining workers who are affected by the changes and who can be transferred to other parts of the firm, or even to jobs in other companies. These benefits could even be based on plans for product or market shifts. The role of the Employment Security Council in this effort is to "spread the ideas," provide advice, support, and as needed, half of the money necessary for implementation of the plan. In 1983, 3,000 workers were involved in the council's dismissal-prevention projects at a cost of about $7 million.

In talking about dismissal prevention, Hans Ursing stresses that the program is not foolproof. Certain preconditions must exist if it is to succeed. High on his list is the complete commitment of the executive management. It will not work, he says, if only the personnel department is interested. Backing must come from the top. However, the personnel department must be involved, and it must be both adept and professional. In addition, it must have independent control of enough money to fund the project. Although the council will help to finance the program, it cannot do the whole job; some of the funds must come from the company itself. Moreover, the overstaffing problem cannot be too big, too overwhelming. However resourceful the planners, however strong the commitment, dismissal prevention has its limits. Since much of dismissal prevention often turns out to be more akin to dismissal conversion, that is, shedding surplus workers by gradual, voluntary means rather than by abrupt authoritarian methods, a successful program requires a stock of vacancies into which people can move. These can be created through early retirement, a hiring freeze, or other methods, but they must be there. Finally, it is important that the pool of surplus workers include all grades of workers and not become merely a dumping ground for the least able. If that occurs, the ability of the program to successfully place, or even to retrain the surplus will be severely constrained. Not only will the specific program fail, but the entire effort will acquire a bad reputation, affecting other companies in similar situations.

New Businesses

Closely related to both the dismissal-prevention program and the personnel-clearing service is the fourth activity of the council, namely the program to help its members start new businesses. In Sweden, about 10 percent of those who either are laid off or are persuaded to leave their jobs voluntarily want to become entrepreneurs and start their own businesses, most of them small, service-type businesses. The Employment Security Council stands ready to help these people. In its first ten years it helped 2,000 companies get started, companies which today employ over 10,000 people, with annual sales of over $500 million. According to the council's own research, the survival rate of these firms is impressive. Seventy percent of the companies started seven years ago are still going. To help these would-be entrepreneurs, the council arranges for them to receive their severance pay—usually doled out on a monthly basis—in a lump sum. This can be a considerable amount, which in many cases can provide the initial capital necessary to start a new business. The council also provides a liaison function between the entrepreneurs and the government programs which exist for the support of small business.

Job Creation

The last field into which the council has moved is also in the realm of job creation, but on a much more generalized basis. Like many groups in Western Europe which are currently wrestling with problems of employment and unemployment, the council is searching for what it sees as the golden fleece of innovation and invention. Taking the United States as a model, and particularly U.S. inventiveness, innovation, and advanced technological development, many Europeans have concluded that they too can develop a Silicon Valley, if only they can find a way to encourage innovation. The Employment Security Council is trying to do just that in a variety of ways. Perhaps its most unusual undertaking is its school for inventors, a kind of seminar in which inventors are instructed in the procedures necessary to get their inventions into production. The council also provides scholarships for inventors who need additional financial support to further develop their ideas. Well aware of the benefits that have accrued to new high-technology businesses in the United States through close university connections, the council has also undertaken efforts to encourage closer cooperation of this kind in Sweden. Regional seminars based on travels abroad have provided another means for introducing Swedish employers and union leaders to practices that encourage and support innovation in other countries. All of these activities are carried out at a relatively modest cost. The council's 1984 budget called for an expenditure of about $60 million, divided as follows:

	(millions)
Insurance programs	$16
Early retirement	9
Personnel clearing	10
New business	6
Dismissal prevention	7
Job-creation projects	3
Administration and miscellaneous	9

To cover these costs, it is necessary to increase the normal employer contribution by an additional 0.4 percent of payroll. However, even with the increase, the amount that is being levied is only ten cents a worker-hour.

Successful Programs

Ursing thinks that perhaps the council has had too much money or, at any rate, that it may have been spending it on the wrong things. He would like to see less going to insurance and to early retirement, and more spent on dismissal prevention. Two examples illustrate why he favors this program.

In late 1976, the Domnarvet Steel Works, which had been affected by a series of crises in the European steel industry in the 1970s, made a decision to reorganize and to close down a part of the company's operation—specifically, stainless-steel production, an electro-steel mill and the heavy-plate mill. Although it was decided that the closures would be implemented gradually, altogether the reorganization and the closures would require a cutback of 650 blue-collar workers and 170 white-collar employees.

A joint labor-management council, such as those present in all large Swedish manufacturing establishments as part of their system of codetermination, was already in place at Domnarvet. The Domnarvet Council had union representation from both the blue-collar and the white-collar unions. The three white-collar unions involved were the Engineers, the Clerical and Technical Employees, and the Foremen and Supervisors, all of which are affiliated with the PTK. To cope with the problem of the cutback, the Domnarvet Council appointed a special joint committee, called the Main Committee. The task of this committee was to determine the consequences of the planned closures and reorganization, and to develop and assess proposals for redeployment of personnel under the reorganization. Since the committee members were already used to working together—both the union representatives with each other and management with the unions—the committee was able to proceed smoothly and without major problems to the principal issue, namely how to solve the problems of the redundant employees. Two principles were quickly adopted.

First, it was agreed that solutions for the redundant workers had to be found before the reorganization and staffing plans were finalized, that is, individual plans for surplus workers had to be considered before the reorganization was fully implemented. If they did not do it this way, the new organization might be left with skill gaps that it could ill afford. Strict application of the "last in, first out" principle could mean that highly qualified specialists would leave the company—an outcome which neither the unions nor management wanted.

The second principle adopted was in fact a precondition for the first: There would be no dismissals. No one would be dismissed unless unforeseeable difficulties arose, such as a further deterioration in the general economic situation. To avoid dismissals it was decided to explore all other possible approaches, specifically including the resources of the Swedish labor-market board (which supports a variety of security programs focused primarily, although not entirely, on blue-collar workers) and the SAF-PTK Employment Security Council. Early retirement and natural attrition over a reasonable period of time were other avenues that were to be explored.

By March 1977 the committee had made its recommendations, and implementation of the dismissal-prevention project began. The goal was to complete all necessary staff reductions and the company reorganization over a period of two years—by July 1979. In addition to the management pledge not to dismiss anyone, the plan called for several adjustment measures. Affected personnel were required to accept reasonable suggestions for internal and external transfers, with retraining provided as necessary. Funds for the retraining were to be subsidized by the Employment Security Council and the labor-market board. A recruitment and hiring freeze was imposed. Voluntary early retirement was offered all during 1977 to all white-collar employees between the ages of 60 and 62 and to a selected group aged 55 to 59. All vacant positions within the firm were to be advertised internally, and appointments to those jobs were to be made in consultation with the PTK so that the organization could keep track of the total restructuring program. Joint team's worked with selected employers, including government agencies, to develop new jobs for displaced white-collar employees on an individual basis. Training, whenever it took place, was oriented toward specific identified jobs. It was never simply an upgrading exercise of a general nature. Finally, individual plans were drawn up for each redundant white-collar worker, in consultation with the individual and with the PTK. No one was to be taken off the payroll until a personal development plan was approved by all of the parties and implementation was assured.

All employees were made aware of the plan through newsletters, public announcements, and both group and individual meetings. Most of the actual implementation of the plan was handled by the company's personnel department, but it was followed closely by the labor-management committee and by the representative of the Employment Security Council, who visited the steel works at least once a week over the two-year period to follow up on individual cases. Nobody was left "hanging in the air." Every opportunity for new jobs, training, or transfer was followed up daily and taken advantage of.

The results were good. The number of redundant white-collar employees dropped from 179 in the fall of 1976, when the first decision was made to close the mills, to 12 at the end of 1978; three of those twelve were chronically ill and not expected to return to service. In fact, destaffing took place more rapidly than had been planned, partly as a result of the creation of 26 new jobs within the company during that period. Some 25 persons took advantage of the early-retirement program, and 20 switched over to part-time work. Of the remainder, a very large proportion were retrained for new permanent jobs in the company.

The Domnarvet story has a postscript. In 1978, the three big Swedish steel companies merged into one, with the result that by the fall of 1981, Domnarvet again had an overstaffing problem. This time the Domnarvet Works had to reduce its white-collar staff by an additional 225 workers. Using its previous experience, the joint labor-management council prepared a new plan, setting a goal of no forced dismissals and completion of the necessary staff reduction by March 1984. The new program looks much like the old—an offer of early retirement to persons between the ages of 58 and 62; a freeze on hiring; internal advertising of job vacancies; training and retraining with pay; internal and external transfers with job-placement assistance for those who move outside the firm; help in starting new businesses; and preference for reemployment for those trying outside work. At last report it seemed clear that the council's goals would be met.

Another example of a successful dismissal-prevention project is provided by the experience of the Trelleborg Group, a large industrial rubber company. In 1978 the company was suffering its third and worst consecutive year of poor performance, actually showing a loss of more than 60 million Swedish crowns for the first three quarters of the year. The problem was high fixed costs and an inability to reduce them in line with the declining volume of sales. It was clear to all that costs had to be cut. Decisions were made concerning a better focus of marketing efforts and a greater concentration on the company's more profitable, specialized high-technology products. But the most important cost-cutting measure had to be a reduction of personnel, particularly in the number of white-collar employees. Rumors were rife, and news stories warned that 200 jobs were going to be cut. Initial uneasiness and unrest among the employees was replaced by resignation. Everyone accepted the inevitable. However, both company and union management had had a previous favorable experience with the SAF-PTK Employment Security Council, and together they decided to approach the council again to ask for assistance in exploring all possible alternatives to the prospective layoff.

In this instance, the first step was to hold a general meeting of all parties in the company to discuss what could be done to avoid dismissals. As in the Domnarvet case, a joint committee was established to look at the alternatives and, specifically, to consider the potential role of training or retraining. Within a month the committee reported its conclusions. Natural attrition and scheduled retirement, it was felt, could lead gradually to the necessary adjustment of the white-collar labor force over a period of 18 to 24 months. But to allow this to happen, the group stated, would put too great a strain on the company's finances. Therefore, external help was necessary. To solve the problem, the committee suggested that full-time training be made available and, they reasoned, if 100 employees could be induced to accept such training, the problem could be resolved. During the training these employees would receive normal pay, but it was hoped that the money would be provided from another source, specifically from the local labor-market board and/or the Employment Security Council.

The two organizations were approached. Both were interested but, as might be expected, the labor-market board had to operate within certain constraints, the most important being that the "last-hired, first-fired" principle be followed and that only unemployed redundant workers be considered eligible for assistance under their program. This was acceptable to neither the company nor the joint committee. They were trying to avoid dismissals, retain younger well-educated workers, and keep everybody usefully occupied until the company's fortunes improved. Since the Employment Security Council was more flexible, it could support a program more attuned to the needs of the company. In the end, it was decided that training would be conducted on a voluntary basis, with all employees of the company eligible to participate. This would allow persons who already had attained a high level of education and training to further improve their education, and persons with less education to receive the basic training they needed in order to retrain or upgrade employability. Work was to take precedence over training, but once a person started a training program, studies were not to be interrupted in the middle of a term. The cost of the training was to be shared by the Employment Security Council and the company. In addition, government training subsidies were to be utilized whenever possible.

During the first half of 1979, training subsidies were paid for 43 individuals. The drop-out rate was insignificant. Most of the trainees were reabsorbed into the company without difficulty at the end of their training period. Many changed careers and went on to new employment, some within the company, some elsewhere. The drain of young well-educated staff, which the company had feared, did not take place, and no dismissals were necessary. The required staff reduction was well under way.

The comments of Trelleborg's personnel director point up the significant aspect of the Employment Security Council's program. "One of the reasons we dared to choose this path [training instead of dismissal] was the impression we got of the Employment Security Council. That it would be possible to work in a fairly unconventional manner. That we wouldn't have to stick to any rigid regulations, but instead be able to adapt solutions to our special needs."[15]

The fact that the Swedish Employment Security Council has this flexibility and knows how to use it is what makes the institution both unique and worthwhile. However, it must be noted that Sweden has a vast network of government programs designed to deal with labor-market problems, including both cyclical unemployment and structural dislocation. The Employment Security Council's program is both a complement and supplement to those programs. It demonstrates in a most creative way what can be done—not only as a result of cooperation between labor and management, but also with collaboration between the public and the private sector.

DANA CORPORATION

Describing outplacement, the relocation of displaced workers, as a strategy for protecting employment security seems like an anomaly, but not if employment security is understood to mean the preservation of an individual's ability to continue to work, even though at a different job or with a different employer. Change is endemic in a dynamic economy. Businesses are transformed, falter, or fail; plants close. The issue then becomes how to provide continuous employment for workers affected by such changes. The Dana Corporation provides an interesting example of how outplacement and relocation services can be used to help workers adjust to change and retain a degree of employment security.[16]

Dana is a large multinational manufacturing corporation, headquartered in Toledo, Ohio, but with more than 100 plants in the United States and over 500 throughout the world. In 1979 Dana employed about 36,500 people worldwide, of which about 30,000 worked in the United States. During the recession of 1981–82, however, domestic employment dropped to about 18,200. The company supplies components and parts for the automotive industry, such as axles, frames, transmissions, and clutches. It also produces related products for general industrial use. One-third of its sales are to General Motors and Ford. Obviously, what happens to the auto industry affects Dana. When car and truck sales are up, business is good; when they decline, Dana feels the crunch.

Dana is a well-established company, with a reputation for good management and good labor relations. But like other companies in the automotive industry, the company has had to close plants from time to time. In 1980, Dana found it necessary to close its Edgerton, Wisconsin, plant, which manufactured axles for light trucks, particularly front-wheel drive trucks such as

Blazers and Broncos. The Edgerton plant had only opened in 1972. Dana had two other light-axle plants but needed the Edgerton plant when its main light-axle plant in Fort Wayne, Indiana, could not keep up with demand. All went well at the new plant until June 1979 when the worsening economic situation, combined with the impact on consumers of the OPEC oil crisis and the influx of energy-saving imports, severely cut into the market for U.S.-made light trucks. Dana found it had to cut back production and begin to lay off some of its 1,600 workers. For several reasons—one being the relative newness of the operation—the Edgerton plant was selected as the target for work-force reduction. The first dismissals took place in July 1979. These were followed in February 1980 by additional layoffs that cut the work force in half. In May 1980, Dana announced the permanent closing of the plant.

Dana workers in some plants have been represented by the United Automobile Workers (UAW) for more than 30 years. Workers at the Edgerton plant were involved in a Scanlon Plan, under which employees shared in the benefits from any changes in the plant that resulted in improved productivity. Company and union representatives met regularly on a monthly basis, thus creating an ongoing system of open communication between the two groups. The plant was recognized as being very productive; it was, in fact, a model plant: The workers were highly paid, labor turnover was under 1 percent, and absenteeism ranged from 3 to 5 percent. In the eight years since the plant opened, the union, in this case UAW Local 1838, had negotiated three contracts, with no strikes. It was in this atmosphere of generally harmonious relations that the union and management sat down to negotiate a closure agreement immediately following the plant-closing announcement.

Edgerton, the town of about 4,500 in which the plant was located, is a small community about ten miles from the larger manufacturing center of Janesville in the southern part of Wisconsin. It is primarily a farming area, but more than 40 percent of the county's labor force work in manufacturing jobs. Dana was the fourth largest employer in the area. The educational level of the area's labor force is high, even by Wisconsin standards, and Dana's employees reflected these characteristics: the work force was young, educated, and skilled. For the most part, the laid-off workers were males about 30 years old, with a high school education or more. Eighty percent were married, with most couples having only one child or none. In other words, they were more likely to be mobile and able to shift into other jobs. Under the circumstances, outplacement was a reasonable solution to the problem.

Long before the shutdown of the Edgerton plant, Dana had established its philosophy and policy for handling closure situations. A basic tenet of this policy was that when and if Dana workers were displaced, they should be given priority for openings at other Dana facilities. To implement this policy, one of the first measures the company took was to set up a program, called the Preferential Hiring Program, to move displaced Edgerton workers to other jobs. The program provided each worker who agreed to move an amount equal to two months' pay which he or she could use for relocation assistance. Eligibility for participation in the program was kept open for five years beyond the layoff date. In addition, it was possible, depending on the facility, for an Edgerton worker who was rehired at another Dana facility within the five-year period to have vesting and pension rights, as well as seniority, fully protected. As it turned out, despite the theoretical mobility of the Edgerton work force, very few of the workers took advantage of this opportunity—for the very good reason that the recession had affected Dana operations everywhere and there were very few openings to which they could be referred.

More successful was the company's Job Search Program. The nucleus of this program was an 18-hour course, conducted by Dana employees over a period of four-and-one-half days. The object was to give Dana workers the skills they needed to find new jobs. About 300 Dana employees, both white and blue collar, participated in the Job Search Program. Designed to build self-confidence and to teach people how to market their skills, the course started with an inventory of each individual's skills and interests, and went on to the development of communication abilities. It included instruction in such practical matters as how to write a resumé, how to contact a prospective employer, and how to manage an interview. It was a classical self-help approach. One Dana official compared the program to fishing, explaining, "Getting as many lines as possible in the water is the best way to catch fish. We can give them the fish, but how long will it last? We can teach them to fish and they can use it for the rest of their lives." For workers who wanted and needed it, there was also assistance in financial planning and, if appropriate, in retirement planning.

The entire program was paid for by the company and was carried out on the premises of the plant. This proved to be an important factor. Although the program was coordinated with the Wisconsin State Job Service, the workers apparently preferred using the Dana Job Search Center to the state agency's local office. Resources at the Dana Center were easily accessible and did not require the help of any outside third party, counselor, or interviewer, a situation workers found less embarrassing. The resources included a microfilm of job openings (and instruction in how to use it), a bulletin board with job listings and other information pertinent only to Dana workers, and a bank of telephones which could be used free of charge to call potential employers, even long distance. In some instances the company also paid travel expenses so that employees could go out on interviews in other localities.

Workers seemed to like the program. A University of Wisconsin survey of those who had participated indicated overwhelming approval, particularly in terms of building self-confidence and constructing resumés.

Perhaps the most useful feature of the Job Search Program, and certainly the most ambitious, was the effort the company itself made to find new jobs for its displaced workers. Not only did the company advertise the availability of the workers in newspapers and journals, but it contacted over 3,000 employers through phone calls and letters on behalf of the workers in the search for job openings. The result or this massive effort was that 95 percent of the white-collar workers and 86 percent of the hourly workers who participated in the Job Search Program were placed by mid-1981. However, about half the workers took over six months to find new jobs.

The closure agreement negotiated with the union helped Dana workers to bridge this gap. Medical insurance coverage was continued at company expense for up to one year after layoff, and qualifications for pension vesting were made easier by giving an 11-month extension of seniority to the hourly employees.

Outplacement is sometimes criticized as being a cop-out, too late and too little. At the Edgerton plant, the full involvement of the union in the effort helped to avoid such criticism. Perhaps the Dana program could have started sooner, but then, hindsight is always better in such cases. On the whole, the Dana experience is generally credited with having contributed to the long-term employment security of its employees and of those it had to lay off.

NOTES

1. Audrey Freedman, under the supervision of Edgar Weinberg, *Report on Case Studies of Telephone Operators*. Bulletin #1574 (Washington, D.C.: U.S. Department of Labor, Bureau of Labor Statistics, 1968).

2. This case study discusses the UAW-Ford Employe Development and Training Program as it existed between the signing of the 1982 Collective Bargaining Agreement between United Automobile Workers and the Ford Motor Company and the UAW-Ford contract negotiations concluded in the fall of 1984. As a result of the 1984 negotiations, the Ford Motor Company greatly expanded its commitment to employment security, building on the experience of the company and the union in working together to develop the jointly operated Employe Development and Training Program.

3. Information for this case study is drawn from a joint presentation by Thomas J. Pasco, executive director, and Richard J. Collins, associate director, UAW-Ford National Development and Training Center, to the President's Commission on Industrial Competitiveness, April 1984; on published information supplied by the National Center; and on an interview with Marshall Goldberg, associate, Retraining and Reemployment Services, National Center, August 1983.

4. Presentation by Thomas J. Pasco and Richard J. Collins to the President's Commission on Industrial Competitiveness, April 1984.

5. UAW-Ford documents establishing the UAW-Ford Employe Development and Training Program and the UAW-Ford National Development and Training Center.

6. See page 91 for further information on the Education and Training Assistance Plan for active workers.

7. The 1984 Distinguished Performance Award presented by the National Alliance of Business was given to the San Jose plant joint committee in recognition of its "exemplary contribution to create training and hiring opportunities" for the nation's unemployed.

8. Information for this case study is from a report entitled *Retraining and Economic Development for California* (Sacramento: California Employment Development Department, 1984, and an interview with Steve Duscha, executive director of the Employment Training Panel, April 1984.

9. In administering its unemployment insurance program, each state uses a system of experience rating in which employers with records of frequent layoffs and quits and, therefore, substantial withdrawals from the insurance fund, are penalized by having to pay a higher tax. Conversely, employers with records of employment stability are rewarded by having their tax reduced.

10. Since 1981 a change in California's Unemployment Insurance code has allowed laid-off workers to collect full UI benefits while participating in training programs. The usual UI eligibility standards that require unemployed workers to seek and be available for work are waived. Workers who have lost their jobs due to plant closings, technological change, foreign competition, or lack of demand for skills may enroll in these training programs.

11. Information for this case study is drawn from an interview with Roger Niven, training manager, Operations Department, British Airways, London, January 1984.

12. Information for this case study is drawn from materials provided by the Manpower Consultative Service in Ottawa and from interviews with Allan Jacques, director general, Labour Market Planning and Adjustment Branch, Employment and Immigration, Ottawa, and various members of the MCS Toronto staff, specifically Ken Gelok, D. Allan Watson, Edward Kearns, and Allne Revoy.

13. Interview with Ken Gelok, assistant regional director, MCS, Toronto, December 18, 1983.

14. Information on the Swedish Employment Security Council was obtained from materials provided by the council and from a presentation made by Hans Ursing, president of Trygghetsradet, at a meeting of the National Advisory Committee for Work in America Institute's national policy study "Employment Security in a Free Economy," Dearborn, Michigan, November 10, 1983.

15. "Reports and Assessments of Dismissal Prevention Projects," an unpublished progress report prepared for Trygghetsradet, Stockholm, Sweden, September 14, 1983, and *The SAF-PTK Employment Security Council* (Stockholm, Sweden: Trygghetsradet SAF-PTK, 1980).

16. .Information on the Dana Corporation was obtained from a report prepared for the U.S. Department of Labor entitled *Plant Closings: What Can Be Learned from Best Practice*, by Robert B. and William S. McKersie, 1981, and from a report by TASC, the Team for Analysis of Social Concerns, University of Wisconsin, entitled *Some Social Consequences of the Dana Corporation's Plant Closing in Edgerton*, December 1980.

6.
Easing the Adjustment
to Technological Change

The rapid pace of technological change in recent years has made it necessary for both companies and unions to develop adjustment strategies specifically aimed at helping workers adapt to the new world in which they find themselves. Changing technology is not a new phenomenon, of course. It is a continuous process and, indeed, most industrial companies have long-established internal training programs for their employees to enable them to learn to handle and operate new machinery as it comes on-line. What is different today is both the speed at which technology is being introduced and the radical nature of the change, particularly in respect to the computerization of manufacturing and other industrial processes. Along with this is a drastic reduction in the worker hours required to produce manufactured goods. Although this means a parallel improvement in productivity, it also means permanent displacement for many workers who thought their jobs were secure.

Companies and unions that were content before with a moderate or even large-scale in-house training program to keep employees and members up-to-date in their skills and able to continue in their jobs now find that much more needs to be done to ensure employment security. Several interesting cases that illustrate different approaches to easing the adjustment to technological change are presented here.

The first is a joint program developed cooperatively between the Buick Division of General Motors and the United Automobile Workers. The program focuses on workers who are scheduled to be displaced by the introduction of new technology and enables them to take up to two years, at full pay and with full benefits, to retrain and prepare themselves for other jobs and even new careers. A second case describes the bold initiative taken by the Amalgamated Clothing and Textile Workers Union to develop—with the cooperation and support of several companies in the apparel and textile industries—a new technology for the industry that will enable it to compete with foreign imports and thus save jobs for some—but, of course not all—of its members.

In Great Britain, concern about new technology has led many unions to push for collectively bargained new-technology agreements, or NTAs. These agreements are discussed in this chapter, with particular reference to the Job Security Agreement negotiated between the British Post Office and the Post Office Engineering Union, the union representing most of the employees of the telecommunications arm of the Post Office. The British Post Office agreement is regarded by the union primarily as a work-force planning agreement, giving the union advance notice of any proposed technological changes and establishing a mechanism for full participation of the union in planning for the change.

Work-force planning, particularly planning in advance for the adjustments necessary to adapt to changing technology, has long been assiduously and effectively practiced by the Ruhr Coal Company in West Germany. In fact, the company has earned a worldwide reputation for maintaining its competitive position by utilizing the most advanced technology available. Planning for employment security for its employees has always been an integral part of the process of change in this company. It is included here as a good example of preplanned adjustment practice.

BUICK EMPLOYE DEVELOPMENT CENTER

The Buick Employe Development Center in Flint, Michigan, a joint undertaking of the Buick Division of General Motors and United Automobile Workers Local 599, is an outgrowth of the commitment by both parties to cooperative efforts to solve joint problems. In this case the problems were, and still are, technological change in the auto industry, the need to maintain and improve competitiveness, and the impact of both on Buick employees. The Employe Development Center (EDC) is an innovative attempt to solve these problems. Essentially it is an institution for the retraining and further education of workers who are, or will be, displaced by productivity improvements and by the introduction of new technology in Buick plants. However, the EDC is much more than that.[1]

It all started in late 1975 when Buick, with almost 7,500 workers on layoff and only 9,000 people still employed—reduced from a high of 16,000 a few years earlier—recognized that something drastic would have to be done to enable the company to stage a comeback from the plight in which it found itself following the 1974 recession. Up to that time, the history of Buick's labor-management relations was one of confrontation and almost continual conflict. Not only was the production of Buick vehicles suffering, but the division was also losing its rightful share of the corporation's business: the manufacture of engines, components, parts, and the like. Buick managers knew that productivity had to be improved and felt that the skills and knowledge necessary to do so could be found within the company itself. But they also knew that nothing could be done without the understanding and cooper-ation of the workers. The managers therefore approached the union to see whether something could be done to improve their relationship. There was, and Buick and the union then took the first steps toward what has become standard operating procedure in working together to solve their joint prob-lems. Since then the company and the union have cooperated in a quality-of-work-life program involving thousands of meetings, a high degree of information sharing, and the building of trust between the two parties at all levels. The new approach has worked. productivity has improved, and so has the ability to compete. As a result, Buick is regaining both its position in the market and its share and more of the corporation business.

However, by the fall of 1982 Buick, together with the rest of the auto industry, was reeling from another recession, and the company again found itself in the position of looking for ways to improve its competitive position. An intensive period of self-examination convinced Buick's managers that much could be done to improve productivity and maintain competitiveness. At least there were enough good ideas on paper to bring about this result. But, in the words of W. J. Rowland, Buick's director of Personnel, "A significant part of this management thrust to become competitive and increase our busi-ness opportunities would require the active and dedicated effort of our em-ployees and Local 599. The challenge then became: How can it be [made] acceptable to the union? How can we expect an employee to go along with something that could cost him his job?[2] The answer was found in the concept underlying the Employe Development program, namely, that whenever and wherever the company improves its competitive position by changes in work practices or the introduction of technology that eliminates particular jobs, the people "who would otherwise go to the street" go instead to a new Develop-ment Center where they can gain the skills and education necessary to enable them to compete successfully in the changing labor market.

Unlike the UAW-Ford retraining program described in chapter 5, the Buick Employe Development Center is not the result of formal collective-bargaining negotiations between the company and the union. Instead, it is the outcome of eight years of joint efforts to deal with particular problems, an evolving interactive process between the company and the union. In fact, establishment of the EDC came about through a handshake agreement. It is an experiment in which change and accommodation to the needs of the people involved are the order of the day.

Certain elements are fixed, however. In June 1982, the Buick Joint Council, which consists of an equal number of persons representing the union and the company, signed a simple document establishing the Employe Development Center and promising that any individual whose work was affected by changes in work practices or technology would have the opportunity to enter the center. The agreement came, however, only after a lengthy process of discussion and consultation with the workers themselves to determine if the concept was viable and in accord with their interests and concerns.

It was agreed that employees who enter the center can retain the same base rate of pay that they had in their last job and that they will be entitled to all fringe benefits. On entry, enrollees must sign a contract agreeing to remain in the center for a minimum of one year, but they can stay longer if their individual development plans require it.

The company and the union had already established a cooperative approach to training when the discussions concerning the EDC first began. Two years previously the two parties had jointly set up an in-house Buick Skills Training Center to retrain skilled trade workers, such as electricians, millwrights, carpenters, and machine repairers, to work with new advanced technology equipment. The skilled trades workers themselves were and are heavily involved in that training program, designing the curricula, serving as instructors, and conducting the training. However, no issue of employment security was involved in the case of the skilled trades workers. The new program, the Employe Development Center, was designed to open up opportunity for retraining to the unskilled workers, who would otherwise have been laid off, probably permanently.

The center itself is a large unused junior high school building belonging to the Flint Board of Education and leased by the program for a period of five years. In addition to a director and an administrative staff, the center's staff consists of both academic and vocational counselors and instructors. The EDC program is designed to encourage each enrollee to pursue the program of training or education that is most appropriate for him or her. Some who come into the center lack basic educational skills, such as reading, math, and in some cases, the ability to communicate easily in English; for these, the center can provide basic literacy training. Others have specific vocational goals they wish to pursue. Some of the courses are taught directly at the center, while others are provided by outside vendors.

Since the school was in bad repair at the time the program actually got under way in the summer of 1983, the first enrollees helped with the redecoration, repair, and landscaping of the facility. It was a cooperative affair and a learning situation for all those involved. By early 1984, there were more than 120 enrollees in the center; ages ranged from 25 to 55, and all levels of attainment and interest were represented. Many of the enrollees selected courses in computers and related fields, but there are also others, in basic education classes or working toward the high school equivalency diploma, the GED. Some are enrolled in associate degree programs at nearby institutions, and others are in full-time college courses. The location of the center in Flint, the hub of Buick's activity and employment, means that the enrollees are drawn exclusively from the Buick facilities in or near Flint. Asked whether it was anticipated that on completion of their courses, some of the enrollees would be reemployed at Buick (they retain their seniority ranking throughout their participation in the program), Rowland indicated that there was always such a possibility, particularly since the skills being learned were, for the most part, useful to Buick as well as to the individuals involved.

Entry into the center is regarded by the employees as a valuable opportunity. In keeping with normal union practices, selection of enrollees for the program operates in a manner fully consistent with the seniority system. When a change is made in a particular Buick plant or factory that will result in the displacement of one or more employees, the corresponding number of opportunities to enroll in the center are offered to all workers at the same level in that plant or factory. The most senior person or persons applying for entry gets the opportunity. Participation in the program is voluntary, and apparently there has been no shortage of volunteers. The center program, however, is used only for dislocations that occur as the result of proposed technological changes that are linked to the necessity to improve productivity and to enhance the company's ability to compete. The center program is not applicable to dislocations or layoffs that occur as the result of economic considerations, cyclical fluctuations, or the ups and downs of the market. In such a case, the regular "flow-chart system" that is part of the negotiated agreement between the UAW and the company comes into play, and the people with the lowest seniority are laid off first.

Both the union and the company are convinced that the EDC has succeeded in making it possible for the company to improve productivity with the full help and cooperation of the union. Rowland describes a situation in which the employees in one area designed a new and different approach to taking inventory. The system they recommended eliminated 20 jobs, but the workers supported the change because they knew that no one would be thrown out of work as a result of the change. In fact, 20 workers from the affected group were enrolled in the center, where they are preparing themselves for new employment.

Clearly there are costs involved. Keeping an unlimited number of workers in training with full pay and benefits, for as long as two years while paying the costs of administering a complex and varied educational and training program, is no small item. However, Buick believes it is worth the expense and that the benefits of increased productivity, maintenance of the ability to compete, and smoother labor relations exceed the costs. Moreover, as Buick points out, with the supplementary unemployment benefits, or SUB program, and other negotiated job-protection measures, the cost of unemployment is already very high and with no offsetting benefits. In addition, the company feels there is a substantial cost in *not* providing this form of employment security for Buick employees.

The cost of the EDC is a budgeted cost borne directly by Buick. The EDC does not receive funds from any other source—local, state, or federal government. Neither is the program supported by the national five-cents-per-hour-worked fund established in the 1982 negotiations between the UAW and General Motors. The EDC program does use money which comes to the company from the so-called ten-cents-per-hour-worked fund that was also part of the 1982 negotiations. However, this is not really a fund but represents an agreement by the corporation to allocate a certain amount of money each year to its division for the purpose of training and retraining.

One of the problems that the union had to face, at least in theory, was that the retraining program, if successful in terms of what it could do for the individual, would take some workers into new careers, out of the union and perhaps even into the ranks of salaried as opposed to hourly wage workers at Buick. It is a problem about which the union appears to have little concern. Local 599's interest is in providing employment security for its members, and if that means preparing for nonunion jobs, that is something that has to be dealt with in other contexts. Al Christner, the president of Local 599, is enthusiastic in his support of the EDC program. "It's great to know that we can have this type of program by mutual understanding. This thing came about . . . because over the past eight years we had been building trust between the parties—which was not there before . . . But I can assure you that it is there now."[3] Christner can well be proud of the record of eight years of cooperative, joint effort to solve mutual problems. Since 1975, when the quality-of-work-life program began, the membership of Local 599 has grown from about 8,500 members to over 14,000, a growth which the union itself ascribes in part to the growth and strength of cooperation at Buick.

In Christner's view, the EDC program offers a kind of employment security to his members that was simply not possible before. As he says, "I never thought that something like EDC would happen during my lifetime at Buick. I never thought that people could be guaranteed a job."[4] The EDC is, of course, not a guarantee, but it is a strong commitment on the part of both the union and the company to continued employment for Buick workers.

It is interesting to note that other companies and unions are thinking along the same lines as Buick and the UAW. In Italy for example, the remarkable recovery of the huge auto company Fiat, whose history of labor relations would make Buick's earlier experiences look like a textbook model of good personnel management, is attributed in large part to an agreement between Fiat and the unions on a two-year paid retraining "leave," at company expense, for workers displaced by technological and other changes needed to enable the company to compete in the international market. More recently the Italian program has become the model for a French government proposal for a similar two-year "reconversion leave" to smooth the way for a necessary restructuring of its major industrial companies. The Buick program is, of course, still too new to provide answers as to the effectiveness of this approach. But if commitment, trust, and dedication to a fully cooperative approach are the ingredients necessary for success, the Flint program will make it.

AMALGAMATED CLOTHING AND TEXTILE WORKERS UNION

For trade unions today, the issue of employment security for their members has become increasingly important, if not critical. The issue was never treated lightly, but in recent years fierce import competition, repeated recessions, and the computer-led technological revolution have moved the issue of employment security ahead of the usual bargaining issues, such as wages, benefits, and working conditions, on the priority lists of many trade unions. This has been so particularly for unions representing workers in basic industries such as steel and autos, as well as in the textile and apparel industries, where employment declined from almost 2.4 million in 1973 to 1.9 million in 1983. One union that has been in the forefront of efforts to promote employment security has chosen a particularly bold and imaginative approach to the issue. The Amalgamated Clothing and Textile Workers Union (ACTWU) has joined with employers in supporting the development of new, advanced technology to enable the textile and apparel industries to compete with imports. The objective is to save the industry, even if it means losing some jobs and some of the union's members.[5]

The ACTWU represents 349,000 workers, employed primarily in the male apparel and textile industries, but also in other businesses affected by imports: those producing shoes, headwear, and chemical fibers. Another ACTWU-represented firm, the Xerox Corporation, is also affected by imports. While continuing its efforts to persuade government to take the steps necessary to restore a fair balance in international trade through the negotiation of such orderly marketing procedures as the Multi-Fiber Agreement, quotas, and other trade-control measures, ACTWU recognized that additional measures had to be taken if its industries were not simply to disappear.

In the men's and boys' suit and coat industry, improving productivity and the ability of domestic firms to compete was seen as the key to the problem. The solution proposed by the union was the establishment of a new nonprofit research and development corporation, the Tailored Clothing Technology Corporation, or TC, to be funded by the federal government, companies, and the union. Its purpose was to develop technology that would allow the U.S. men's and boys' tailored clothing industry to compete with its foreign challengers.

Building on an industry-wide collective bargaining relationship that goes back 40 years, TC was launched in 1979. The idea for the research and development project grew out of a study of the impact of imports on the tailored clothing industry, research which the union had committed itself to conducting during the 1976 round of negotiations. At that time, the union asked John T. Dunlop, a Harvard professor and former U.S. Secretary of Labor—well known not only for his vast knowledge of U.S. industry and labor relations, but also for his skill at bringing together groups with disparate interests to work together to solve common problems—to undertake a thorough study, looking at current trends in the apparel industry and its future prospects. The study, which was conducted in association with his colleague, Professor Elisabeth Allison, confirmed that the future looked bleak. While in 1965 the apparel worn by American men was almost all U.S.-made, ten years later nearly one-third of the shirts and sportcoats and 18 percent of the trousers were made overseas, accounting in part for the 25 percent decline in employment in the industry during the same period. If things continued on the same track, by 1987 almost half of all apparel worn by American males would be foreign-made.

In 1979, the union again approached Dunlop. He thought that the industry could become competitive with foreign imports, but in order to do so, it would have to concentrate on finding a way to gain a technological lead. He suggested a joint investment in new-technology development. The union embraced the idea and then approached some of the large apparel employers to ask them to join in sponsoring such an effort. A men's clothing manufacturer, Hartmarx, was very interested in the idea, as were some of the other large apparel companies. Employers in the textile and yarn industries were also approached—Burlington Mills, J. P. Stevens (the union's old enemy), and Du Pont, which produces man-made textile fibers. The response was good. With support and funds from both sides, and with an additional grant from the U.S. Department of Commerce, the Tailored Clothing Technology Corporation was established. It is a unique organization, a joint venture in which rival competing companies and the dominant union in the industry have pooled resources to solve a market problem. This has been accomplished with the government's support and participation, but it is not a government program. The Tailored Clothing Technology Corporation is run by an executive committee on which sit representatives of both the union and the major industry employers. To date about $3 million to $4 million has been spent on the project.

Actual development of the technology itself is being carried out by an engineering research firm in Cambridge, Massachusetts, the Charles Draper Laboratories. Ordinarily, this firm is involved in such projects as designing guidance systems for missiles. In this instance, however, it is concentrating on developing automated machinery to improve productivity in the men's tailored clothing industry, perhaps a less glamorous but potentially more rewarding task.

As Jack Sheinkman, secretary-treasurer of the ACTWU, explains the project, "We felt that we had some time to become competitive." Several factors lay behind this thinking. First is the shift of employment in the United States from blue-collar to white-collar work. The apparel industry, including the ACTWU, has taken note of the fact that the working costume of the future, for both men and women, is more likely to be a suit, than overalls. The

project planners noted that the number of "young, upwardly mobile profes-
sionals" is growing fast, and these people wear suits to work. The market for
tailored clothing therefore appears to be expanding. Second, it is known that
menswear retailers do not like to order too far in advance. Eight weeks has
been the normal time between order and delivery. It was reasoned that if this
time could be shortened by reducing the time needed for the manufacturing
process itself, the U.S. domestic industry could improve its competitive position vis-à-vis foreign suppliers, who have to cope with the transportation time
lag. What had to be done was to find a way to exploit the U.S. industry's
geographic advantage. The planners recognized that although it would be
possible to speed up the sewing machines, that would not be enough and
would not get at the real problem. In the manufacture of tailored clothing,
about 70 percent of the time is spent in handling the material and garment
pieces, getting them into the right position to stitch the parts together. Only 10
percent of the time is spent in the actual sewing. With that in mind, Draper
Laboratories set out to develop robots that could take over the materials
handling.

Obviously, the adoption of this machinery by the apparel manufacturers
will cause some workers to lose their jobs. It has been estimated that the new
equipment can perform one-quarter of the handling and sewing done on a suit
coat, replacing as many as 20 percent of the workers now required to produce
that coat. "If that's all that happens," says Murray Finley, president of
ACTWU, "we'll have 15 or 20 percent less people. But, if it enables us to
become more competitive, to substitute what we make for imports, we could
make up that loss in jobs. And, if we don't do it, I'm convinced we'll lose the
jobs anyway."

By the spring of 1984, the new equipment was being tried experimentally in
several apparel factories. So far, it appears promising and is reported to be
getting a good reception from the workers who are being asked to use it. The
employees understand that it's a matter of accepting the robots, even if there
will be fewer workers than before, or facing the possibility that there may be
no jobs. After the trial period, the machinery will go back to Draper Laboratories for further refinement and then it will be marketed by TC. Full use of
the new equipment will, of course, be dependent on how much of the industry decides to adopt it, but the union is confident that acceptance will be
widespread.

There are some clouds on the horizon, however. Development of new
technology for the industry is not confined to the United States. Japan and
others among our technologically advanced trading partners are reported to
be spending considerable sums on research and development projects in the
clothing and textile industries. Although the exact nature of their research is
unknown (Sheinkman says, "We don't know what they are doing, and they
don't know what we're doing."), clearly they are outspending U.S. industry. In
addition, the time advantage that the union originally felt was on its side has

evaporated somewhat under pressure of the international trade skewing that has taken place in recent years as a result of the strength of the dollar. Despite these problems, the outlook for improving the competitive position of the men's and boys' tailored clothing industry is good, and it is certainly better than it was before this project started.

There are factors which made this joint technology development venture uniquely suitable for the men's and boys' suit and coat industry. For one, through their national association, the Clothing Manufacturers Association of the USA, the firms in the industry have had a sustained, fruitful, and peaceful collective-bargaining relationship with ACTWU. Also, this segment of the apparel industry is not as fashion-sensitive as others, and the leading firms are more stable and longer-lived. In part, their longevity is nurtured by the durability and wardrobe life of their products; not uncommonly, a man gets more years of wear from a suit than he does from his car. In some of the other branches of the apparel trades, marketing strategy and other industry-specific factors tend to reduce the contribution that research and development can make to a firm's balance sheet.

Consequently, the Amalgamated Clothing and Textile Workers Union has utilized other initiatives to improve the employment security of members in the other industries in which it represents workers. The union has pioneered in what Sheinkman calls "creative bargaining" to protect employment security. Through collective bargaining, it has negotiated prenotification of plant closings and compensation for technological displacement. Quality bonuses have been negotiated in some instances. In an agreement with Xerox, the company said that there would be no reduction in personnel for three years while technological improvements were being made to meet the competition from Japan.

The union has also looked for ways to cooperate with employers in finding alternative solutions to proposed plant closings. Xerox, for example, felt that it would have to reduce operating costs by $3 million in order to remain competitive and proposed the elimination of one operation to achieve that goal. Some 180 workers would be laid off and the work subcontracted out. Instead, at the union's urging, a joint union-management study action team was established to find an alternative to the threatened layoffs. After six months, the team proposed cost-cutting recommendations, totaling $3.2 million, more than the cost-reduction target. No one had to be laid off.

In industries where the workers are not highly paid, where many are women and/or minorities, and where the union has had to work hard to win its organizing victories, it might have been expected that the union would take a negative stance on the issue of new technology, resisting change and trying to hold on to every job. It is a tribute to the leadership of ACTWU that this union is taking a long-term view of the employment security problem, becoming an advocate of change, and moving in innovative, even radical ways to meet the problem.

NEW-TECHNOLOGY AGREEMENTS IN GREAT BRITAIN

Many trade unions in Great Britain have turned to the collective-bargaining process and the execution of new-technology agreements (NTAs) to help protect the employment of their members who are threatened with displacement by changing technology. The Trade Union Congress (TUC), the collective organization of the British labor movement, has developed model agreements and encouraged affiliated unions to bargain for such agreements. In general, the white-collar unions have been more successful in negotiating such agreements than those representing blue-collar workers, although one can find technology agreements in both groups. Business, as represented by the Confederation of Business and Industry (CBI), has expressed its opposition to any form of new-technology agreement, claiming that it will hinder the modernization of British industry. But experience with the NTAs so far does not seem to support that prediction.[6]

A survey of new-technology agreements conducted by the Work Research Unit of the Department of Employment in 1983 uncovered some 225 separate agreements which had been negotiated on the introduction of new technology, providing an indication of their general acceptance by both unions and employers. In addition to a review of the agreements themselves, the Work Research Union distributed a questionnaire in companies where new technology had actually been introduced to determine how the agreements affected employment. One of the main points that emerged from the survey was that the unions had been successful in making the introduction of technology a subject for consultation, and more than half had been able to ensure that the workers would in fact receive detailed information concerning the impact of any additional technology.[7] Perhaps more important, many of the agreements stipulated that no one would lose employment as a result of the introduction of technology. Redeployment, it was found, had in most cases safeguarded the position of the people affected by the new technology.

New-technology agreements are generally fairly broad in scope and cover the full range of the potential impact of new technology on employment. They often start with a guarantee of continued employment for the existing work force, or at least a promise that no one will lose a job on technological grounds alone. This guarantee, however, is usually tempered with an "escape clause," permitting the employer to lay off workers in cases "beyond his or her control," such as a worldwide recession. The employer's interpretation of such a clause becomes the critical element, of course, in determining the real value of the guarantee.

The agreements also describe the steps that the employer must take in order to mitigate the possible adverse impact of new technology. These steps generally start with the imposition of a hiring freeze and end with a procedure for the implementation of an early-retirement plan. Steps in between include the

elimination of overtime; the callback in-house of work previously subcontracted out; and redeployment, but with seniority, salary, and grade protected.
The agreements also provide for training and retraining at the company's
expense. Many of the agreements, particularly those negotiated by the white-
collar unions, also include provisions for monitoring the impact of the new
technology on the health of affected workers. In the case of the white-collar
workers, the new technology most often introduced is word processors, computers, and other devices which require that the worker sit and look at a video
display unit (VDU) for long periods of time. Since it is not yet known what
the long-term effect of these VDUs may be on workers' health and especially
on their vision, many of the NTAs include provisions for frequent health
examinations for these workers. Finally, to guard against exploitation of computerized personal records, many of the agreements also include privacy-
protection provisions.

One example of a new-technology agreement was signed in October 1983
between Cossor Electronics, the British subsidiary of U.S. Electronics, and
four white-collar unions, representing some 700 workers in a manufacturing
plant in Harlow. The agreement guaranteed prior consultation with the
unions before any new systems were introduced. In addition, it pledged no
enforced redundancies and provided for full training on the new equipment.
This training was to be made available to all workers without discrimination.
The agreement also gave full recognition to health and safety matters that
arose in connection with the new technology and set up a committee representing the four unions to monitor developments. Since the new system would
also affect some 1,300 shop-floor blue-collar workers, the company had begun negotiations with the two unions representing these workers.

The NTA negotiated between Swan Hunter Shipbuilders and the white-
collar union APEX, the Association of Professional Executive and Clerical
and Computer staff, provided for full consultation, no enforced redundancy,
monitoring procedures, training, health and safety protection, and the safe-
guarding of personal information on the computer files. In still another case,
the association representing graphics and reproduction employers and the
National Graphics Association, the major union for print craftsworkers, negotiated an agreement in which, in return for its cooperation on the introduction of word processors and other new technology, the union obtained
guarantees on job security, while the employers accepted certain restrictions
on the use made of the word processors. The agreement promised that there
would be no redundancies and established wage rates that assured that some
of the cost savings would be passed on to the employees.

Perhaps the most successful of the NTAs is the one negotiated in 1980
between the Post Office Engineering Union (POEU) and the Post Office. This
agreement, called the Job Security Agreement, is credited with playing an important role in the modernization of the British telecommunications system.

The POEU has about 130,000 members; 121,000 of them work for British Telecom (separated from the Post Office in 1982) and approximately 9,000 work for the Post Office. About 100,000 of the POEU members are engineers or mechanics working in jobs below the supervisory grades; the others are primarily in clerical occupations. The Job Security Agreement covers both groups. It was conceived originally to protect against displacement caused by modernization, not by economic factors or competition. However, the recent decision of the British government to return the telecommunications part of the Post Office operation to the private sector and open the field to competition will no doubt mean that the Job Security Agreement will take on added significance.

Insofar as the union is concerned, the Job Security Agreement is viewed as a work-force planning agreement in which the union has an important role to play. Consultation and cooperation are the key factors in making the agreement work. Like many of the other new-technology agreements, the POEU agreement starts with a guarantee that protects workers against compulsory redundancy. It includes all of the measures typical of most such agreements, including a freeze on hiring whenever there is a jointly recognized surplus of workers, followed by restrictions on overtime, redeployment and relocation (along with protection of the transferred workers' seniority, salary, and grade); retraining and, finally, voluntary early retirement for workers over 50 years of age. In addition, the POEU agreement establishes a mechanism to ensure that the provisions are carried out. The agreement specifies the officials who will be held responsible for the implementation of the agreement. These are special regional and local "redeployment liaison officers," named by the general managers in consultation with the regional or local union branch representatives. It is those liaison officers—whose names are made known to all Post Office employees—who have responsibility for making sure that every individual worker whose job is affected by the introduction of new technology or by the threat of displacement for whatever reason, receives the attention and services required under the agreement. Anyone not satisfied with the resolution of his or her particular work situation can go to the regional or local liaison officer who is then obliged under the agreement to work out a satisfactory solution. Other provisions in the agreement are also of interest. One entitles a worker who is reassigned or redeployed to a four-week trial period to determine whether the new job is suitable. If not, a new solution must be offered. Another is a provision ensuring that if a worker must be moved to another location in order to retain employment with the company, total moving costs, including such costs as redeeming a mortgage or making overlapping rental payments, are reimbursed by the company. Few American companies provide such extensive relocation reimbursement.

The POEU is organized into 61 local areas and, understandably, performance under the new agreement is not uniform throughout the country. One problem for the union has been to get its local leaders to understand and fully share the responsibility of work-force planning. In order to become effective partners in such advance-planning exercises as they are carried out at the local level, the union's local leadership must be given special training. The national union has developed and is providing such a training program, but participation is voluntary and at last report the program had not yet been fully utilized by all local leaders. Where the local unions have not felt comfortable with their new role as partners in planning, the national staff has become involved.

In the past the union members have benefited from changes in technology. Real-pay levels for engineers have increased significantly over the past 20 years. Moreover, relations with the Post Office have been good. Consultation between the union and management is widely accepted and practiced. At the present time the union is somewhat apprehensive about the upcoming change of the Post Office from a public-service enterprise to a private-sector organization, but it is hopeful that the experience gained under the Job Security Agreement will permit the transition to take place without detriment to the workers or to their union.[8]

RUHR COAL CORPORATION (WEST GERMANY)

A crucial element in the success of adjustment policies in providing employment security for workers is the extent and quality of the planning that goes into the program. This is true not only in regard to short-range plans, such as those for individual workers who are affected by some sort of personnel-management crisis, or a cutback or plant closing, but also in regard to long-range planning, as practiced by the Ruhr Coal Corporation in West Germany. This company is presently looking ahead; planning today to provide employment security both for its current employees and for its employees in the future.[9]

Ruhr Coal is an integrated coal company based in the lovely Ruhr Valley, the site of one of the world's largest hard-coal fields. The nucleus of the company's operations is its 24 collieries and 14 coking plants scattered throughout the area. It also owns and operates several power plants and participates in the production of natural gas. Chemical, merchandising, engineering, and service subsidiaries complete the corporate structure. Until the late 1960s ownership and operation of Ruhr-area mines were widely dispersed among 30 to 40 small independent companies, in addition to Ruhr Coal. When problems in the steel industry began to force many of the mines to cut back production and to lay off miners, the unions, concerned with the impact of the cutbacks on their members, became convinced that they would have a stronger negotiating position if they could deal with one large company instead of having to negotiate with so many. The unions therefore began to press for consolidation of mining operations. Backed by the government, this did in fact occur, and today Ruhr Coal is the operator of all but three of the area's mines.

As the chief supplier of coking coal for the West German steel mills, Ruhr Coal has long been tied closely to the steel industry. As a result, the company has suffered from the same cyclical swings that affect steel. Fortunately, however, the steel industry is not Ruhr Coal's only customer. The company is also an important supplier of fuel to German utilities, as well as to many factories and mills (Ruhr Coal has 20-year contracts with the utility companies). In addition, the German coal industry enjoys a state subsidy.

Compared to many other companies, Ruhr Coal's market is secure. Nor is there any immediate danger that the coal will run out. Recent exploration indicates that there is more than enough coal underground to last for another century or more, although the new areas are somewhat farther to the north than the present coalfields and they are also at much deeper levels, making the coal more costly to extract. To get at it, the industry has already begun to shift toward the North Sea.

Technologically Ruhr Coal has always been on the leading edge of new developments. Its coal-digging and other mining and milling operations are entirely mechanized, making the company's work force among the most productive in the world. The effect of this mechanization, however, has not only led to a gradual reduction in the work force, but also changed the nature of the miner's job. If at one time muscular strength and endurance were among the chief qualifications, today the miner must be a highly skilled technician, who has undergone from three to five years of specialized training to learn his profession.

Fifteen years ago Ruhr Coal had 186,000 employees; by the end of 1983 there were only 122,000—a 35 percent reduction over the period. Klaus Stockhaus, the personnel director of the company, explains that since the attrition rate was high during that period, the reduction was accomplished without great difficulty. Today, however, the company is facing two new, more difficult problems. One is the need for further reduction of the labor force. This is, in effect, a short-range problem. The second, and more difficult, problem concerns the need to ensure that there is a reliable, secure labor force in the future, ten years from today. The short-range reduction results from both the current economic recession in West Germany and additional technological advances in the mining industry. The long-range problem stems from the demographic situation that exists in West Germany, and in other European countries as well—the foreseeable decline in the population in the future which, in turn, is the result of the low birth rates during the past decade. By 1990 West Germany's chief labor problem will be a labor shortage, not a surplus.

Since Ruhr Coal is a subsidized industry, the government has some control over its management. Last year, the company was ordered by the government to close three pits that were not operating at an economically justifiable performance level. The order was to be effective immediately, thus eliminating the jobs of approximately 16,000 workers. The company, working with the union, determined that about 7,000 of these could be absorbed by other operations of the company. This, however, was the maximum of what could be done without resorting to layoffs, an unacceptable outcome for both the company and the union. The company therefore proposed that the reduction take place gradually and on a widely diffused basis. Production and employment would be cut back in all of the mines, and not limited to just three. The reduction would be spread out over a five-year period, ending in 1988. Obviously costs are involved in following such a procedure, but in the company's view the gain in terms of worker satisfaction and loyalty to the company would be worth it.

The government agreed and, in cooperation with the union, social plans were developed that described exactly how the reduction would be implemented at each facility. Generally speaking, the plans relied on attrition and early retirement, but redeployment of personnel was also involved. The plans called for workers to be shifted to ten different collieries, some of which were from 12 to 15 miles from their present work sites. Each worker was allowed to select three preferred sites and, as it turned out, nearly 50 percent of those redeployed were given jobs at their first-choice site. Moving allowances were provided and, working in concert with the works councils, great care was taken to resolve all problems at the local level.

Clearly underlying the company's interest in phasing the planned reduction and in finding new jobs for the displaced workers was its concern with what might happen in the future. At the present time, Ruhr Coal's work force is relatively old. In 1982, 47 percent of its employees were over 40 years of age—admittedly younger than eight years previously when 53 percent were in that age bracket—but still not a reassuring state of affairs. Anticipating the projected labor shortage in about six years' time, the company's first concern is to hold on to its younger skilled workers who were trained at company expense. Clearly, the company was not anxious to do anything to jeopardize the employment security of the current labor work force, and so undermine the loyalty that has been so carefully nurtured. And in view of the technological nature of the work, the company was not eager to follow the normal system of "last in, first out." But although this particular incident was apparently well handled, Ruhr Coal's managers are not content to stop there. Planning for the future while continuing to emphasize employment security is serious business for them. Explaining how they approach the problem, Stockhaus makes the point that by 1990, 60 percent of Ruhr Coal's work force will be from 20 to 35 years of age. These will be young men and women who have grown up in the 1970s and 1980s. Ruhr Coal's management is very sensitive to the need to understand how these workers will think, what their life-styles will be, and what they will expect and want from their work. With this in mind, the company is concerned that work will have to be organized in different ways to meet the new workers' expectations.

One idea that is under consideration is to make it possible for workers to enter into some form of partnership with the company. That decision, and how it is to be enacted, will have to come from the workers themselves. The company has no desire or intention of imposing a new system. "There are no real solutions," Stockhaus says. "We don't want to manage it. We have no right to do that."

Since underground coal mining is by necessity dirty, dangerous, and frequently uncomfortable work, and since there is a limit as to what the company can do to improve conditions underground, Ruhr Coal has always followed a policy of trying to make its workers' lives above ground easier. That this leads to somewhat paternalistic attitudes, there is no doubt. Pay is high, but the company feels that the monetary reward does not offer sufficient stimulus and that, therefore, it is necessary to introduce other rewards, other motivations. Employment security is one such reward.

Apparently the policy has had some success. In many families in the area, succeeding generations find employment with Ruhr Coal. Each year, from 4,000 to 5,000 young people come to work with the company—one out of five of those leaving school in the Ruhr Valley. However, if the company is to continue to be able to maintain its labor force, this proportion will have to increase in the future.

One practical approach that the company has taken to retain its employees is to provide them with housing. This is especially important as the coal industry moves northward, since in the areas where new mines are being opened up, frequently there is a shortage of housing. To correct this situation the company is constructing new housing and making it available to its workers. One out of ten housing units in the Ruhr Valley is currently controlled by Ruhr Coal, and more will be in the future.

It will be interesting to see if Ruhr Coal's concern with the future, and particularly the steps the company is taking now to ensure a secure labor work force, will pay off. Certainly, if planning is the key, the Ruhr Coal program will be successful.

NOTES

1. This case study is based on presentations made to a meeting of the Work in America Institute National Advisory Committee on "Employment Security in a Free Economy," by W. J. Rowland, director of Personnel, Buick Motor Division, and Al Christner, president, UAW Local 599, Dearborn, Michigan, November 10, 1983. Information was also drawn from later conversations with Rowland.

2. Ibid.

3. Ibid.

4. Ibid.

5. This case study is based on an interview with Jack Sheinkman, secretary-treasurer, Amalgamated Clothing and Textile Workers Union, June 1984; on a speech made by Sheinkman to the Cornell University School of Industrial Relations Conference on Dislocated Workers, Washington, D.C., April 1984; and on an article in the *Washington Post*, "Alterations Ahead in Apparel," by Peter Behr, May 13, 1984.

6. Information on new-technology agreements was obtained from interviews with Oliver Tynan and David Grayson, Work Research Unit, Department of Employment, and with Vicky D. Kidd, assistant secretary, Post Office Engineering Union, January 1984.

7. United Kingdom Department of Employment, Labour Research Department, *Bargaining Report: Survey of New Technology* (London: United Kingdom Department of Employment, Labour Research Department, 1983).

8. Comments of Vicky Kidd, assistant secretary, Post Office Engineering Union, Greystoke House, London, January 1984.

9. This case study is based on an interview with Klaus Stockhaus, chief of Personnel Planning and Development, Ruhrkohle AG, Essen, West Germany, January 1984.

7.
Job-Replacement Strategies

Many European companies have experienced large-scale work-force reductions as they restructure their operations to improve productivity and maintain the ability to compete. Some of them have undertaken special efforts to create jobs in new enterprises to replace those eliminated in their own companies—a practice that has not yet caught on in the United States. To the extent that these job-creation strategies are successful, the companies' efforts certainly help to contribute to the employment security of their workers.

The job-replacement strategy is especially prevalent in France, but it occurs in other European countries as well. Two French programs are described in this chapter: the job-creation program of Rhone-Poulenc, the large French chemical company, and another program being carried out by the electrical and electronics conglomerate, the Thomson Group. These two programs are illustrative, but they are not unique. Almost every large French company has a similar program, including Usinor, the nationalized steel producer; Péchiney-Ugine-Kuhlman, one of the world's six biggest aluminum companies; Boussac, the textile giant; and BSN-Gervais Danone, the food processing multinational. The mechanism used by all of these French companies to foster job creation is a subsidiary company, usually known by its acronym. Although these subsidiaries are theoretically independent, they are usually staffed by a small number of senior personnel drawn from the parent company, and they are supported by a contribution which shows up in the budget of the sponsoring corporation. Their activities are aimed at attracting, encouraging, and supporting the development of new businesses and new investments in the areas affected by the parent company's personnel cutbacks or plant closures.

Several large British companies have also established subsidiaries to encourage the development of new enterprises in areas where they formerly dominated the labor market. Indeed, the concept was apparently pioneered in Great Britain. One of the first and perhaps the best known of these is British Steel's subsidiary, BSC Industry. After almost a decade of activity, BSC Industry is moving into a new phase and merging its local operations into those of the new Enterprise Agencies being established throughout Great Britain. In fact, it is BSC Industry's success in pulling together all of the resources of the community to encourage the development of new industry that has provided a model for the new Enterprise Agencies' approach to job replacement.

Another case, that of the Landskrona Finans Company in Sweden, represents a unique blend of public and private interests in implementing a job-replacement strategy. In this case, a shipbuilding company that was forced to close one of its facilities joined with the local government authorities and with other private-sector employers in the area to start a job-creation organization aimed at bringing new business into the abandoned shipyard to provide jobs for the ex-shipyard workers.

Not only companies, but also community-based organizations, have initiated job-replacement programs. One of the best examples of such a job-replacement strategy is in Michigan, where a dynamic community-service organization, the Downriver Community Conference, has evolved from being solely a provider of training to disadvantaged workers to being a successful community enterprise broker. Downriver has been responsible for bringing new business to the area, thereby increasing the opportunity for productive and secure employment benefits to the community as a whole.

Another interesting example of community sponsored job replacement is provided by a program in Munich, West Germany, where the union and local government worked together to initiate a new problem-solving institution to deal with recurrent employment problems in the area. By bringing together all of the parties affected by sudden changes in the labor market—employers, unions, national and local government authorities—this informal employment council, meeting on a regular basis, has been able to contribute in significant ways to employment stability in the community.

A final case illustrative of the community-based approach to job replacement is the development of the local Enterprise Agencies in Great Britain. Spearheaded by an independent nonprofit organization, Business in the Community (BIC), these agencies represent a blend of the public and private sectors, bringing together multiple resources to encourage the development of new jobs in a local area. One of the most active and successful of the Enterprise Agencies is the New Work Trust in Bristol, which is constantly searching for and finding new ways to promote employment security for the community it serves.

RHONE-POULENC—SOPRAN (FRANCE)

One of the first of the big French companies to institute a separate job-creation subsidiary was Rhone-Poulenc, France's leading chemical and pharmaceutical conglomerate. Established seven years ago, the new organization is named SOPRAN, an acronym standing for Society for the Promotion of New Activities. Its purpose is to develop new uses for Rhone-Poulenc's disbanded plants and to create new jobs for its former employees. No doubt self-interest played

an important part in the original decision to establish SOPRAN, but it is clear
that the company was also motivated by a traditional concern for the welfare
of its employees and for the communities in which its facilities were located.
Cultural and social factors also had a significant impact.

Rhone-Poulenc is a multinational corporation, with its headquarters and
most of its operations located in France, but with plants and other facilities
throughout the world.[1] It employs 82,000 people, 51,000 of them in France. In
1982 consolidated sales amounted to 37 billion French francs, or about $4.6
billion. Exports and foreign-produced goods accounted for 70 percent of the
company's total business. In addition to basic chemicals and pharmaceuticals,
the company produces agrochemicals, man-made textiles, film, and communications products and systems, such as magnetic tape and other media for
data processing. The corporation's headquarters are located in Courbevoie
just outside of Paris, in a newly developed area where many of the world's
largest companies have established offices and where one large, shiny building vies with the next in eye-catching elegance, architectural daring, and sheer
bulk. Rhone-Poulenc's manufacturing establishments, however, are found in
much simpler surroundings, mostly in small- and medium-sized towns
throughout France. At the present time there are 65 such plants. There used to
be more.

During the late 1960s the company went through a period of expansion,
particularly of its production of man-made fibers. Many smaller factories and
companies were acquired in this period and then, as more advanced technology was introduced, Rhone-Poulenc began to consolidate some of these
smaller plants into more efficient larger operations. By the mid-1970s, the
economic recessions resulting from the oil crises plus increased foreign competition had made an impact on the company's textile and chemical business. In
the words of Philippe Lecerf, spokesperson for SOPRAN, "We were the first
industry to face the need for reconversion, for restructuring. We found we had
to close some plants and to modernize others. The question was how to do it;
what to do about the people." SOPRAN was the answer.

From the beginning Rhone-Poulenc was committed to a no-dismissal policy; the work-force reduction had to be made without any involuntary layoffs. Adherence to such a policy is not unusual in France, and for good
reasons, some of them rooted in French custom and sociology, and others the
result of government regulation. In the Rhone-Poulenc case it is probably
correct to say that custom and tradition counted more than did government
fiat. As indicated earlier, the Rhone-Poulenc facilities are for the most part
located in small towns. Often they provide the only or the largest source of
employment in the area. Many of the company's plants have been in the same
location for many years, with generations of the same families working for
the company.

Beyond that, it is important to recognize that, in France, dismissal or layoff
is not taken lightly. To be laid off is to be stigmatized. Even though the layoff

is the result of economic factors and not because of poor performance or poor conduct on the part of the worker, other employers shy away from hiring a person who has been dismissed. Neither is change for the sake of change accepted easily in France. What is acceptable is to stay in one town or village, to work for one employer, and to bring up your children to do the same. As an official of the big French steel company Usinor stated, "Employment security is not only security in employment, but in life."[2] Such loyalty and stability are generally rewarded. As in most large French companies, Rhone-Poulenc's employees enjoy a system of bonuses based on longevity. Although there is some mobility, particularly among the younger workers, even in this group the urge to move to another place or another job is not as strong as in the United States. "Mobility is very weak here," according to Lecerf. Those who quit their jobs, even if it is to seek a better job, are often targets of considerable scorn and disapprobation. In some places such job leavers are even treated as pariahs. Then, too, dismissal can bring real financial hardship to those who are let go. At Rhone Poulenc, for example, a full pension is dependent on a continuous work association with the company until retirement age. Dismissal also means that the longevity bonus has been sacrificed.

"When a person decides to come to work for Rhone-Poulenc," Lecerf explains, "he or she makes a choice between security at some sacrifice in earnings, and risk, with perhaps higher earnings." Therefore, when the time came to restructure its operation and reduce personnel, the management of Rhone-Poulenc felt that it had to honor the security promise that was implicit when its employees made the choice to work for Rhone-Poulenc. For all of these reasons, "the ambience, the humanitarian aspects, and because we are French and do things the French way," the company adopted its no-dismissal policy. SOPRAN is the organization that was set up to implement the policy. The way it works is this:

Whenever a factory closes or its staff is cut back, SOPRAN becomes immediately involved. Although it is regarded as an independent subsidiary, SOPRAN's funds come entirely from the parent company, as part of Rhone-Poulenc's annual budget. (In 1984, for example, SOPRAN received 25 million French francs, its entire budget, from Rhone-Poulenc.) In addition, the SOPRAN staff is drawn almost entirely from Rhone-Poulenc. It numbers about 15 and consists primarily of managerial and technical staff, most of whom have had at least 20 years' experience with the company. The head offices of SOPRAN are located in the Rhone-Poulenc building outside Paris, but most of its staff is located in regional offices throughout France. In addition, SOPRAN has offices in New York and San Francisco, which have responsibility for promoting new American investments in the French communities where Rhone-Poulenc's operations have been curtailed.

After the decision is made to reduce personnel in a particular location, the first step is the classification of all the individuals affected. All those who are 55 years of age or over or who have worked for at lest 37 years are offered early retirement. When the company first began its restructuring efforts, about 90 percent of those eligible accepted the offer. Recently, however, that percentage has declined, so that today only about 60 percent retire voluntarily. To encourage an active job search by the other workers, Rhone-Poulenc pays a premium to those who find and take another job on their own. Then the management of the local plant, often with SOPRAN's help, canvasses the region to locate other employers who can offer jobs to displaced Rhone-Poulenc workers. In many cases employers have signed agreements with the unions to give priority to laid-off workers; although such a contract may discriminate against new entrants into the labor force, especially young people seeking jobs for the first time and older women reentering the labor force after an absence, it does help to alleviate the impact of the closure. Employers who hire displaced Rhone-Poulenc workers are paid a premium by the company of 30,000 French francs, about $3,750. The government also helps by supporting some retraining and by providing mobility grants in certain cases. The major responsibility for finding new jobs for Rhone-Poulenc workers affected by reconversion has been assumed by the company and by SOPRAN. It should be noted, however, that the division of responsibility between government and the company is not entirely clear-cut. Like most big French companies, Rhone-Poulenc was nationalized by the present French government. Although, for the most part, nationalization has made little difference in the way companies operate, still it does mean that company losses can be covered by government subsidy. The bottom line for Rhone-Poulenc and for its subsidiary SOPRAN, therefore, does not have quite the same meaning as for a U.S. company operating in the private sector.

If a laid-off worker wants to start a new business—and SOPRAN works hard to encourage its workers to do this—the company will do everything possible to support the effort. In some cases SOPRAN has encouraged new entrepreneurs to develop some of the company's own research ideas or its new products, with a buy-back guarantee if the project does not work out. SOPRAN can lend money to the individual and, through its local contacts, can arrange local or government loans to supplement a SOPRAN loan. In addition, the SOPRAN staff is available to provide technical support, for example, in setting up an accounting system, organizing production, marketing the product, or other aspects of managing a business. SOPRAN will also pay for from three to six months of training for new entrepreneurs or, for that matter, for any workers who want to be retrained in order to improve their chances for reemployment.

SOPRAN also develops new jobs for former Rhone-Poulenc employees. If a worker wants to try out such a job for a period of time, SOPRAN gives the worker three months to decide if the job is satisfactory and gives the new employer the same grace period to accept the worker. If either party is not satisfied, Rhone-Poulenc will take the worker back and try again. If the new employee stays, the employer receives the 30,000-franc premium. If the new job requires training, either on or off the job, SOPRAN will foot the bill, thus providing a further inducement to employers to hire its displaced workers.

The activity for which SOPRAN is probably best known is its effort to encourage new investment in the areas affected by the company's withdrawal, using former Rhone-Poulenc facilities where appropriate. To do this SO-PRAN offers a variety of inducements to the would-be investor, starting with the plant itself, at favorable rates of sale or rent, and followed by assistance with financing, help with the selection and training of personnel, marketing feasibility studies, sometimes a guaranteed purchase of the product to be produced by the new investor, and finally, expert guidance through the French bureaucratic maze, a formidable task under the best of circumstances. However, as Lecerf says, "To find the money is not a problem. The problem is to find the ideas and the people who want to put them in action." SOPRAN does not limit its search for new investment to France, but has staff looking all over Europe as well as in the United States.

In putting together a financial package for a new investor or entrepreneur, SOPRAN utilizes all possible resources, including money from the government, regional banks, and other investors. If the new investor still needs additional money, SOPRAN itself will provide as much as 50 percent of the total cost if the investor promises to replace at least 20 percent of the jobs that were lost by the Rhone-Poulenc reconversion. To further sweeten the inducement, SOPRAN will supervise the plant renovation or new plant construction, install equipment, train labor, and even find a plant manager. In other words, it will do everything possible to get the new enterprise off to a good start. But this is not a solution that comes about overnight. Generally speaking, it takes a minimum of 18 to 24 months to get a new plant going; at best, the new plant will provide employment for only half as many people as the old Rhone-Poulenc facility.

SOPRAN officials, as well as officials of the parent Rhone-Poulenc, believe that the program has been well worth the effort. Over the past six years, Rhone-Poulenc has reduced its employment in France by 14,000 jobs. SO-PRAN's activities in promoting new investment have resulted in the creation of over 1,200 new jobs. About half of these have gone to former Rhone-Poulenc employees, a proportion that is much higher than, for example, the proportion of British Steel workers that find jobs in the new enterprises established with the help of British Steel's BSC Industry, Ltd. The cost to Rhone-Poulenc has been a relatively modest one, about 65,000 French francs per job. It may not seem an impressive record to American readers, but to the communities in which the new SOPRAN-supported businesses are now in operation, it has provided a much needed boost.

THOMSON—GÉRIS (FRANCE)

Like Rhone-Poulenc and many other large companies in France, Thomson, or more accurately the Thomson Group, has established its own job-creation subsidiary as a means of coping with the problems caused by the process of reconversion, or restructuring. Reconversion is another name for the kind of streamlining that is going on throughout the French economy and, in fact, in large industrial companies in all Western European countries. As is typical with the French companies, the name of the Thomson subsidiary is an acronym, GÉRIS, for (in French) Grouping of Economic Activity for the Reconversion of Industries and Services.[3]

Although the basic design of GÉRIS is much the same as that of the job-creation subsidiaries of other French companies such as Rhone-Poulenc's SOPRAN, there are significant differences between Thomson's GÉRIS and the other organizations. One concerns the nature of the Thomson work force compared to that of other companies. The Thomson Group, which includes Thomson-CSF, Thomson-Brandt, Bonnet, and many other companies, both large and small, is one of the world's most important producers of electronics products, including consumer electronics. Much of the work that is done in Thomson factories has required the employment of many semiskilled workers who are engaged in assembly work. As Thomson restructures itself to better compete in world markets, it is precisely these workers who are being replaced by new machines that perform mechanically the tasks formerly performed by hand. For Thomson then, it is these workers, many of them women, for whom new jobs must be created.

The second important difference between the activities of GÉRIS and some of the other job-creation subsidiaries flows from the first. This is Thomson's commitment to small- and medium-sized enterprise since, in the Thomson view, this is the best and perhaps the only solution to the particular reemployment needs of Thomson's target population. A third difference concerns an innovative operating strategy adopted by GÉRIS called a "progressively phased agreement," or PPA—involving a sort of reverse subcontracting procedure between an outside entrepreneur and the Thomson Group and designed to complement the incentives to new businesses provided by the French government.

The Thomson Group—nationalized since 1981 along with other large companies—is the leading French industrial corporation in domestic appliances, professional electronics, telephone switching equipment, radiology and medical electronics, lamps and lighting, and general engineering. It also produces military and defense equipment under contract with the French government. Thomson is highly decentralized, with each of its many subdivisions and subsidiaries operating more or less independently. The company has both production and commercial facilities all over the world, but its operations are concentrated in France and in West Germany where most of its 130,000 workers are employed. In the Paris area alone, the corporation has more than 50 separate facilities. In all of France, there are about 170 industrial units, technical and research centers, and service and commercial agencies. Sales for 1980 amounted to over $8.5 billion, putting the company in the top 50 of *Fortune*'s list of the largest industrial companies in the world.

The company has had the reputation of being fairly conservative in its management, especially in regard to its personnel policies. Moreover, until recently it has enjoyed a somewhat protected market because of the predominance of government contracts for defense and for the French postal system. In economic downturns, this part of the company's business could serve to shelter to some extent the consumer side. That situation has now begun to change. Technological advances, increased competition from industrialized nations such as Japan and the United States and the newly industrialized nations of the Third World, as well as recent world recessions, have forced the company to restructure in order to improve productivity and thereby maintain its ability to compete in world markets.

Insofar as personnel policies are concerned, the corporation faced a double problem. GÉRIS Director General E. P. Courtillot explains, "On the one hand, the company has a pressing need for specialized personnel—engineers, technicians, and skilled workers that are very hard to recruit. In 1983, Thomson had to hire 1,000 people in these categories. On the other hand, the elimination of repetitive tasks by automation is removing thousands of jobs at the bottom of the skill ladder, and most particularly those jobs held by women."[4]

To solve the second part of its problem, Thomson started by introducing a large-scale retraining program that provided more than 5,000 workers with education and training courses designed to improve their qualifications. But clearly this was not enough, since Thomson's managers estimated that roughly 75 percent of the workers made redundant by the restructuring process would not be eligible for "reclassification" by this means. It was primarily to help this group that GÉRIS was established, although it is clear that Thomson also hoped to gain new business from its activities in promoting small- and medium-sized enterprises in the areas where Thomson plants were located.

Like its counterparts, GÉRIS is an independent company, with a board of directors that outnumbers its small staff. It is owned jointly by three companies in the Thomson Group—Thomson-Brandt, Thomson-CSF, and Thomson CSF Telephone. GÉRIS has been in business only four years, but by the end of the first two it had already amassed a notable record, helping to start 19 new businesses, which led to the creation of more than 600 new jobs. The GÉRIS staff is a team of four managerial experts drawn from the company itself and based in Paris. The organization operates on a budget of about 4 million

French francs, or about $500,000, some of which is contributed by the parent companies, supplemented by additional funds as needed from local Thomson companies where the actual restructuring is taking place and new businesses are being established.

GÉRIS offers three basic types of assistance to its customers. The first is the progressively phased agreement, or PPA. The PPA is designed to help those enterprises which want to increase or expand their business but who cannot because of limited manufacturing capacity and/or lack of financial resources to enlarge that capacity. A GÉRIS-sponsored PPA provides a way for such an outside employer to solve these problems at a minimum cost, the important condition being that the jobs created by the expansion will be made available to the Thomson employees whose jobs are slated to be eliminated. The PPA proposes a two-step procedure. In the first step the outside employer subcontracts to Thomson the production that cannot be undertaken in the outside employer's own plant. (Obviously this program is only useful where the products that the outside entrepreneur manufactures are the same or compatible with products manufactured by Thomson.) During this stage of the agreement, while the subcontracted production is under way in a Thomson unit somewhere in France, the outside employer is helped by GÉRIS to determine the feasibility of setting up an independent operation, preferably in the same area where a Thomson facility is being cut back or closed down. If it is determined that the project is indeed worthwhile, the second step is undertaken. This is the transfer of the real assets used by Thomson for the subcontracted production to the outside entrepreneur. This can include everything from the buildings to the equipment to the workers themselves who are involved in the production. With the transfer of the workers goes a reemployment incentive, paid by Thomson and which, if necessary, can be prepaid. Of course, the transfer of other assets involves a cost to the outside entrepreneur, but the rates are reasonable and often accompanied by some form of government assistance. The personnel who are likely to be transferred under this arrangement are kept fully informed of the proposed operation, and the actual transfer is on a voluntary basis.

Use of the PPA actually involves two agreements: the subcontract between the employer and the Thomson unit, and the PPA itself. The PPA usually calls for a variety of support services, which GÉRIS agrees to arrange. These include the training of Thomson workers and supervisory staff to undertake the subcontracted work, a feasibility study, a marketing study, arrangement of the necessary financial backing for the expansion, performance of the administrative tasks necessary to take advantage of the French government incentives to new and expanding businesses, and assurances that the buildings necessary to house the new expansion are available. Except for the payment of the reemployment incentives, which apply to any former Thomson workers who are transferred to the new enterprise, there is no other direct financial support from Thomson. Regular banking and other financial organizations are expected to provide the necessary capital on the basis of performance under the first step of the process.

A second type of assistance that GÉRIS can offer is in cases where an existing business decides to establish a new unit, warehouse, or maintenance service center in an area affected by a Thomson reconversion. The kinds of assistance that GÉRIS can offer in these circumstances include the basic management necessary during the start-up period, tools and other necessary equipment, required buildings or offices, data processing or other administrative services, and, if necessary, the training of the new work force.

Assistance to help launch an entirely new business is the third kind of help offered by GÉRIS. In this case the GÉRIS staff focuses on providing the would-be entrepreneur with a professional feasibility study, as well as helping obtain the necessary financing; advising on fiscal, legal, and administrative matters; and intervening with the public authorities to obtain required authorizations.

The GÉRIS team would be very pleased if its efforts could always be directed entirely at helping former Thomson employees become entrepreneurs and start their own businesses. And in fact this has occasionally occurred. But, for the most part, the new entrepreneurs come from outside the group of displaced Thomson workers since the attributes which make a worker valuable in a large enterprise are apt to be quite the opposite of those that characterize a successful entrepreneur.

One of the problems that GÉRIS has had to face is the reluctance of former Thomson workers to go to work for a new small business, even when it is supported by the Thomson program. In many of the small towns and villages where Thomson has its facilities, working for Thomson was considered an honor, and a degree of status was attached to such employment. In the eyes of some of the redundant employees, to go to work for a small- or medium-sized business is to lose status. In order to overcome this prejudice, GÉRIS has found it necessary to carefully present and discuss each new project with all of those who may be affected. It is also important for GÉRIS to very carefully select the entrepreneurs it wants to back. Under these circumstances, it cannot afford any failures. Fortunately for the program, thus far only two new ventures have failed.

The experience with one "area of reconversion" illustrates what GÉRIS can accomplish. In this case, Thomson planned to reorganize an electronic component factory in Montville, near the city of Rouen, in the north of France. The reorganization meant the elimination of some 700 jobs in that plant. As a result of the efforts of GÉRIS, eight businesses were either newly established or expanded their operations in the area of Montville, with five of them actually setting up in business on the site of the electronics factory. The number of jobs created was 503, about half of which were held by former Thomson workers. The new businesses were as follows:

Company	Business	Number of jobs
SNEP	Electronic components	30
Varimaille	Knitwear	60
Sagem	Electrical equipment	16
Marechal	Electrical equipment	28
Sovecore	Furniture	50
S.G.E.P.	Repair shops	150
Euroterminal	Electronic printing	166
T.R.T.	Electronics	3
		503

The furniture company provides a good example of the kind of enterprise which GÉRIS likes to encourage. The owner had worked for several years, first with a shoe company, where he had been in charge of setting up new factories in developing countries in Africa, and then as an agent for an Italian furniture company, opening up new markets throughout Europe. He had left that company two years before to start his own furniture company. Having determined that the market for small furniture made of wood was dominated by imports from the Far East, this entrepreneur decided he could compete successfully, taking advantage of the fact that there was a good supply of the necessary raw materials in Europe, that he was located closer to the market, and that demand was sufficient. After 18 months of operation, he felt he could easily expand his production, except that he did not have enough space or the necessary capital. With GÉRIS' help, he got both. Fifty new jobs were thus created, with the expectation that additional personnel could be hired within the next two years.

What does Thomson get out of all this? It is not easy to quantify. Courtillot says that the average cost of creating a new job is 200,000 French francs. If the job is in a highly automated industry, using the most up-to-date computerized equipment, a single job could cost as much as 500,000 francs. The contribution of GÉRIS to a new job in a small- or medium-sized enterprise ranges from 5 percent to 10 percent of the total cost. Banks, other financial institutions, and the government provide the rest. In return for this contribution, GÉRIS and Thomson can take some credit for helping to reduce the high rate of unemployment in France, which is expensive not only for the government, but for business as well. Second, Thomson can hope that one day one of the small businesses that the company helped to get started will turn out to be an Apple or a Wang, allowing Thomson to be in on the ground floor. Finally, through its activities, GERIS is contributing to the unemployment security of all Thomson workers, a worthwhile objective in itself.

BRITISH STEEL CORPORATION—BSC INDUSTRY, LTD. (GREAT BRITAIN)

Given the widely accepted need for British companies to improve efficiency and productivity in order to be able to compete in world markets, perhaps the most interesting current development in Great Britain is the effort by large companies to promote new small businesses in communities where they have had to reduce work forces or to shut down plants. Certainly this development will have a lasting impact on the structure of business and employment in that country. It may be a back door to the goal of employment security for workers, but it is nevertheless a door and, under the circumstances, one that appears to make the most sense to most people. The British Steel experience is perhaps the best known of these ventures and provides the best example of some of the problems associated with a job-creation approach to employment security.

In the ten years since 1974, British Steel Corporation has reduced its work force from a high of 220,000 employees to approximately 75,000. The communities in areas where British Steel was forced to close plants have been hard hit by these cutbacks. To help these communities cope with the problems they faced as a result of the steel layoffs, British Steel created a new subsidiary, BSC Industry, Ltd., in 1975. The new, wholly owned but independent subsidiary was designed to help create new jobs in the most affected areas in England, Scotland, and Wales. Over a period of ten years about £50 million has been committed to BSC Industry by British Steel. However, BSC Industry is a separate company, with its own board of directors and its own budget. The goal it set for itself was to help create 25,000 jobs by March 1984. A year before this scheduled date, BSC Industry had helped 1,400 businesses, thus creating about 20,000 current jobs and pledging another 16,000 before 1986.[5]

It is important to note that BSC Industry was established to promote new business and thus new jobs in areas hurt by British Steel's restructuring. It does not consider itself in the business of finding new jobs specifically for displaced steel workers. "We don't see that as our responsibility. If a man is made redundant, well that's very bad. But giving him a job is not what we're trying to do. By creating new jobs in the community, he *may* get a new job, but if it helps his son or daughter or cousin or uncle or neighbor, that's all right too."[6] As a matter of fact, entrepreneurship cannot correctly be considered a practical solution for most laid-off steel workers. One official of BSC Industry estimated that not more than 2 percent of the steel workers made redundant by British Steel were themselves of an entrepreneurial bent. It should also be noted that of the total number of laid-off British Steel employees, about half took advantage of the early-retirement offers made to them.

Others were able to find new jobs on their own. The job-creation efforts of BSC Industry were and are intended to facilitate and stimulate that process.

During its first eight years, BSC Industry operated through local offices situated in most of the areas where steel plants had been closed. Relying mostly on word of mouth, but also with some active promotion and advertising, BSC Industry served as a catalyst to help new enterprises get established in the affected areas, and it had a range of services to make that possible. These services included arranging financing; providing technical assistance, including marketing and training and retraining for workers; and, at times, making available appropriate facilities at a reasonable cost. What BSC Industry did was to put together a package that made it possible for the new enterprise to get over the initial hurdles involved in getting started. Not all of the enterprises that BSC Industry helped, however, were actually new; some were already-functioning companies that were considering expansion and were looking for a good location. For example, BSC Industry is credited with playing a major part in bringing the European headquarters of the Canadian telecommunications company Mitel to South Wales, where it will employ some 3,000 workers.

When a potential entrepreneur asked for help, the first thing the BSC Industry staff did was to decide whether or not the idea appeared viable. If the decision was favorable, it designed a package especially tailored to the entrepreneur's needs. If financing was required—and most of BSC Industry's clients did need such help—it was arranged by BSC Industry staff, who drew on the variety of resources available to them. Since most of the British Steel-affected areas were also designated Government Assisted Areas, the government-sponsored development programs which offer grants and low-interest loans provided one such resource. Another resource was the European Steel and Coal Community, which can provide loans at favorable interest rates for job-creation purposes in coal- and steel-closure areas. The resources of local banks were also tapped and, if necessary, BSC Industry itself had funds which it could lend to fill any gaps that could not be taken care of by any other means. If technical assistance was needed, BSC Industry, which at the peak of its operation had a staff of more than 70 people—some lent, or "seconded," by other organizations (e.g., banks) to BSC Industry for a short period of time—provided such expertise. This covered the whole gamut of business-related problems, from accounting to production, including legal questions, marketing advice, organizational structure, dealing with government regulations, and taking advantage of government assistance programs. If the company did not have the necessary resources, BSC Industry arranged and paid for consultants to come in to deal with the problem. If training or retraining was needed, BSC Industry could make the necessary contacts and arrangements with the Manpower Services Commission to obtain training funds and/or to arrange classes.

In 1983 BSC Industry changed its method of operation. Since then, its local offices have been merged into local Enterprise Agencies (for a more complete description, see pages 170 to 175). The agencies bring together public- and private-sector resources to support local teams, which carry out the same functions as the former BSC Industry local offices. BSC Industry supports such teams in 18 areas in Scotland, England, and Wales; it continues to market these areas and to provide gap-filling financial support for new or expanding businesses.

Frequently new businesses need facilities in which to operate, so to accommodate this need, BSC Industry has established workshops in eight of the areas affected by closures of British Steel plants. These workshops are often located in the same buildings that formerly had been part of the steel plant. A highly successful workshop is located in Cardiff, South Wales, the site of British Steel's former East Moors Iron and Steel Works.[7]

In 1974, the East Moors Works employed 4,500 people and was a major employer in the area. In 1978, however, the works was closed and demolition of the plant begun. It is a huge site, adjacent to the Bristol Channel and not too far from the center city. Originally the Welsh Development Agency proposed to make the entire site available as a new industrial estate, but when BSC Industry indicated that it wanted to use some of the old buildings to establish a workshop, the Welsh authorities agreed. Some 15 of the old buildings, including administrative buildings, the health clinic, train sheds, and several workshops were converted, providing space for up to 94 separate new businesses. Space was made available for every kind of enterprise, from a large machine shop to small operations providing employment for only one or two people. In developing the workshop concept, BSC Industry started from the premise that the availability of appropriate space was itself an important ingredient for the success of a new enterprise. The BSC Industry management believed that anyone thinking about taking the plunge into a first-business venture would not want, and could not use, a large custom-built factory, with long-term rent and/or other property commitments. They felt that they had to offer new entrepreneurs the chance to get into business easily and, equally important, the chance to get out easily. Instead of a lease, therefore, tenants of the Cardiff Workshops get a "license" giving them the right of occupation for an indefinite period. If they want to leave, all that is required is three months' notice. Rents are about average for the area and include all site services, such as building maintenance, insurance, site clearing, and landscaping; in addition, the tenants pay fees for services such as heating and power. They also have available the use of a conference room, a mail drop, and such clerical services as a copier and access to a telex machine, plus—an important part of workshop facilities—on-site management advice.

To be accepted by Cardiff Workshops, the potential entrepreneur must submit two personal references, as well as one from a bank. But the deciding factor is a personal interview with the workshop manager. BSC Industry considers the workshop environment to be comparable to a plant nursery, a seed bed for budding firms, so it looks for small operations with growth potential. As originally conceived, BSC Industry workshops were not intended to be profit-making operations; however, the Cardiff Workshops have produced a profit, which has been used to help subsidize other, smaller BSC Industry workshops.

In the three years it has been in operation, the Cardiff Workshops have sheltered and supported some 73 new businesses. Of these, 28 have already left the premises. Sixteen moved out because they grew beyond the nursery stage and needed additional space—and probably more sophisticated surroundings—to expand. Nine tenants, having decided for one reason or another that entrepreneurship was not for them, retired gracefully either to continue their businesses on a reduced scale elsewhere or to take a job. Only three really crashed and went into liquidation. Of those that have made it and remained in business, some have been notable successes: One business, a photo-printing operation which started out as a two-person, husband-and-wife operation, today employs 25 people.

Because of the range in size of workshop units and the nature of small start-up businesses, a wide variety of companies have been attracted to Cardiff Workshops. There is a sophisticated biotechnology company, a steel fabrication and machine-shop operation, and a small office-stationery distributor. One company specializes in producing sterile hospital supplies. Inevitably there are also several new businesses connected with the new telecommunications and computer industries, such as one that produces tailor-made circuitry for specialized-process computers. Indeed, Cardiff Workshops have been so successful that they have become a model for private developers trying to ride the "small is beautiful" wave.

At the time of its formation in 1975, BSC Industry was designed to act as a catalyst organization to promote and support new businesses in communities affected by the crisis resulting from British Steel's restructuring process. It was not necessarily expected to become a permanent institution. It has, however, operated for nearly a decade and, since 1973, has moved into a new and different phase. During this period, it has progressively merged its local operations with those of the new Enterprise Agencies that are being established throughout Great Britain, not only in the steel-closure areas, but in many other communities as well. By doing this, it has found a way to assure both continuity and a broadening of its early operations.

LANDSKRONA FINANS (SWEDEN)

The Landskrona Finans Company, or LAFI, of Sweden presents an interesting example of a successful cooperative effort between government and private industry to create new jobs replacing those lost in a declining industry, in this case the shipbuilding industry.[8] Although the original idea for LAFI came from the management of the government-owned shipbuilding company and its union, the organization obtained and has operated with broad support and financial backing from other companies located in the same region, and from both local and national governments. As such, LAFI represents a cross between the French corporate-sponsored job-development subsidiaries and the British community-backed workshops for new enterprises.

The crisis began in 1978 for Landskrona, a town of 36,000 people in the southern part of Sweden, when a decision was made by the government which owned the Oresund shipyard, located in the town, to substantially cut back capacity and personnel at the yard. Oresund was one of several shipyards owned by Swedyard, the nationalized Swedish shipbuilding corporation. The original decision was to reduce the nearly 3,000 workers employed by Oresund at that time to about 2,500. It was at this point that management and the union began working together to (1) make the company more efficient and thus, it was hoped, stave off any additional reductions, and (2) find a way to bring new replacement jobs into the community to provide employment for workers who would have to be dismissed. Throughout the next 18 months the Oresund shipyard suffered from a welter of serious problems: changes in top management, anger and frustration and even wildcat strikes among the workers, lack of clear direction from the government, and declining business. The result of all this was that in May 1981, the Swedish Parliament, acting at the request and with the support of the parent company, decided that the Oresund yard should be closed down completely. The shutdown was to be accomplished on a gradual basis, with the final termination date set for June 1983.

As it happened, during the months preceding the closure decision by the Parliament, some important activities were going on at Oresund. The parent company, Swedyard, had decided as early as the fall of 1980 that the Oresund facility should be closed, and soon afterward this recommendation was accepted by the government. The act of Parliament was merely a ratification of these earlier decisions, although the action of the legislature did stretch out the time before final closure took effect. Planning for the shutdown therefore had begun long before the final decision was made public. As early as mid-1980, a community report had suggested that a development company be established as a way of promoting replacement jobs. And later that year a report from a consultant identified at least 30 new business possibilities that might be located within the shipyard facilities. As a result of this preliminary activity, by February 1981, several months before the parliamentary decision, the Oresund yard management, working with the union, had made a preliminary decision to establish a development company—in effect, a regional new-business venture company—which would be called Landskrona Finans. Moreover, through the combined efforts of the shutdown planning group, several new companies had already set up operations within the shipyard.

When in May 1981 the Parliament made its decision, Landskrona Finans was officially established and immediately began operations on its own.

The organizational structure of LAFI is a unique blend of public and private interests. LAFI is owned by 19 different organizations, including two towns, the government-owned parent shipbuilding company, a regional investment company, and 15 private industrial companies in the region. The Swedish government has contributed most of the capital, about 100 million Swedish crowns, but the private sector controls the majority of the votes. Why this interest from other local employers and businesses in the region? The answer must be found in the importance of the shipyard to the region's economy. For many years Oresund was the biggest industrial employer in Landskrona. Obviously, the shutdown and the resulting unemployment would have a disastrous impact on the local economy, as well as on the welfare and even the stability of the government. This last point may have been partly responsible for the large contribution that the Swedish government made to LAFI to get it started. In any case, the shipyard, including not only the land but also the buildings and all the equipment, was sold to LAFI for the token sum of one Swedish crown, although the assessed valuation was about 140 million Swedish crowns. With these assets, plus the direct capital grant from the government, LAFI was in business.

LAFI has taken a very practical, business-like approach to its tasks, which it defines as the support of regional industry, the development of new products and new activities, and the encouragement of research and development. Insofar as it is possible, LAFI tries to develop complete assistance "packages" to support new businesses getting started in Landskrona. However, it will only support those businesses which promise to be successful. No subsidies are involved and no extraordinary risks are taken. Rentals are in line with the regular market. Financing from LAFI is available only to supplement that obtainable through normal financial channels. Projects are judged on their ability to contribute to sustained profitability within the region; LAFI is not interested in short-term projects. The company will take some risk above and beyond that taken by the banks and other financial institutions, but even the risk taking is somewhat circumspect. As could be expected, LAFI operations are limited to the Landskrona area. It will not support new ventures outside the area in which it has chosen to operate. And, finally, LAFI will not support any activity which is in any way involved in shipbuilding.

Results are reported to have been very good. By April 1983, only two months before the final closure date for the Oresund yard, 63 companies and projects were operating under the LAFI umbrella. Together they provided jobs for 775 workers, one-fourth of whom were former shipyard workers. Since there were about 2,400 employees at Oresund when the parliamentary closure decision was made and LAFI became fully operative, this may not seem very impressive. However, of the 2,400 workers who lost their jobs, approximately 1,300 found new jobs on their own or with the help of the Labor Market Board, the Swedish version of the U.S. employment service. Another 350 persons accepted an early-retirement pension or were covered by other government support programs. No one remained on the unemployment rolls very long. Without Landskrona Finans, however, the story would have been quite different.

The number of jobs created by each of the 63 new-business ventures ranged from one to as many as 200. The latter is an industrial enterprise, a plastic manufacturing company. Another large employer is a heavy-engineering enterprise which in April 1983 employed 110 people, but was planning to expand to 150. Many of the new companies manufacture such products as packing materials, windows, kitchen equipment, plastic pipes, pallets, and bicycles. Service industries are also well represented, with several waste-disposal companies, two moving companies, machine and vehicle repair shops, a guard duty company, a hearing aid company, and a law firm, among others. The new information sector is represented by companies providing research, system development, and data processing. Other LAFI-supported enterprises cover traditional building and construction trades, including building construction, painting, plumbing, and carpentry. In other words, the new businesses run the gamut of industrial and commercial activity.

Several factors are credited with contributing to the success of LAFI. First among these is the early and effective cooperation between the management and the union in conceiving the program and in getting it going even before the final decision on closure was announced. This pattern of a close working relationship between the company and the union was replicated by a similar pattern of cooperation between the local community and the company. All of the interested parties were accustomed to working together long before the crisis and certainly before LAFI began its operations. They not only wanted to cooperate, but they knew how to do so. Another factor was the small, flexible nature of the organization. LAFI operates with a permanent staff of only five persons: a managing director, comptroller, technical analyst, secretary, and administrator, who handles the real estate management of the company. Instead of hiring additional people, LAFI uses professional and technical consultants, drawing from both industry and academia as needed and appropriate. With this small staff, LAFI can make its decisions easily and quickly. In addition, the organization is strengthened by its adherence to a market approach to new ventures. There is no doubt that the initial capital grant from the Swedish government and the turnover of the Oresund facilities made the LAFI task easier and, indeed, possible. It is also clear that LAFI's position as a going concern before the yard was shut down entirely has helped it build on the infrastructure that was already there. Finally, as pointed out in the report issued by the Organisation for Economic Co-operation and Development (OECD) on the Landskrona Finans operation, the success of the project is due in large part to "the people involved. Thanks to them, and all their commitment, strength and hard work of taking care of a future that in the beginning of the eighties looked like a huge black cloud, the situation has now . . . turned into an opportunity."[9]

DOWNRIVER COMMUNITY CONFERENCE

The Downriver Community Conference is a consortium of 16 communities that make up a portion of southeastern Wayne County, Michigan—located "down the river" from Detroit. It is a mixed suburban-industrial area of about 350,000 people, with some large plants and many small- and medium-sized factories and workshops involved primarily in the steel, chemicals, and automotive industries.[10] A public nonprofit community-service organization, the Downriver Community Conference was established in the mid-1960s, more or less in response to the Detroit riots of that period, in a mutual-aid pact for police and fire protection. This original concept was soon extended to cover a broad range of other public-policy areas. The agency did not get directly involved in operating job-creation programs, however, until 1977 when Downriver received a grant from the Ford Foundation to develop an experimental program in intergovernmental relations. Out of this initiative came the organization's direct operation of a variety of economic and social projects. In addition to employment and training, some other areas covered are youth projects, help for senior citizens, economic development, health, transportation, housing, and even support of the arts. Today, the employment and training aspect of Downriver's work has become the largest and perhaps the most important area of activity.

The Downriver Community Conference is governed by a board of directors made up of the mayors of all of the 16 member communities. The board reviews and has veto power over all of Downriver's projects. The organization is funded for the most part from grants provided on a project-by-project basis. Initially it received no formula funding from either the state of Michigan or from the federal government, but that has changed somewhat. At the present time, Downriver has been designated a "service-delivery area" under the federal Job Training and Partnership Act (JTPA), a designation that entitles it to an established flow of funds from the state to carry out its employment and training programs. Each of the member communities also contributes a small amount of money each year, but this is more in the nature of "dues" than of meaningful support for the organization's programs.

The Downriver Conference considers itself, and is regarded in the community as, an action agency, an agency that gets things done. Unlike the Private

Industry Councils (PICs) established under the JTPA to oversee the federally supported employment and training programs, Downriver is not a planning organization, nor does it have responsibility for monitoring or coordinating other local programs. It does, however, work closely with other community organizations and, in fact, some of the Downriver staff sit on the boards of other community agencies, thereby enhancing its ability to function effectively within the community. Projects are carefully selected by the staff and reviewed by the board to maintain its reputation as a can-do organization. As one staff member said, "We couldn't do what we do if we didn't have these mayors supporting us all the way."[11]

Downriver's first experience with employment and training came in 1979 when the mayor of one of the member communities, the city of Wyandotte, told the organization that BASF Southworks, a multinational chemical company located in Wyandotte, was going to shut down. "What are you going to do about it?" he asked.[12] What Downriver did was to set up a task force that included representatives of business, labor, banking, and governmental and community-based organizations to help it design a program to assist Wyandotte. Within weeks Downriver was in the employment and training business.

In the next few months, several other developments affected this new Downriver program. First, a rash of plant closures and work-force reductions began to overwhelm the area as the world recession began to bite deep into the automotive industry as well as other basic industries. (Within three years, it is estimated, the Downriver area lost approximately 52 percent of its primary industrial jobs.) The other development of special significance to Downriver was that the U.S. Department of Labor under the Carter administration decided to conduct a demonstration program to determine what kinds of employment and training measures could effectively help displaced workers. It was hoped that because of this demonstration the new employment and training legislation being formulated would include a workable program for this group, particularly those who had permanently lost their jobs in declining industries. Downriver was selected as the site for one of the demonstration programs, and the program that was put together with the help of the task force in response to the BASF shutdown became the demonstration effort. The Department of Labor provided a grant of $5.2 million, which was to be used to provide services to 2,000 workers laid off from five plants in the area, including BASF. The project began in July 1980 and was in operation through December 1982.

In developing its program, the Downriver Conference made some important decisions that set it apart from other employment and training programs. The first was to set up an information and referral network so that even those workers who never got involved in training could be immediately directed to appropriate sources of help in the community. Second, the group surveyed the local situation and decided that, given the workers' previous employment histories, the best prospects for reemployment would come in relatively healthy manufacturing industries that could use their skills. Despite the ravages of international competition and the recession in the Detroit area, the staff of Downriver found that there were still about 6,000 manufacturing firms within a radius of 50 miles, its operative area. These firms, then, plus the growing number of enterprises in the service sector became the market to which the Downriver organization addressed itself. Third, and most important, the Downriver Conference early on took the position that the employers should be considered the organization's customers. If Downriver was going to be able to persuade employers to hire the unemployed workers streaming through its doors asking for help, it had to be able to convince those employers that it could provide them with whatever they needed. This concept is in contrast to most employment and training programs supported by community organizations, where it is the participant, the unemployed worker, who is the agency's client, not the employer. Instead, Downriver saw itself as a marketing organization with a "product line" to sell. Instead of focusing on improving the general employability of the unemployed workers who come to the agency, Downriver focuses on the jobs. And since jobs come from employers, it is the employers' needs which are paramount. Obviously, this requires a fairly rigorous screening system.

In carrying out its demonstration program, Downriver developed a three-track system, which is still used by the organization even though the demonstration has been completed. Under this system, the organization requires that everyone who comes to it asking for employment assistance first take part in a three-stage, two-week orientation program in which each applicant is tested, assessed by a counselor, and then enrolled in a job-seeking skills workshop. The window shoppers, those not really committed to following the program, usually drop out at this point on their own. Those who remain are then divided into three groups. In the first group are those who already have marketable skills and who only need some help in finding a job. This is provided through the information network and resource center which Downriver maintains. The second group comprises those who have demonstrated high test scores but who do not have a marketable skill. These people are given classroom training geared to occupations and, indeed, often to specific jobs for which a real need has been identified. The third group includes those who have not scored high enough on the tests to warrant the investment in classroom training. This group is placed in Downriver's on-the-job training program, which involves subcontracts with local employers and workshops. None of this training, however, is conducted in limbo. It is firmly tied to jobs. For example, before the Downriver Community Conference organizes a classroom training program, the staff work with their customers, the employers, to determine whether jobs are available and, if so, exactly what sort of training is needed to fill the jobs. Based on the employer's described needs, the appropriate educational institution—usually a local community college—is asked to prepare a curriculum, which the employer is then asked to review. "Is this what your people need to know?" the employer is asked. The curriculum is revised and then taken back to the educational institution with the question, "Is this what you can teach?" The proposed curriculum is passed back and forth until a solid course is developed that is acceptable to both parties. Most classroom training programs are from six to nine months in duration; longer programs are avoided as being too expensive and often too frustrating for the participants.

The results of the Downriver employment and training program have been impressive. Of those who participated in the demonstration program, 72 percent were reemployed, compared to 50 percent and 60 percent of the control groups of workers who did not receive services from Downriver. Those reemployed obtained jobs that paid an average of $8.20 an hour, about 10 percent less than they had been getting in their old jobs, but about $2.00 higher than the wage received by the workers in the control group. The average cost per participant in the program was $1,750, but this included those who were in the first group and received only minimal help from the organization. Costs for those placed in jobs after training were higher, averaging about $4,500 per placement—an amount which might be compared with 25 to 30 weeks of unemployment benefits.

For Downriver, however, this program was only the beginning of its adventures in job replacement. Freda Rutherford, the director of the Downriver Community Conference Employment Programs, describes it this way. "Believe me, we did not start out with any intention except running a retraining program. However, what we turned out to be was a catalyst in the community. When you start involving the education community, the private sector, all of the bankers, the health-care-services people, you find that you get a lot of direction that you have never had before. What we needed to do was intervene both in the supply side of the labor market, by retraining dislocated workers, and intervene in the demand side of the labor market. If you feel that there is a demand side to the labor market, then probably you are going to become involved in job creation." That is exactly what has happened at Downriver.

By 1981 the organization was being swamped as more and more plants shut down and unemployment in the area rose relentlessly. Desperately looking for other ways to help dislocated workers, Downriver began to consider how to develop new jobs—a job-replacement strategy. According to one report, the idea for becoming directly involved in job creation began when a staff member attended a U.S. Defense Department procurement conference held in May 1981.[13] The staff member was impressed by the fact that most of the 200 companies attending the conference had never before been involved with federal defense contracting. He saw an opportunity for the Downriver Community Conference to provide them with a service. A list of those attending the conference was obtained, followed by a Downriver market survey asking these employers if they would be interested in receiving some type of assistance in respect to defense contracting. Almost all of those answering the survey indicated interest. Since the processes used by the small manufacturers in the automotive, steel, and chemical industries are often the same or very similar to those used in manufacturing the products and equipment purchased by the Department of Defense, the Downriver staff believed they had a natural. They further reasoned that the small manufacturers with whom they were dealing would have a better chance as subcontractors than as prime contractors. In setting out to learn the ropes of defense contracting, Downriver found that it already had a head start because of its considerable experience in dealing with the U.S. Department of Labor, which operates under the same rules and general procurement procedures and regulations. "We don't know anything about building parts for Defense, but we sure can put together all the government paperwork that goes with that activity, and we know whom to call to get information," explains Rutherford.

Still feeling a little anxious about its expertise, the Downriver Community Conference opened its Business Assistance Center in February 1982, advertising to the companies that it would act as broker in the business of government contracting, particularly in defense contracting. If the companies would provide the information and do their own costing, the new center would deal with the federal bureaucracy and do the packaging.

One of the key features of the center is a microfiche of the bidding specifications of the Defense Supply Service and the General Service Administration, the two main federal government procurement agencies, as well as a reference library where bidders can identify who is likely to buy what they manufacture. As Rutherford explains it, "A vendor provides us with the microfiche of everything the government buys. It's updated every two weeks. The cost of that service is about $7,500 a year. That's fine for GM, but it's not fine for the little employer. If you don't have that kind of money, and you read in the *Commerce Business Daily* about something you'd like to bid on, you have to send to a clearinghouse in Philadelphia to get those bid stacks. The bid is usually due in 30 days, but the clearinghouse takes six weeks to send the microfiche. That's the kind of thing we help them with."[14]

The service seems simple enough, but it has been effective. In its first 20 months, the Business Assistance Center provided more than 700 Michigan firms with orientation on how to bid on defense contracts. Of these, 81 bidders were successful and received 190 contracts, totaling $41 million. The number of jobs created through this effort has averaged about 18 per contract, so clearly the economic impact on the community has been very positive.

Rutherford says that the Business Assistance Center has also had a favorable impact on other elements of Downriver's program. "What has happened," she says, "is that instead of our agency going out to private businesses to ask if they could help place our disadvantaged or dislocated workers, all of a sudden, businesses are walking through our doors every day. We are at the point where private businesses have approached us with more projects than we ever would have thought of on our own."

The Downriver Community Conference has not stopped thinking of new areas of activity, however. With some support from the U.S. Department of Commerce, the Business Assistance Center has now greatly expanded its services. In addition to defense contracting assistance, a variety of other services are offered to small businesses in the area, including tax-credit seminars, help with loan applications to the banks, and even assistance in developing a marketing plan. In 1983, the Downriver Conference moved to new facilities, taking over a local high school that had been closed. This encouraged Downriver to experiment with a new concept, the development of small business "incubators" in the building. By November 1983, four new companies had been launched as part of the new project called, Make It in Michigan. The Downriver Community Conference provides space at a low rent and central administrative services, such as accounting, clerical help, and a telephone answering service.

The organization also began planning a venture-capital project: the projected Michigan Investment Fund, to be located in the same building, will offer venture capital to the companies that use other Downriver services—Downriver's "customers." Another program still on the drawing boards deals with the provision of health care.

How can one account for the success of the Downriver Community Conference? Several reasons can be suggested. First, the primary reason for the success of the organization has to be the energy, dynamism, and entrepreneurial nature of the staff, which is remarkable in every respect. But it is also clear that this has been a two-way street. True, the staff has made the organization what it is, but also the organization was such that it attracted this particular kind of staff—a staff which felt comfortable there, able to do their jobs in a productive and effective way.

Second, the structure of the organization has helped make it possible for Downriver to be an effective action agency. The fact that it has a clearly defined and, in a sense, homogeneous constituency—the 16 neighboring communities share similar characteristics and similar problems—is very important. The mayors of these 16 communities make up the board of directors. All of them share the same burden, carry the same responsibilities, and must answer to similar constituencies of their own. Unlike many other community organizations, there are no built-in divisions; no "outside" or different groups are represented on the board. There is no need for trade-offs or debilitating compromises. There is a commonality of interest that certainly must enhance the organization's effectiveness.

Third, the Downriver Community Conference has been performance-oriented from the start. The organization has kept its sights firmly fixed on the ultimate objective: jobs. By focusing its efforts on providing services to employers, the organization has earned and retained a reputation as a reliable service agency. It has perfected its techniques for effective intervention in the labor market, to the benefit of both the demand side and the supply side.

Fourth, by relying on grants and other non-tax-based financial sources for funding, the organization has avoided becoming bureaucratized and kept its entrepreneurial character. Its budgets do not have to be reviewed and approved in competition with other organizations. There is no pressure for conformity. This has made it possible for Downriver to maintain a certain freedom of action, which in turn permits and encourages experimentation and organizational growth.

There may be other factors that also contribute to the success of the Downriver Community Conference. Whatever they are, it seems clear that Downriver will continue to exploit every potential for new job creation. As Employment Program Director Rutherford has said, "I am starting to be able to say with great confidence that Downriver is going to make it. That area will recover." As it does so, it can thank the Downriver Community Conference for helping make the recovery possible.

MUNICH EMPLOYMENT COUNCIL (WEST GERMANY)

To the casual observer, Munich, the capital of Bavaria in the south of West Germany, is a prosperous, thriving, and comfortable city. Well-dressed, well-fed burghers throng the streets and shops early and late. Munich is a center of high-technology industry in West Germany, and its air of prosperity is not illusory. The unemployment rate for the Munich area is much lower than it is in West Germany as a whole and, indeed, business and industry are doing well. Nevertheless, the Munich area is not without its employment problems. As in the rest of West Germany, and indeed among all industrialized nations of the world, much of the older Bavarian industry is faced with the twin problems of a lack of productivity growth, increased competition, and the need to adopt job-displacing technological advances. Munich-area companies have had to reduce their work forces and, in some cases, to shut down entirely. Young people entering the labor market are having a difficult time. Employment security is a problem for Bavarian workers, just as it is in other areas of the country. In Munich, however, a unique informal community council exists to deal with the problems of employment security. The council does not even have a formal name, but it is functioning and it is making a singular contribution to employment stability in the Munich area.

The council was started through the efforts of the local district office of the large metal workers' union, I.G. Metall and especially of the district's energetic president, Alois Laus.[15] It is an informal, unofficial group chaired by the mayor of Munich and it includes representatives of other local governments in the area, both large and small employers, trade unions, and the federal labor-market agency—in short, the movers and shakers in the Munich-area world of work. What the council does is to provide a framework within which solutions to current employment and labor-market problems affecting the entire community can be worked out on a cooperative basis. Primarily an information-sharing body, the council has no power or authority of its own, but the people who take part have authority within their own organizations. Through cooperation and coordination of their activities, they can make things happen in Munich to make it a better place to live and work.

I.G. Metall, the metal workers' union, is the largest industrial union in West Germany, comprising some 2.5 million members, or more than 10 percent of West Germany's entire labor force. It is this union which holds representation rights for workers in the automotive, machinery and mechanical equipment, electrical, and electronics industries, among others. I.G. Metall is one of the member organizations which make up the German Federation of Labor, the DGB. Because of its size and importance to the labor movement, it is both economically powerful and socially influential. It is I.G. Metall, for example, which spearheaded the push by German trade unions in the spring of 1984 for a reduction of the workweek from 40 to 35 hours, with no decrease in weekly wages. Like other West German unions, I.G. Metall is a national union, with geographically defined district offices representing its members in a particular area. The Munich district office represents some 60,000 workers. Within any particular company or plant or shop, the relevant union body is the works council. But this is not where collective bargaining takes place. In West Germany, as in many other European countries, collective bargaining is done on a truly collective basis, between employers as a group and the unions. The real nuts-and-bolts bargaining takes place at the regional and district levels, between the local branch of the National Federation of Employers and the regional office of the DGB, or its constituent elements. Thus, it is at the district level that the action and interaction between employers and unions takes place; and, in Munich, that solutions to employment security problems are developed.

Establishment of the Munich employment council was a gradual development, growing out of a series of events that were potentially disruptive to the community and very disturbing to the union. The first of these was a decision by the MAN company, a West German multinational company manufacturing trucks, buses, diesel engines, and other heavy equipment, to reduce the

number of workers in one of its Munich-area plants. MAN had been especially hard hit by the recession due to several factors, some of its own making,
some not. In October 1982, it became known that the company planned to cut
its local work force by 450 workers. Under West German law, a company
planning a large-scale staff reduction must notify both the federal labor-
market agency and the union well ahead of the proposed reduction so that a
"social plan" can be worked out that provides reasonable alternatives for all
of the affected workers. However, this requirement is waived if the reduction
represents less than 5 percent of the employer's total work force. In this case,
the proposed reduction of 450 was slightly less than the required 5 percent.
Taking advantage of this provision, MAN waited until the last minute and
then informed the government office of its plans on the same day that the
union works council was notified. Mr. Laus, who represented the I.G. Metall
district office, says, "We knew, we could feel it, that more than the first 450"
would be let go. Feeling that the employment security process was being
short-circuited to its disadvantage, the union first went to City Hall, then took
it's story to the press, and finally organized a demonstration. The effort was
partially successful; although the cutback remained in force, a social plan was
negotiated and implemented. "But," says Laus, "that doesn't bring in any
other jobs."

At about the same time a crisis arose with another I.G. Metall employer,
AGFA, the international camera and film manufacturer. The company operated a plant in Munich that made both cameras and film and employed
approximately 3,800 workers. The top manager of the plant had only recently
been brought in—some now believe solely for the purpose of shutting it
down. In any case, when it became known to union leaders that the plant was
to be closed, it was a surprise and shock to everyone concerned. Even the local
plant managers apparently did not know of the proposed closing until they
heard about it from the union leadership. At first they didn't believe it, but
when the story was confirmed, they wept. Based on his previous experience,
Laus again went to City Hall to get assistance in keeping the plant open. The
mayor agreed to try. A shutdown of the plant would have a serious economic
impact on the entire community and could add as many as 5,000 workers to
the ranks of the unemployed. It was a situation that the city and the union
wanted to avoid if it could.

In the union's view there were very good economic reasons for keeping the
plant open. Through its participation on the company's board of directors—
codetermination is provided by law to employees in West Germany—the
union had access to important management information. On the basis of such
information, the union felt that the Munich plant was not in desperate enough
straits to warrant closure. The company's original idea had been to integrate
the production of camera equipment and film in one plant. When camera sales
lagged because AGFA could not compete with the Japanese, the company

decided to shut down the plant, even though the film business was still satis-factory. The union opposed the plant closure, arguing that there was no real reason to keep the two parts of the business together, or to sacrifice the entire Munich plant because one part of the operation was doing poorly.

With this information, and with the full cooperation of the mayor, the union took a series of steps to force the company to keep the plant in opera-tion. The first was a public relations campaign, orchestrated with the mayor. This was highly successful, resulting in the outspoken support by all of the Munich press and broadcast industry of efforts to keep AGFA in operation. Second, the union put in motion the procedures provided under West German law; it argued its case in the labor court and began negotiations with the company. In due time a social plan (a plan to manage the reduction of the labor force) was developed and agreed to by all parties. Meanwhile, however, the mayor had called together, on an informal basis, the representatives of all the affected groups: employers, officials from neighboring towns, the unions, and the federal labor-market office. This was the beginning of the present employment council. Through the actions of this group it was decided that the city could and would enact an ordinance preventing the land on which the plant stood from being sold unless the new owner could provide employment for two-thirds of those who were displaced by the plant closing. For AGFA, enactment of such an ordinance meant a drastic change in the company's cost-benefit equation. If they could not sell the facility the economic benefits the company expected to gain from closing the plant could be nullified. In the end, the plant was kept open, although at a reduced capacity. At the present time, the plant employs 1,500 workers.

The informal employment council has also continued to operate. Chaired by the mayor, the council meets regularly once every two or three months to exchange information about employment-related problems in the area and to map out plans to deal with them. For example, in early 1984, the council was busily involved in planning for the annual June influx of school leavers into the labor market. At the union's suggestion a survey of all employers in the area was under way to determine how many and what kinds of jobs would be available when school closed, and what kinds of training and apprenticeships would be necessary to accommodate the expected flow.

What the council is trying to do is to head off trouble before it develops. So far, it seems to be working. One interesting aspect concerning the council is the relationship between the union and the mayor. In West Germany, there is a close political alliance between the trade unions and the Social Democratic Party. The mayor of Munich, however, is a member of the opposing party, a Christian Democrat. But that has not hindered the union and the mayor from working together to improve employment security for Munich workers. Shar-ing a common concern, together they have forged a unique and apparently effective new institution.

ENTERPRISE AGENCIES IN GREAT BRITAIN:
BUSINESS IN THE COMMUNITY AND
THE NEW WORK TRUST COMPANY

Motivated by the conviction that the key to economic growth and a reduction
of the continuing high levels of unemployment lies in the development of
small- and medium-sized businesses, many large British companies have become involved in the business of establishing and nurturing new enterprises.
In doing this most are also moved by a sense of social obligation to the
communities where they are or were located and which for years have been
dependent on them.

   One of the first attempts by a big company to establish new businesses and
new jobs for its laid-off workers was a community Enterprise Agency started
by Sir Alistair Pilkington, former chairperson of Pilkington Brothers, a large
glass company located in the town of St. Helen's in Lancashire. Sir Alistair, a
relative of the founding fathers of Pilkington Glass, conceived the float process, a much more efficient and less labor-intensive method of making glass
than that previously used. Although during the 1960s and early 1970s the
discovery of this process was the basis for the company's expansion, by the
end of the decade, international competition and the recession made it necessary for the company to trim its work force from 16,000 workers to approximately half that number. Pilkington was one of the most important employers
in the community of St. Helen's. The impact of the cutback was disastrous for
the area. With a strong tradition of company involvement in the community
behind him, and a sense of obligation to his former employees, Sir Alistair
started St. Helen's Trust, a wholly owned subsidiary of the glass company and
the first such organization dedicated to the promotion of new small businesses
and the creation of new jobs for displaced workers. Since the organization
began in 1979, more than 100 new businesses have opened their doors in the
community, creating about 2,000 new jobs. The key to the success of St.
Helen's Trust is the partnership that exists among all elements in the community: other established businesses, the banks, government agencies, and the
local authorities, as well as the Pilkington Company itself. This experiment,
now six years old, and the similar successful venture of the British Steel
Corporation, have become the models for the new community Enterprise
Agencies that are now beginning to spread throughout Great Britain.

Business in the Community

   The moving force behind the Enterprise Agency movement is a new organization, Business in the Community, or BIC. This organization, formed in
1981, is a national consortium of 76 large companies, trade unions, and
employers' organizations. Sir Alistair Pilkington and Sir Charles Villiers,

chairperson of BSC Industry—another dedicated believer in business-community cooperation to solve community economic and social problems—were prime movers behind the establishment of BIC. The new Enterprise Agencies operate in much the same way as St. Helen's Trust and BSC Industry, pulling together company, community, and government resources to provide the kinds of support required to get new businesses going.

BIC's purpose is to persuade business to take a real interest in the social, economic, and environmental needs of the communities in which they are located and to take an active part in undertaking programs that will improve conditions. The principal means for achieving this purpose is the local Enterprise Agency. At the beginning of 1984 about 150 of these Enterprise Agencies had been established. BIC's goal is to have at least 200 going by the end of the year.[16] A small staff headquartered in London helps to guide the local Enterprise Agencies through the initial planning and start-up and then monitors performance, lending a hand as needed.

The Enterprise Agencies are cooperative ventures, but with a very simple format. Each one is an independent incorporated body, a non-profit company limited by guarantee, that is, without share capital. Under the limited-guarantee format, the liability of the corporation's members is limited to the extent of their individual pledge. For most Enterprise Agencies the membership fee is £1 per year, with funds for the administration of the company and for the operations it undertakes raised by subscription from the members. The most important resource offered by the enterprise agency is its staff, which for the most part is made up of personnel loaned or "seconded" by the members. The government supports the Enterprise Agency movement both directly and indirectly. In 1983 about £1.5 million was provided to BIC in direct grants, out of a total £9.5 million expended. The government's indirect support may be more important, however, since companies can deduct for tax purposes the cost of the seconded employees as well as any cash or other in-kind contributions.

What do the companies get out of participation in the Enterprise Agencies? Perhaps one of the strongest motivations is simply a desire to do good. As a BIC spokesperson put it, "Don't underrate altruism." Another factor is certainly enlightened self-interest. The riots that hit some British cities in the summer of 1981 were very disturbing for most Britons and no doubt caused many companies to look for ways to help resolve the underlying causes. The riots also led to a degree of political interest in the Enterprise Agency concept and the development of bipartisan political momentum. In addition, since a thriving community is better for business than a depressed one, no doubt many of those who lend their support, time, and effort to struggling new businesses through the Enterprise Agencies expect that to some extent this effort will in time be rewarded. For example, an accountant who helps a new entrepreneur set up a bookkeeping system might expect some day to be called upon for additional accounting services from that client. Free advice can lead to paid advice.

Is the Enterprise Agency movement just another gimmick, another cosmetic approach to the problems of unemployment and economic distress that is affecting so many British communities? Perhaps so in some cases. At this juncture, the movement is still too new to make a final judgment. It should be understood, however, that BIC does not consider and has never claimed that the Enterprise Agency movement is a panacea for all that ails the British economy. But already there are some notable successes. Overall, the new businesses that have been helped to get started by the Enterprise Agencies have a failure rate of only one in 20, compared to a national failure rate for new enterprises of one in four. In terms of cost, each job created with the help of an Enterprise Agency has required an expenditure of about £500 compared to a social cost of ten times that amount to maintain an unemployed person on the dole for one year.

New Work Trust Company

One of the most successful of the Enterprise Agencies is the New Work Trust Company in Bristol, in the southwestern part of the country.[17] Although Bristol was the site of some of the worst of the 1981 riots, it is not a particularly depressed area of Great Britain. Indeed, it is in an area with a tradition of small business, where new firms, particularly those involved in new technology, are located. The unemployment rate, although still high, is lower than the national average. Nevertheless, the original sponsors of the New Work Trust Company felt there was sufficient need for an Enterprise Agency to justify its creation.

A variety of both private and public bodies were involved in the early planning for an Enterprise Agency, and in September 1981 the New Work Trust was legally constituted. Starting with some 30 sponsors, within two years the list had grown to 256 sponsors, representing the full range of interests and capabilities within the Bristol area. Some very large companies (British American Tobacco, Cadbury's, Imperial Chemical) are members of the New Work Trust, as are banks (Barclay's, Lloyds, National Westminster Bank) and several unions (the Transport and General Workers Union, the largest in Britain and the Associated Engineering Union). Law firms, accounting firms—Arthur Andersen, for example—and, of course, the local authorities and local universities and technical schools have also joined. Even the churches are included. It is truly a cooperative community undertaking.

Like other Enterprise Agencies, the New Work Trust Company chose the limited-guarantee form of organization. Although in this case the members were permitted to pledge up to £100 each, the New Work Trust selected this form because it wanted to adopt a businesslike approach and demonstrate the characteristics of a public company from the start so as to attract broad support. It also felt that this format would permit the company to obtain access to the full range of services needed to be effective, without having to meet a heavy initial capitalization cost. At last report, over 250 institutions and individuals had provided support for the organization.

The challenge that the new corporation set for itself was to develop practical ways for new and existing small entrepreneurs to minimize their risks and to quickly learn the best management practices. In the three years since it began, the New Work Trust has developed several different activities to accomplish this purpose.

Appropriate space at a reasonable cost was the first and most obvious need for the new businesses. To meet this need, the Avondale Workshops were established in a derelict factory located in the Kingswood area of Bristol, a factory which had been bought for reconversion but whose sympathetic owner agreed to lease the part of the building that he did not need to the New Work Trust under very favorable terms. With cash and other support gathered from a number of sources—including two local authorities, private donors, bank loans, and the government's Manpower Services Commission, which agreed to provide the labor for painting, minor repairs, and other improvements—the building was renovated and opened for business in the fall of 1981. Eleven weeks later the Avondale Workshops had begun to generate revenue. By the end of the year, the building was 70 percent occupied and the workshops had achieved a break-even point. Run on an "easy-in, easy-out" basis, with tenants paying a monthly license fee that can be terminated with only 30 days' notice, the Avondale Workshops currently maintain an 85 percent occupancy rate. During its first two years of operation 72 different companies were located at one time or another at Avondale, creating approximately 210 jobs. Some of the companies have grown and moved on to larger space. The business failure rate for the entrepreneurs has been extraordinarily low—only 4 percent. Among the types of businesses that got their start in the Avondale Workshops are engineering, fabrication, circuit-board manufacture, pottery, ceramic tiles distribution, electronics, packaging, and printing companies. One of the most successful businesses is a manufacturer of billiard cues and tables. So successful have the Avondale Workshops been that the New Work Trust has recently bought another building to convert into additional workshops. Unlike the BSC Industry workshops, such as the Cardiff Workshops in Wales, the directors of the Avondale Workshops shun the nursery concept because, they say, "that implies too much hand-holding, and we are not doing that here." However, the kinds of services provided by the BSC Industry workshops and Avondale are very similar. In addition to space, they all provide access to a variety of business services, as well as training for new employees and assistance in putting together a viable financing package.

For the New Work Trust Company, the creation of the Avondale Workshops was only the beginning. Almost immediately it began to branch out into other activities. In so doing, the company regards itself as an economic development agency committed to the growth of small business, and not simply as an agent for fostering job-creation. However, most of the organization's new activities represent a natural outgrowth of the need to provide specialized services for the tenants of the Avondale Workshops. For example, in addition to providing the typical business services to workshop tenants, such as a telephone switchboard, an answering service, and photocopying, the agency found that many of its tenants also needed more sophisticated office services, such as data processing, telecommunications, and other computer services. Again, with help from the Manpower Services Commission, a center was established within the workshop complex to provide that kind of support. This center operates with a full-time staff plus a complement of trainees. Training is provided not only to the personnel of the client organizations but also to groups of unemployed youth referred to the agency. As a result of this activity, when the government decided to establish and fund "new-technology centers" on a national basis to encourage the use of new technology by small business everywhere, the New Work Trust Company already had such a center in operation and, therefore, quickly became one of the government-designated centers.

Another New Work Trust program that flowed from the expressed needs of the workshop tenants is the Small Firms Marketing Center. The Marketing Center is located in a restored Victorian building leased by the Trust for this purpose and provides marketing assistance not only to the workshop tenants, but also to any small firm requesting such help in the Bristol area. In addition to consultation and technical assistance, the Marketing Center also provides space where advertising exhibits—prepared with its help—can be shown.

Research and development is still another area of activity for the Trust. In this case, the organization undertakes market surveys for potential entrepreneurs or for existing small businesses considering expansion. As a result of such surveys, it became apparent that a directory of small businesses in the area would be helpful, not only to help new small enterprises determine the competition for their product or service, but also—since small businesses often patronize each other—to foster an exchange between the many small businesses in the area. Preparation of such a directory is now a regular feature of the organization's activities.

From the start, the provision of training for new employees has been an important activity of the Trust Company. Recruitment and training is always a major problem for a new company starting out. For the most part the New Work Trust has provided the training in conjunction with the Manpower Services Commission and with the local technical schools. However, in many instances, the Trust has arranged for on-the-job training programs, many of which have taken place at the Avondale Workshops. The company's latest initiative is the establishment of a second workshop in another redeveloped building.

A challenge down the road—and one that the director and his dedicated staff are already working on—is to find ways to encourage the development of new export businesses so vital to the recovery of the British economy. If enthusiasm plus hard-headed practicality plus a willingness to innovate and improvise can do the job, the New Work Trust will no doubt find some interesting and worthwhile solutions to this problem too.

NOTES

1. Information on Rhone-Poulenc and SOPRAN was obtained from an interview with Philippe Lecerf of SOPRAN, Courbevoie, France, January 1984, and from materials provided by the company.

2. Interview with M. Rosat, director of Personnel and Social Relations, Usinor, La Defense, January 1984.

3. Information on Thomson GÉRIS was obtained from materials supplied by the company; from an interview with Pierre Frachot, director, CÉRIS, in Paris, January 1984; and from a speech describing the activities of GÉRIS presented by E. P. Courtillot, director-general of GÉRIS, March 3, 1983.

4. Speech by E. P. Courtillot (see above).

5. Information concerning the activities of BSC Industry was obtained from materials provided by the company and from interviews with the chairman of the board, Sir Charles Villiers, London, October 1983, and with Neil Piercy, marketing manager, Croydon, January 1984.

6. Comments of Sir Charles Villiers, London, October 1983.

7. Information concerning the operation of the Cardiff Workshops was obtained from material provided by BSC Industry and from interviews with Brian Margrett, regional manager, BSC Industry, Cardiff, and G. R. Blackburn, general manager, Cardiff Workshops, January 1984.

8. Information for this case study was taken from a report, *The Landskrona Finans Project*, prepared by Carl-Johan Asplund and Erik Hafstrom of the University of Lund, Sweden, and published by the Organisation for Economic Co-operation and Development in Paris, April 1984.

9. Ibid., p. 9.

10. Information on the Downriver Community Conference is drawn from a presentation made by Freda Rutherford, director of Employment Programs, Downriver Community Conference, to the National Advisory Committee for "Employment Security in a Free Economy," a Work in America Institute policy study, November 1983. Material was also taken from a two-part report prepared by ABT Associates for the U.S. Department of Labor, *Reemploying Displaced Workers: The Implementation of the Downriver Community Conference Economic Readjustment Program*, September 1982 and May 1983.

11. ABT Associates, *Reemploying Displaced Workers*, p. 75.

12. Presentation by Freda Rutherford, November 1983.

13. ABT Associates, *Reemploying Displaced Workers*, pp. 24–25.

14. Presentation by Freda Rutherford, November 1983.

15. Information on the Munich employment council was obtained in an interview with Alois Laus, president of the Munich District, I.G. Metall, Munich, West Germany, January 1984.

16. Information on Business in the Community and on Enterprise Agencies is drawn from material provided by BIC, and from an interview with Christopher Norman-Butler, Executive Unit, BIC, London, January 1984.

17. Information concerning the New Work Trust was obtained from materials provided by the organization and from an interview with Managing Director Michael Winwood, Bristol, January 18, 1984.

Index

About the Author

JOCELYN F. GUTCHESS is an economic analyst and employment and training consultant with special interest and expertise in policies and programs to deal with mass employment resulting from structural changes in the economy. From 1969 to 1981, Gutchess was a senior associate and partner in Ruttenberg, Friedman, Kilgallon, Gutchess and Associates of Washington, D.C., an economic research, manpower, and labor-relations consulting firm, with special emphasis on serving clients within the labor movement. On leave from this firm in 1978–79, she acted as a consultant with the Organisation for Economic Co-operation and Development (OECD) in Paris. Within OECD's Manpower and Social Affairs Directorate, Gutchess undertook policy studies, with special responsibility for work in positive adjustment policies. Earlier in her career, she held various positions in the U.S. Department of Labor, including special assistant to the administrator of the Neighborhood Youth Corps, executive assistant to the Assistant Secretary of Labor for Manpower, and senior analyst for the Office of Policy Planning and Research. Other areas in which Gutchess has worked extensively include international economic policy; pension-fund investment policy with particular reference to labor-union participation in pension-fund management; labor-movement policy, programs and organizations; and international commodity supply policy. Gutchess is the author of *Report on Union Involvement in the Investment and Management of Union Pension Funds* (1980) and *Raw Materials for America* (1975). She is the co-author of *The Federal-State Employment Service: A Critique, Manpower Challenge of the 1970s: Institutions and Social Change,* and *Needed: A Constructive Foreign Trade Policy.* Gutchess is a graduate of Bryn Mawr College and was a Fellow in the National Institute of Public Affairs.